CONVERSATIONS ON AWAKENING

Part One

CONVERSATIONS ON AWAKENING

Part One

Interviews by

IAIN AND RENATE McNAY

www.whitecrowbooks.com

ALSO AVAILABLE

CONVERSATIONS ON AWAKENING: PART TWO

featuring interviews with

Susanne Marie, Debra Wilkinson, Richard Moss, Mukti, Miek Pot, Reggie Ray, Aloka (David Smith), Deborah Westmorland, Russel Williams, Jurgen Ziewe, Martyn Wilson, Jah Wobble

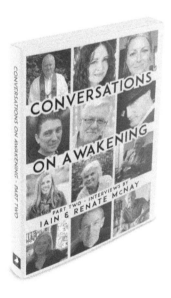

Paperback ISBN: 978-1-78677-095-0
eBook ISBN: 978-1-78677-096-7

Available from Amazon and other bookstores.

CONTENTS

FOREWORD

When I first became involved with these interviews several years ago I wondered how the transcripts would add anything to the filmed recordings, but I quickly became fascinated by the richness and pace of experience offered by reading, rather than listening or watching.

These valuable and engaging dialogues are a wonderful gift for those who find themselves curious about their own and others spiritual unfolding. Such an apparently diverse range of guests appear in these dialogues with Iain and Renate: intuitive glimmerings sensed in childhood, chance meetings with teachers, rigorously disciplined and traditional paths contrasted with intuitive and spontaneous awakenings. Each one of these illuminates a different facet of the search for wholeness and authenticity or, as A.H. Almaas puts it: 'the real truth of all of this that we experience?'

Reading these accounts has opened me up to a deep appreciation of different voices and different strategies – the dialogues invite us to explore, and importantly, trust our own journey beyond the conditioning of society to our deepest, authentic being.

Julian Noyce,
founder, Non-Duality Press

INTRODUCTION

This book contains twelve unique accounts of Awakening. They are all taken from transcripts of interviews that were made for Conscious.tv. People used to talk of 'Enlightenment' or 'Self-Realisation' but these days it is Awakening that people tend to speak of. What does Awakening mean? What form does it take? How does it affect ones practical life? How is it integrated? These are all important questions that are addressed in the chapters in this book. Some of the subjects are renowned spiritual teachers and others are completely unknown having never lead a seminar or written a book.

The beauty of the spiritual path is that no two stories are the same. There are a myriad of paths up the mountain and we all end up finding our own way.

So many of us realise that we are much, much more than just a human being. There are so many levels of our existence. This book will hopefully encourage you, inspire you, and maybe even guide you to find out who you really are.

Iain McNay,
founder, Conscious TV

PART I

A.H. Almaas –
Endless Enlightenment
Interview by **Iain McNay**

*P*eople talk about non-dual, boundless. This is not non-dual. It is beyond non-dual, beyond dual. And that is just an example, another way that the enlightenment realisation can happen. So, I'm inviting people not to box it in. Each tradition tends to box it in as one thing. And it's true, each thing is freedom and liberation. But freedom and liberation can be even further freedom and liberation – even freedom and liberation from those freedoms and liberations. So, the freedom liberates itself from being anything in particular.

Iain: Today my guest is Hameed Ali.

Hameed is also known as A.H. Almaas, which is his pen name. And he's written about twenty books altogether. I have a few of them here. *The Unfolding Now: Realising Your True Nature through the Practice of Presence, Diamond Heart: Book Five* – which obviously indicates there is a Book One, a Book Two, a Book Three and a Book Four as well.

Hameed: The last of the series, yes.

Iain: And *Essence: The Diamond Approach to Inner Realisation*, and *The Point of Existence* which is quite dense, but also very fascinating. So, Hameed, it's interesting, I was realising earlier that last time I was in Amsterdam I came for a conference and it was quite a difficult time in my life. I was going through some changes and I'd left one spiritual school and I wasn't quite sure where I was. I had dinner with somebody who said, "You know what? The Diamond Approach" – the Ridhwan School, which is your school – "could be the right thing for you now." And I found out there was a group happening in Northern Germany, near Bremen, so I went. That was just a few weeks later that I went to the first group. And that was very instrumental for me in understanding where I was, and also very much a catalyst for change in my life. And when we were talking earlier you were saying to me that at age thirteen you became interested in finding out more about life and at that point you thought that maybe science had the answers for you.

Hameed: That's what I thought and for a long time; I became a scientist. But it really started for me by just feeling. I didn't think about it, it was just a feeling that I wanted to know what it is. Reality – what is all this about? What is the real truth of all of this that we experience? And I thought science will give me an objective knowledge, not somebody's opinion, not somebody's story. I knew about religions and all that, but what I knew were like stories. I couldn't tell whether they were really true. But I thought science would provide the answers at that time. And partly the influence of my teachers, I had good science teachers. So I got interested in mathematics, physics and chemistry. First, I thought, "I will be a chemist." But I turned out to be more of a physicist. So when I went to college I went to the US and studied physics in Berkeley, California.

Iain: Thirteen is quite early for someone to have this desire, this calling to ask these deep questions. Was that something you could share with your contemporaries? Or was this quite an isolated thing for just you?

Hameed: No. I think maybe we all feel that in different ways. And for me it wasn't exactly an explicit kind of question in my mind that was driving me. It was like part of my life. I was just that way. You know, I felt that way. I wanted to know, what is this reality? We had religion classes and science classes, different kinds of psychology classes. I was interested in – what is it, what's it all about? And I thought, physics, especially deep theoretical physics, can go deep into what is it – what's happening –that is not anybody's opinion or idea. I wanted to know the truth as it is.

Iain: You wanted to know the truth as it is.

Hameed: And at that time I thought, science will do it. And I went into science very far. I was at the point of getting my Ph.D. in nuclear physics when I realised that's not what I'm looking for. And it was an interesting story. I don't know if you ever heard how I realised that. I used to work in graduate school in Lawrence Rad Lab, in Berkeley. That's where they first did the research on the atom bomb and all that work. I had my office there and I was in the cafeteria for lunch with all the professors and graduate students. I was sitting having lunch and at some point, for some reason, I was looking around. And I looked and all those brilliant physicists and mathematicians who were some of the top in the world. And it struck me, I don't want to be like that. And I felt that way because I saw something. I saw those brilliant big heads and nothing else. And I realised, no, that's not the kind of truth I'm looking for. That's not the kind of life I want. Big head, great intelligence, but the rest is almost gone. It's not there.

Iain: So it was like knowledge without depth, almost.

Hameed: Yes. Well, knowledge without completeness. It's partial, it's part of being human, part of the truth. And it was an intuitive thing. Partly it was like recognising the truth I'm looking for isn't going to happen that way, I realised at that time. It was my intention to get my Ph.D. and become a professor and teach and do research in physics. Then. I realised, no. My research is not that, I learned at that point. And then I lost complete interest in physics. And I'd go to my office to do research and every day, every morning, I'd go and sit at the desk to write all these equations and within half an hour I'm asleep. That happened for weeks. Finally, I went to my professor and told him, "I can't do it."

Iain: So what were the clues that took you to the next stage? I know you still had to do some experimental workshops.

Hameed: Then what happened is that I got interested in various kinds of workshops, different kinds of individuals. I even went to Esalen, for instance, in California and I did various workshops. I went to various events. I learned meditation. I learned transcendental meditation, TM, for a while. That was one of the first meditations I ever learned.

Iain: Did that work for you?

Hameed: I liked it. I still like it, you know, but I didn't go deep into that school. Because you can go deeper if you followed Maharishi. I didn't do it that way but it was one thing I learned. But I did a lot of psychological therapies. Gestalt therapy, bioenergetics, I actually got a bioenergetic therapist. I did several years of it. I did Reichian therapy for several years and I worked with the various Gestalt groups and therapists. It was called the human potential movement, I was pretty involved in it and learning various things. Until of course I met Claudio Naranjo at an Esalen workshop he was leading on meditation and Gestalt therapy. He approached me at some point during the workshop and said, "You know, I'm forming a group in Berkeley to work more on that thing, if you want to be involved" – because he knew I was living in Berkeley. And I said, "hmm". So I went to that group. And of course, Claudio taught a combination of psychology – he worked with psychology and meditation. He taught different forms of meditation and he worked with psychology by using the Enneagram of Fixations. And he has a lot of psychological background because he was a Karen Horney student. She emphasised self-analysis so he taught self-analysis, basically. So, he did two directions – psychology and spirituality – side by side.

Iain: And hardly anyone was bringing those two things together at the time.

Hameed: He was one of the pioneers, I will say, of seeing that psychology and spirituality can go together.

Iain: And he had a great title. He called it "Seekers After Truth," which must have really appealed to you.

Hameed: That's what Gurdjieff called his work. He got it from Gurdjieff, yes.

Iain: I'm looking at my notes here ... you were involved with the Fourth Way teaching as well.

Hameed: What happened is that Claudio Naranjo was instrumental in some sense in my development. Not in terms of my realisation or my liberation, but in terms of going in the right direction. Because he knew he had something, but he didn't have everything. So he introduced us to many other teachers. He brought many other teachers – he brought Rinpoches, he brought Taoist masters, he brought Hindu masters, he brought Sufi masters. So, I got to work with many of those people. Through one of the Rinpoches, for instance, a Tibetan lama I worked with for several years, I learned a lot about Tibetan Buddhism. And I worked with E. J. Gold who had more of a Fourth Way orientation as well as a Sufi orientation. I worked with another person who was more Gurdjieffian, Fourth Way; I worked with him for several years. And at the same time, I was still continuing my Reichian therapy. I was doing my psychological bodywork, too. Breathing, energising, liberating the body at the same time that I was learning with those various teachers. And by the time I was working with the Fourth Way teacher, at some point I was beginning to have experiences of what I call essential nature. When I talked to him about it, he didn't recognise them. He dismissed them.

Iain: So what kind of experiences were they?

Hameed: I was experiencing something that I felt as truth. I was feeling, "I am experiencing truth." But I could feel it, sense it, see it. And it was like a pretty palpable sense of the presence of truth. Which is so present, it's like a conscious mass of twenty-five carat gold. I became like a statue of gold. And just like the gold statue you see of the Buddha, I felt like that. I felt, I am gold. I am truth. And I recognise that gold, what the alchemists call gold, is truth. True truth. The truth I was looking for. I was looking for what is objective truth. So when I talked to this teacher about some of those things, he didn't recognise it. And I began to have a peaceful, congenial separation from his work and then went on my way because things weren't developing in me. And I think one other influence at that time was the sixteenth Karmapa, Rangjung Rigpe Dorje, whom I met.

Iain: I don't know what that is.

Hameed: The Karmapa is one of the leading figures in Tibetan Buddhism. He does what's called the Black Hat Ceremony where he transmits the teachings of his lineage. It's called Mahamudra. He is the head of the Mahamudra lineage and he does an initiation where he transmits that state, so I went to his transmission. That was the early '70s and I got a headache. Many people had clarity and light. I had a headache for several years. It reminded me of Krishnamurti who had headaches for many years at the beginning. I had a headache and I went from one person to another – doctors, and I went to yogis, a Hindu yogi who said, "Oh, this is just some kind of gas" and he gave it some name. When I talked to the Rinpoche I knew, he taught me, "This is light." And I didn't know exactly what it meant. But in time, when I started working psychologically on what is this? Like an obstruction in the head. At some point there was like – even when doing the meditation – things like something flowed down, descended. And it was light, but it wasn't light the way people know it. More like liquid light. And I felt it as my presence. That is my being. Presence. And that was the discovery of presence, which I then talked to my friends too, like Karen.

Iain: Karen Johnson?

Hameed: Johnson, yes, I talked to her. She'll talk to you later about how she received it. And she got it, right away. And I thought other people would get it right away. That was the beginning of the Diamond Approach. That presence, which is the truth of reality, the truth of what I am, didn't just stay that way. It developed and grew and manifested so many things about itself and the rest of reality and what I am.

Iain: How did that realisation, that manifestation, influence you in your day-to-day life? How you interacted with other people, how you went out and about? Was that always with you, and how did that change things on a personal basis?

Hameed: Very good question. At the beginning, when I was first learning, I noticed I was not interested in people. I was married, right, we had a house and I had a small group I was working with. But I was not interested in social contacts. My wife would invite people and I would stay in my room. I wouldn't go.

Iain: Really?

Hameed: Yeah. I might say hi and then go back to my room. I wasn't interested in what was happening and I saw that all these other things would be distractions. For several years it stayed like that. I didn't dislike people or anything, I was friendly and fine. But I didn't want the usual social practices to dominate. I just was that way. And that allowed this truth, this presence, this awareness, to grow and develop and teach. Teach me, teach my mind and teach other people. Then of course it changed – then it started impacting my behaviour and my relationships to people. And one of the ways it presented itself is personalness. What we call 'the pearl beyond price'. How to be not just this consciousness conscious of itself as presence, but how it can be a person who interacts with another person, like I'm interacting with you. I am the true nature but I'm also a human being. It showed me not only how to be a human being but what a real human being is.

Iain: Yes, that reminds me, when I got the first book of yours, the line I read that really hit me was being man in the world, but not of the world. I think you're touching on the beginning of that in terms of you were beginning to find that, yes, there was presence there. And also being in the world was important, living the potential of a human being.

Hameed: You see that expression – being in the world and not of it – is a Sufi expression which I found very appealing. What was happening, that expression, was appealing and that presence revealed what that means. Which is, I think I didn't want those interactions and those social things because it would've been being in the world and of it. I'll be like everybody else. Lost in the usual, ordinary way of experiencing things and not being in contact with this deeper, more fundamental truth. So being in the world but not of it is like, I am now the presence, the reality, but I'm talking with you. We're discussing things. And I feel that I have a heart and so do you. And our hearts are communicating. And it's amazing wisdom. It shows how to be contactual, how to be personal, how to be aware of the other person and their uniqueness and how to be attuned to them – what hurts, what doesn't hurt, what's useful. So although the truth is sort of impersonal, but also it can present a personal quality that shows what is life and how life can be lived from a place that is outside of life. Like really, being in the world but not of it – not of it means I am not of the physical, I am not an individual

9

human being with a history, a mother and father who has a job and – no, I am something much more mysterious, much faster. At the same time, I am a human being who is a conduit for that. So that mystery works through the individual and lives as an individual. It reminds me of a Christian precept that says "I live not, but Christ liveth in me". So I can say, I live not, but truth liveth in me. That's one way of saying it.

Iain: And the starting point really for being a more real human being is the recognition of presence, isn't it? Because that gives you the reference point. That gives you, as I like to call it, the ground of being. And with that I know for myself of the dangers running off from these automatic programmes. But somehow if there's a groundedness and a feeling of presence – in your books you call it essence a lot of the time – with that essence we have something real to relate from.

Hameed: Something real, authentic. Because usually, in the ordinary sense that I was, and most people are, is to be an individual that is mostly the creation of our history and our mind. Our ideas about ourselves, the programmeming from our childhood. That makes us be a kind of self and we believe we are that self. And we believe we are the body with a mind, physically. So most of us don't know, until we wake up. That's what spiritual work is all about. It's to wake up to – what are you really? What is reality? And so that was the beginning of my waking up. You see, I think that what happened in the cafeteria was the beginning of waking up. I didn't recognise true nature, but I realised that wasn't me. I didn't want to be that way.

Iain: Yes.

Hameed: The next thing is recognising, 'Oh, that's me. That's what I am and that's what everybody is.'

Iain: But why doesn't that spark become more of a flame in most people? Because although there's a growing interest in waking up, it's still quite rare that somebody has the courage and the motivation, the drive if you like, to really follow things through like you have. Why is that? I think you actually said – one of the things I wrote down – is that "Man is asleep, little do we know what this means, the extent of this sleep". And the more I've learned through your work, the more I've realised how man's asleep and how I'm asleep. So how is it that there's not more of what's so obvious when you see it. How is it there isn't more of an interest in this search in most people?

Hameed: Different teachings will explain it in different ways. Some teachings say, "Your karma" – your Eastern teachers of karma. If you come from more Western teachings they will say "God's will. God's grace comes to some people but not others."

The way I understand it – which is just another story because nobody really knows the true reasons behind it – it's a mystery and we can just have approximations of it – is that reality as a whole, the truth I saw, the truth I realised as truth, which then I realised as love, but then I realised as awareness, and consciousness, conscious of itself and its presence. At some point it was revealed that it is not just something inside me, but it is everywhere. Inside you, inside everybody, inside everything. It is not only inside everything, it is everything. It is the inside of everything. The other side of everything. Our physicality, our thoughts, the chairs and the furniture is the outside appearance of something alive and mysterious and conscious. And that reveals itself in different ways, like it's experimenting with different ways it experiences reality. So it experiences reality through the rock, through the tree, through the alligator, through human beings. And then at some point, through some human being, it wakes up completely to what it is. You see. Now, it is not something that chooses to do it one way or another. It is – you know, you hear lately about intelligent design. Scientists realising this universe has a design that seems to indicate intelligence. And some people use it to say, "Yeah, that means God created things that way." I think of intelligent design more as this consciousness, this force is intelligent. And just as intelligence usually experiments with this and that, some experiments work better than others. It is like that. It is evolving and developing different ways it can reveal itself. And in some places it succeeds in revealing itself fully. And in other places it's still working and probably will reveal itself one way or another. So I don't think me as an individual is what did it. I'm not that special as an individual. It is being itself, true nature itself, this mysterious force and power and nature beyond, somehow chose this individual and put them through various karmic experiences. Life made me be born in Kuwait and live there for eighteen years, made me go to the US to study physics so my mind will have the precision and the logic of the scientist. And then made me go and study psychology so I could understand the mind and consciousness. And then oriented me toward particular books, toward particular teachings. It used my mind and consciousness and body to know itself. And now it knows itself and I realise that is what I am. And at the same time I am an individual human being. So the back and the front.

Iain: Yes.

Hameed: The front is the individual that you see. The back is an unfathomable mystery that can reveal itself in many ways. It can be love, it can be truth, it can be awareness, it can be non-dual awareness or it can be dual awareness.

Iain: Could you talk more about the knowing. Is it a knowing that is expanding the whole time? Or is the base of the knowing always there and always basically the same thing?

Hameed: It is more than knowing. It is difficult to say what it is. In fact, there is no way to describe it, to delimit it, because it is unlimited in what it is. It has the capacity to know. Knowing is one of its capacities. Consciousness, awareness is one of its capacities. What people call non-dual awareness is just one of its capacities. It can be aware in other ways, you see. And this truth, this reality that expresses itself through all of us, that's what I see. And it's not just the basis – it is the basis of my teaching, right. And even to say *my* teaching is not accurate. It's not mine. It's true nature's teaching, you know, an instrument. This individual, called Hameed, is an instrument for this magnificent, unfathomable to express itself and to know itself and enjoy life on Earth. How something indefinite, formless becomes a human being who walks and talks and experiences and loves and interacts. That is an amazing thing.

Iain: It's a miracle, in so many ways.

Hameed: It's a miracle. It's always a miracle when we recognise that. When we're just in our usual, ordinary level of experience we don't see the miracle. We think we are those biological entities who are trying to survive and maybe be happy. And when we recognise this, when we recognise our true nature, we realise it's an adventure. It's an adventure of discovery, of learning, of developing. And living life is a matter of discovering and expressing what we discover at the same time. I live it, enjoy it, and I'm also learning all the time. When I use the word 'I' it's confusing because there is no 'I' in the usual sense.

Iain: And the excitement of your learning is coming from consciousness – the expression of your consciousness.

Hameed: I, as a consciousness, enjoy you. I can feel your heart. I feel a sweetness between us and that for me brings us closer because we're already one in a very deep way. From consciousness perspective, which is what my essence is – my true nature, my true condition, my true being – there is no separation between us.

Iain: And in our human form, in a way that's what we're seeking, isn't it? We're seeking this completeness the whole time and we look outside and we try and have more of this and more of that because we want to feel happier and better on the inside. Maybe it's an oversimplification but the way I see it is that's all a way – it's all a false way in its own way – of trying somewhere to get back to the one, to the completeness.

Hameed: I wouldn't call it a false way. I would say a misinterpretation. Because it's natural to want to be happy. Because our nature is happiness and we want to be our nature. It's inherent to us. Every human being wants to be happy. Why would they want to be depressed? You can imagine a race of beings who want to be depressed, or want to be hateful all the time. No, you want to be happy. Why? Because we are moved from deep within us, from the depths to be happy because that is what we are. If we really are relaxed and open and at ease, and being ourselves completely, we're pure delight.

Iain: Pure delight. Yes.

Hameed: Pure delight.

Iain: There's something I want to explore with you in terms of the different stages that you went through and I think other people go through in their own way. I think you say that first of all there was a realisation, there was presence, which you called essence. And you were with essence. And then there was a realisation, or the integration that essence and you were the same thing. And then there was a further realisation that you were the ground of being I think you said containing essence. Can you just talk us through those stages?

Hameed: That's the stages I went through. Some people, some masters, they say they had an awakening and they are suddenly enlightened and they see everything is one. It didn't happen exactly that way with me. For me it was a growing, a presence that grew. It had an infinite mystery in it and it was teaching my mind, my consciousness about it a step at a time. So first I was experiencing something that comes. Something that descends, or arises, you know, sending force. Some people, like Aurobindo, call it something that arises within... it comes from deep within the heart. And I was still being the human individual, what I call the person or the personal or the self. At some point that presence manifested itself in such a way that it made me confront my identity. What am I? Am I really this person experiencing this presence? And I realised that person was a shell, an empty construct of concepts and ideas and memories from the past that my mind has constructed.

Iain: But when you saw that, how was that for you? Because that's quite a devastating realisation.

Hameed: It was. It made me feel ... to be that individual, I realised it felt empty, meaningless, 'Oh, that's why sometimes I feel life is meaningless. That's why sometimes I feel there is no significance.' That's inherent to the sense of the ordinary self, which I call the ego-self, which for me is a stage of development. Being manifests itself gradually, this is one of its first stages. And then I saw a gap between that and this luminous presence. And that gap felt like an abyss – scary. And at some point by knowing the psychology – I was led to study self-psychology, Kohut and others – through that guidance, I saw those books and that's I wanted to read. I saw them in Karen's husband's house who was studying psychiatry. So that's interesting, I wasn't interested in those things before. And I started and learned about self-psychology and how the self develops. And I said oh yeah, that's how it goes. And I realised, but that is not exactly me. That is a fake self, false self.

Iain: It's a reflection of you, I think you talk about it being a reflection.

Hameed: A reflection, it's like a partial expression of what I am but I was seeing that's what I am. And that belief created a separation from the true nature, from the luminous consciousness. And when I saw that disconnection, that disconnection dissolved. And when it dissolved I realised that luminous presence is what I am. And that was it. It continued to be that way, but that luminous presence wasn't just one thing. It kept growing and developing, so what I am is not one static thing. That's what many people believe: they get realised, enlightened, and you become pure awareness or pure emptiness or pure love. I have been those and I still am those, but I am something else also – something more mysterious.

Iain: And are there times in life practically, you look back on the response that you, as Hameed, had to a certain event and you see that could be more refined, that response, so you make a decision or there's a realisation that next time you might act differently? Are those human processes still running?

Hameed: Yes. They're always running. There is a continual refinement of both my understanding of what reality is and how to be skilful in living life. What I do, my choices, my interactions, my communications. I'm always getting better. Or, let's say, reality is learning to hone the instrument and make it a more and more perfect expression. So that it not only enjoys its expression, but it communicates so that other manifestations of the self also begin to enjoy that expression. That's why there's teaching. The teaching is simply sharing this beauty. But it's not me sharing the beauty. It is true nature. It's not 'I' who developed the whole school that I have developed, that people think I co-founded. I didn't co-found. I'm not, as an individual, capable of doing something like that. So being itself, true nature itself, this mysterious spirit developed this individual manifestation and developed the school that we call Ridhwan School. And what is coming through the students and the teachers from our school.

Iain: One of the things that I've been kind of wrestling with over the years – wrestling is probably too strong a word – but I've been intrigued by over the years, is these different people claim awakeness, self-realisation, enlightenment. And it seems from listening to you that the process is never-ending. So there is not a definitive state that somebody can reach, as a human being on this planet at this time. You mention the refinement is always going on. Do you ever feel that you've met someone or you know of someone or indeed you feel in yourself the capacity to reach this, what we might call perfect balance, or perfect expression of the oneness?

Hameed: There are many teachings who teach that you reach a certain place. Like if you're Buddhist it's realising Dharmakaya. In Vedanta you become Brahman, or Satchitananda. They define exactly what it is, you know. And if you're a Sufi you become pure love. Right. And if you're a Christian you become one with Christ or one with the Father. So many teachings have an end point that is well defined although they have different schools, slight variations. And I believe that myself. The teachings, this being showed me these things. At some point I was Brahman for several years. I was Dharmakaya for several years.

Iain: You're talking about in this lifetime or –

Hameed: In this lifetime, as part of the development of this teaching I was the Dharmakaya, non-dual awareness for several years. I was in total stillness of Brahman for several years. All those happened. And I thought at those times, "That's it." I read the books, I study, I read the teachings, and they all say yeah, that's it. And I believe that's it. And I'm happy, comfortable being that and I'll teach it. And then at some point it changes. And of course my mind gets into, what's going on? I'm disoriented – what's going on? I thought that's it! And then what happens – like one time, for one example, I was teaching a group on non-conceptual pure awareness. And as I was teaching, the whole thing was manifesting. Non-conceptual, pure, transparent awareness is filling the whole room, being the whole room, and manifesting. But as I was saying that, I felt myself receding back. Going back. And going deeper. My consciousness was receding back and I could see everybody, I could see the whole room. I see pure awareness and I realise all pure awareness and all this is happening within me. And then I realise the whole universe is happening within me. And that was something different. I wasn't just pure awareness, I was the source of pure awareness. This mysterious, undefinable source of pure awareness. This is just an example of how it changes. That was one of the changes and there's no last change.

Iain: You said your mind was responding somehow – what was that? Was it out of regret or was it basically the excitement of something new, more paramount?

Hameed: Part of it was concern that something went wrong, like maybe there's something in me I haven't worked out, that I don't understand about myself. And yes there was, because what wasn't worked out was a need to be something. To be something. Even though it was formless and formless pure awareness, I was still being something.

Iain: You were still being something ...

Hameed: I was being something. Even though I wasn't an individual self, I was still something that is real. That is still – you can touch it and feel it and it's stable. And everybody wants that stability. And I realized there was a need for stability. And then what I learned by things changing, was the stability is not it. To be stable in one place is a limitation of the freedom of true nature.

Iain: But isn't it basically the mind that is wanting the stability? But that's not the way –

Hameed: Well, that's it. Everybody wants stability in their life. Because it's security, right. But the true nature itself – you see, there are people who reach a place, one place, and they stay at. I've met people like that, like the Karmapa I mentioned – he was expansive, pure awareness. Non-dual all the time, I think he was like that. He might grow bigger or smaller as he lived, but he was that. I could see that. I've met other people who are different things. But in time I learned that for me, it wasn't arriving at a place. For me enlightenment, in the Diamond Approach, the way we learned it, is not recognising a particular condition of reality. It is the freedom for reality to keep discovering itself without restraint. What's the true enlightenment in Diamond Approach, is freedom. Freedom for being to express itself in whatever way it does at any time. It is playing and enjoying and being creative.

Iain: Do you find the human side of you still has to sometimes, in its own way, accept things? Or is acceptance taken for granted now – acceptance always happens inside you?

Hameed: Sometimes, like when I am in physical pain, I don't like it. It's difficult. What's difficult is that discomfort – although I can accept it and I can hold it, and I can be bigger, but it is discomfort. It sometimes takes a while for me to let it be. That happens. Because as an individual, I'm still learning, see. But as being, I'm free.

Iain: I wrote down – it's funny, it just appeared in front of me – I wrote down one of the things you said when I was researching. "Suffering is a heavenly message."

Hameed: Yeah.

Iain: It's not always easy to see at the time.

Hameed: Yes, suffering – you see, in Buddhism the whole approach is how to be free from suffering. The whole approach is inherent to life is suffering. And the teaching is how to be free from the suffering. And the way to be free from the suffering is to be free from the self. And to just be the empty awareness or true nature. I'm not interested in being free from suffering. I am much freer from suffering than – I don't have psychological suffering, let's put it that way. I have physical suffering but not psychological suffering. However, my interest is not freedom from suffering. That's not what I teach.

What I teach is to love the truth and to enjoy the discovery. To enjoy. We are not here just to be free from being here. We are here to fulfil it. To be what it is for. Reality didn't manifest all of this so that to get rid of it. It manifested this so that to experience things in a certain way, to manifest someone's potentiality that hasn't been expressed yet. And that is exciting and it's wondrous and that's what I want to teach people. I want them to catch the wonder and the delight of discovering reality.

Suffering will be dealt with. We need to deal with suffering because that's part of the obstacles to the delight, part of the obstacles to the freedom. Because we're fixated, we're imprisoned by the suffering. It's part of what we need to deal with. But I deal with it and I teach my students to deal with it. We have to. But it is part of the story.

The main thing for me is this luminous delight that comes through, that wants, that lives – to say even wants is human approximation. It just does it. The nature of what I am, what you are, is to express itself. To manifest itself as fully as possible and to know itself more. But it cannot know itself except through an individual consciousness like you or me. Human beings are needed by this mysterious ground to express itself, to be itself, to talk with each other.

Iain: We were talking at lunch earlier and I was just thinking that you love Sherlock Holmes. And really you use that whole world of Sherlock Holmes in this; you say that some of the puzzles that he has to solve are quite difficult puzzles. But you, the vehicle that is you, is really alive by trying to solve this constant adventure of consciousness. Not necessarily trying to solve but exploring this constant adventure of consciousness.

Hameed: It is an adventure of consciousness. And that's what Aurobindo called it, he talked about adventure of consciousness. And I agree with the thing about freedom from suffering because I think there is a lot of suffering in the world. And I see the suffering being manifested as kindness and compassion and wanting to help, to do whatever I can. But I want to help not to be free from suffering – the real help is for them to see the delight of their being. Because their suffering cannot go away without them seeing the delight of their being. See, the disconnection from what we are is the main source of our psychological suffering. And that all teachings know.

Iain: So we only have about two minutes left. Anything you wanted to say in the last two minutes?

Hameed: Not to assume it's difficult, not to assume it's impossible, not to assume only special people can do it. But also, the other thing is not to believe it is something to arrive at. But to continue being interested in what is true, what is real, what is authentic. And it has no end. Like right now, for instance, people talk about non-dual awareness being everywhere. I feel that, but at the same time I feel I am in your heart. I am in your heart. You know why I am in your heart? Because even though I perceive that you are over there and I am here, in my heart there isn't that. In my true heart there is only one heart. It's like being inside your heart. And you are inside my heart. I could be inside the heart of anybody. In a sense, I am feeling their heart. I am the essence of their heart. That's a different kind of realisation. People talk about non-dual, boundless. This is not non-dual. It is beyond non-dual, beyond dual. And that is just an example, another way that the enlightenment realisation can happen. So I'm inviting people not to box it in. Each tradition tends to box it in as one thing. And it's true, each thing is freedom and liberation. But freedom and liberation can be even *further* freedom and liberation – even freedom and liberation from those freedoms and liberations. So the freedom liberates itself from being anything in particular.

19

Iain: Okay. That's a wonderful place to finish, Hameed. Thank you very much.

Hameed: Not being anything in particular (laughter).

Iain: I really enjoyed our meeting. It was very special.

Hameed: It was so sweet. I get to be a being that expresses itself.

Iain: Thank you, Hameed. It was wonderful meeting you here.

Hameed: Oh, it was fun too, Iain.

Jessica Britt –
The Great Alchemy
Interview by **Iain McNay**

*F*eeling the inner spaciousness, inner qualities like compassion, strength, I slowly began recognising they were not just reactive feelings. There was a palpable feeling of kindness and it was like the sense of 'here-ness' took on a whole other texture. Like now, I'm here, not only in feelings and belly, I'm actually here in presence [...] Now I'm in my body, the sense of consciousness, the sense of 'I' was less located in my history, like I could hardly remember my history. Like, self-thought or self-awareness, less and less and less was attached to history and more and more it was a feeling of the simplicity of awareness, a kind of palpable presence that was a new feeling of, "Now I'm really here, and what's here is way more than my history. It's coloured by my history, it's textured by my history.*

Iain: Jessica is a teacher in the Ridhwan School, which I've been a student of for about eighteen years. We're going to hear about Jessica's life, which is a very interesting story. And also hear about some of her work, as well. So, let's start with what we were talking about earlier, before we started recording. You were telling me that when you were around three years old, you were in hospital and you were in a body cast. And you had quite an interesting experience.

Jessica: First of all, this was a long time ago, so hospitals were very different. There were twelve children on one ward and my felt feeling was of being consciousness – it actually touched me saying it – being this consciousness that was hovering, taking care of the children. I had mostly a sense of the children and the suffering. I don't remember having much of a sense of *my* suffering – I was very aware of the other children's suffering and a profound sense of aloneness that was actually very sad. And so it was a sad environment and some part of me rose up to it, literally, and responded in some way.

Iain: It's difficult when you're very young isn't it, and this sense of loneliness.

Jessica: Ah, it's very difficult. It's very difficult. And one of the things I was sharing with you and, looking at different interviews that you and Renate have done, I was really aware of how many of the teachers we love and honour had really good childhoods and I recognised that my destiny is quite different in that I had a really difficult childhood and with a tremendous amount of aloneness and unkindness in it together with a neglect of a certain kind. And so I felt very alone, very isolated and at the same time, determined to figure out what this human life was about ... because my sense of what I was having, wasn't a very good one and I thought, "Something is really off."

Iain: When were you first aware of this determination?

Jessica: Interesting question. Probably around eight or nine ... ten ...

Iain: It must have really impact on your character, because I know for myself, when determination comes in, it really starts to change something.

Jessica: You know, it does, it actually gave me a sense of – which I recognised later – of enquiry, like I really wanted to understand it. What was reality? What was being a human being? I actually, truthfully, didn't know or feel particularly human at that point. I was so withdrawn, but with a very curious, very watchful intelligence. And I can remember at one point, telling my mother I wanted to see a therapist. And I can remember her saying, "Why?" And I said, "Because I'm suffering'" and her response at that time was, "Everyone suffers."

Iain: Yes, yes.

Jessica: She didn't support it so I went into a nursing school and there, my withdrawn nature, my solitude, got the attention of my teachers and they actually opened the door for me to work with my first therapist – a Freudian.

Iain: So it took you quite a long time from eight years old when you first had this feeling of determination to find out what life was about, until what, your early twenties when you were working as a nurse?

Jessica: I was probably around twenty when I started seeing the Freudian analyst and doing face-to-face work. It was a fascinating process. First of all, he responded to my story in such a human way. I still, to this day, feel deeply touched when I remember a tear in his eye when I was telling him something.

Iain: Without going into detail, you were abused when you were a child so you had quite a heavy load to carry and a lot to explore and understand.

Jessica: I had a lot to explore coming from a very abusive atmosphere for myself and my brothers, from a stepfather. That was one of the things – it's a very common story on the planet. So, I found myself turning toward psychiatric nursing and I actually worked with children. I was just very infused with the knowledge of how much suffering there was – emotional suffering for so many human beings.

Iain: But it must have brought you a lot of feeling of compassion for the children you were working with …

Jessica: Totally.

Iain: ... and experiencing this.

Jessica: Totally. Once, when I was still in nursing school, I had to write a treatment plan for a child I was working with – a beautiful, beautiful three-year-old who actually died of cancer, it was very touching – and I remember my nurse supervisor telling me I was too emotionally involved. And I remember knowing very clearly that she was wrong. But I did shape-shift myself to do what she wanted, you know, wrote the report, but I knew inside that I was on to something that was much needed and real and that I needed to let my heart guide me.

Iain: So you were starting to have the therapeutic sessions with the Freudian therapist. How did you find that?

Jessica: Well, I'd say, it organised the chaos of my story. Just telling the story, telling my experiences and having someone listen. It started to break open the feeling of isolation. That was the main thing it did for me, it organised ... so I felt less crazy. It started to make sense of why I felt the way I did, even though I wasn't fully into the feeling level of it yet. That happened when I got to California.

Iain: That's a relief in itself, isn't it? When you start to understand why you feel the way you do?

Jessica: It was a huge relief. And I remember I read like crazy, like I really wanted to understand what a person was, what an ego was. I was just determined and my determination basically got me out of the East Coast to California and there I worked as a nurse, again. I went into psychiatric nursing as my main emphasis and worked with children. And that led to an exploration of Jungian work. The Jungians offer what is called 'sand tray therapy' which is fascinating. The Freudian world *organised* my story and then the Jungian world, kind of, opened up what's known as the world of archetypes – large, governing principles beyond my personal mother and father, like the 'great mother', the anima, the female part of the man. So, it opened up a larger view. And that's what I started feeling, like every new thing opened up a larger view.

Iain: So you were starting a journey weren't you? You took from the Freudian work what you could take from the time. It took you to a certain level and then something else that opens up. So, you move on to Jungian work?

Jessica: Yes, right, and actually, as you say that, what I realise ... I mean I went through a few. The one that really got my interest and has not let me go has been the Diamond Approach work. So, from the Jungian work – long story short – I ended up – and working with children in psychiatry – I ended up at the Esalen Institute.

Iain: Which is in California.

Jessica: Which is in California. It was one of the original human potential centres. And Dick Price, who was one of the co-founders of Esalen, and his wife, Chris Price, had a programmeme where they invited people working in the community ... like for a while I worked with children who had been raped and suffered incest. Very intense work. So, Dick would invite people working in the streets, in the community at large, to Esalen for a week of rest and their own work and that's where I got introduced to Gestalt Therapy.

Iain: This was homeless people he'd invite in?

Jessica: No, no, he'd invite people, people like myself ... the service workers, the nurses, the doctors, the therapists, the social workers, and that's where things really broke wide open. That's where I first started experiencing Gestalt work and so, everything I *talked* about in Freudian work, that I *thought* about, in Jungian work, I actually started feeling in the Gestalt work. It was really quite an eye-opener for me.

Iain: So, you were coming really into your body at that stage, the beginning of a process of discovering your body.

Jessica: I was totally coming into my body and again, in graphic memory, my very first Gestalt group, I remember it with a smile. Chris Price did a guided imagery and the content of the imagery was so based on my history and I was lying there and I was thinking, "That brat [*laughs*], she's going to get me into feelings, right!" I'm a New Yorker, I'm sophisticated and, long story short, the next thing I know, I am sobbing and crying, Chris is one side and Dick's on the other. I mean, I'd never had such an experience, and in that experience, as the sobbing softened, I remember, I remember to this day, that my hands, my body, felt so alive with my presence, with my consciousness. I was startled. I remember just holding my hand up in wonderment. It made me realise how far away I was. It touches me to say it – I was so far away, so far away. So, I just became ... it was like the feeling was, "I'll do anything to stay and find out what this is here."

Iain: That, in itself, was deepening your commitment.

Jessica: That's true, that's true.

Iain: ... to take things to another level.

Jessica: Yes, I became a total explorer of what it is that we are.

Iain: That must have been a very exciting time because I remember interviewing in this studio, maybe a year ago, Claudio Naranjo ...

Jessica: Oh, yes.

Iain: ... who also went to Esalen and worked there and it was a whole new thing, wasn't it, where people were starting to explore themselves and find out more how they ticked, how they worked.

Jessica: Definitely. I was at Esalen in the eighties, so Claudio was there more in the seventies. I did not work with him directly, though of course I'd heard of him. I mean, he's made such an incredible contribution, not only in the Enneagram but also in Gestalt work. But, you know, Stan Grof, R. D. Laing were there, Timothy Leary, you know, John Lilly, the wild ones!

Iain: It was a place, wasn't it?

Jessica: It was *the* place. My focus really was on discovering – along with Chris Price and Dick Price – really working with myself and others, opening ourselves up to what really we're experiencing if we let the masks down; basically, if we really allow ourselves.

Iain: Was that scary for you?

Jessica: Ah … certain feelings were and certain feelings were not. It was easy to get me to cry. Anger was a whole other thing! Anyway, I won't go into all the details, but I had a dream with a very aggressive figure in it and I knew if I worked on it with Dick Price that he'd ask me to become that figure. I had known, for two years, that he'd been working me up to feeling my anger [*laughs*] Directly! And I knew that if I sat on that seat, which he called the 'open seat', something unexpected would happen. So, I ended up on the seat. Something other than my mind put me on that seat and I remember saying to him, "If I tell you this dream, you're going to …" and I started crying. And he said, "Okay, let's just go for it." So, needless to say, I had this very huge experience of aggression and anger at my own bottled up rage.

What's spiritually significant about this, that took on more and more meaning over time, was that, in the middle of feeling rage – and it was a pillow-pounding furious rage – In the middle of it, some inner light of consciousness was there. And it had a sense of 'I' and, I knew, "Ah, I'm experiencing anger and I'm not a killer." And I'm in the middle of raging while this is happening and then the feeling was, "I have anger, but I'm not anger."

You see, what was so powerful there, I would never have known that if I hadn't had the space to feel the anger. I would have pushed it away out of fear of being it. And by allowing it to be fully felt and expressed in this very safe environment with people I loved and trusted, who had a lot of presence, had a lot of integrity, I discovered, "Oh, my God, I have all these experiences, but some part of me is not these experiences." That was a very big door. A very big door … that's kept opening.

Iain: Well, that is the big one, you're right, because for myself, when that started to happen, that intrigued me even more because that was taking me, "Well, who am I really? If I'm not all these experiences, these emotions, then who am I?"

Jessica: Right, right.

Iain: Which is the kind of ultimate question, really.

Jessica: Yes, I get chills when you say that. I feel touched as you say that. Maybe that's why we share a similar path – the Diamond Approach.

Iain: So you mention Diamond Approach, again, and of course, Diamond Approach is a school started by Hameed Ali – A. H. Almaas is his pen name – and you met Hameed at a very early stage, didn't you, before he'd started the Ridhwan School, Diamond Approach work?

Jessica: Yes, yes. As we were talking about earlier, because of my childhood, I felt so fundamentally disembodied. The technical language would be 'disassociated'. I was so in my own mental realm that I needed the body-centred work of practitioners such as Dick Price and Christ
So, I wasn't living at Esalen yet, so I was looking for a Gestalt practitioner to continue my work, up in the Bay area, and I couldn't find one that was body centred. Someone suggested I find a Reichian therapist, someone who works with the breath and the body and emotions and a friend said, "Why don't you start working with Hameed Ali?" And I met Hameed. I actually saw him at a social gathering and he had the kindest face. And the other thing I realise at this moment – as we're talking about bodies – he walks with a cane because he had polio and I remember thinking to myself, "He will understand me" because I'd been in this body cast for three years and I had a very crippled self image. So, I chose him. And I had no idea he was a spiritual teacher. So, the first couple of years, I just would go, you know, lie down, do the breathing work, have different emotions, feel my body more and more, unwinding and opening and then I noticed, he started asking me questions that nobody had ever asked me before.

Iain: Such as?

Jessica: I can remember this one time he asked me during a breathing session, "What are you feeling in your chest?" And I said, "Nothing." Now, in the past, someone would have gone to something, or had me breathe more, so I had something more to report and he said to me, "What's the *nothing* like?" And I can remember just rolling my eyes and looking up at him and saying, "Hameed, what is *nothing* like? Nothing is nothing." So, he's sitting there and in his very kind way, he goes, "Well, is it a light nothing, or a dark nothing?" That was the most outrageous question anyone had ever asked me. He said, "Is it a light nothing, or a dark nothing?" I shut my eyes and began to sense much more immediately and carefully. I remember saying, "It's a dark nothing." And he said, "Well, what's it like?"

In describing the indescribable *nothing*, something opened and I actually recognised a kind of spaciousness in my chest – as if I'd taken acid or something like it. It opened up this other door and over time, I recognised during conversations he'd suddenly go, "Did you notice over here? What about that?" In Gestalt you're not supposed to ask questions, but Hameed's questions opened me up to other realms that made me appreciate at a whole other level that what I am, what you are, what everything is, is way beyond our normal mode of perception and understanding. If you ask the right question, if you slow down enough to sense and feel. Reality reveals things that a young girl from New York never suspected.

Iain: I'm going to read something which really interested me from the comprehensive notes you gave me before the interview me because, from the early sessions with Hameed, you wrote that he was helping you to awaken to the beginning of a recognition of different levels and dimensions of being present. Present in name, present in feeling, present in body, present in consciousness. Can you say something of those different levels of presence?

Jessica: I think it's just a very simple way of saying it. As my own sense of self started being released from just my history, I would recognise for instance that I go to a party and I know my name, I know who my parents are. I could say, "Ah, I'm here, I'm at the party." And then, I noticed, that as I learned about feelings, my sense of this 'here-ness' took on another palpable octave, fullness, richness. It was like, "Oh wow, now I'm really here!" And then my body and my sensing and my recognising – because I'd been out of my body, so now I'm like *in* it – I'm going, "I am my body. Oh my God!" Now, I'm *really, really, really, really* here, right? I'm really here now, full, embodied.

And then, as the inner realms started opening, first really feeling the inner spaciousness, inner qualities like compassion, strength, I slowly began recognising they were not just reactive feelings. There was a palpable feeling of kindness and it was like the sense of 'here-ness' took on a whole other texture. Like now, I'm here, not only in feelings and belly, I'm actually here in presence. But then it became even more interesting, like, now I started noticing, now I'm in my body, the sense of consciousness, the sense of 'I' was less located in my history, like I could hardly remember my history. Like, self-thought or self-awareness, less and less and less was attached to history and more and more it was a feeling of the simplicity of awareness, a kind of palpable [*long pause*] yes, these things are hard to talk about – a palpable presence that was a new feeling of, "now I'm really here, and what's here is way more than my history. It's coloured by my history, it's textured by my history." So, like the light of the awareness itself ... I feel a lot of love right now, actually, as I'm speaking [*Jessica is emotionally moved ...* [*laughs*] ...

You'd better ask me a question. I think I'm on a roll! [*laughs*] Yes.

Iain: What I'm thinking as you talk, is that, in a way this is very different from what other people sometimes say, that the body can be like an entrapment. You get caught and that reinforces the 'I', the kind of a narrowness of the human self. Whereas, your experience has been from your disassociation from your body as a child because of the traumatic experiences and coming back through these different therapies as you did, into the body, and the body not only has started to give you an idea of who you are on a human level, but has expanded it beyond that.

Jessica: Beautifully said, yes. And as you say it, I'm in touch with some sadness for people who see the body as a solid object. I mean, if we take spiritual teachings really deeply, really seriously ... for instance emptiness in Buddhism. What are you talking about? You know they say, essentially, this body can be experienced as transparent, as an open system. I can feel my body as dissolved and just spaciousness. I can feel it, as started happening when I was talking about it, as love. It's not just an emotion. And so the body itself is not something separate from being-ness. We're not just this being that kind of enters the body and we die. When one takes the spiritual perspective and really hears it fully, then it must include the body. It must. The body can't be separate from your true nature.

Iain: And importantly, that was your experience, as well. It was the kind of portal, the gateway for you, wasn't it?

Jessica: It was the gateway for me. Then it was the gateway for me for the miracle of life, for love manifesting. We can talk about awareness manifesting, we can talk about appearance and emptiness co-existing. I mean, there're so many different ways of talking about it. And also I realise, each person's conversation is a contribution because no *one* person can give voice to the miracle of what the totality is, No one single enlightenment can give voice to it. Each one of us has a different purpose, different destiny.

One of the things I've come to realise through the path, is a that part of my function is related to the fact that I made the journey from the most disappeared, dark place to really feeling the luminous goodness of reality and I am so okay. This is in itself helpful for many of the students I work with, especially people who have tough histories.

Iain: But it also took that commitment early on and the courage to follow it through, the determination and the adventure of finding the different therapies that helped you and one thing led to another. It's not always a straightforward, easy journey, is it?

Jessica: [*laughs*]

Iain: You have to follow the clues and stay in there …

Jessica: Right, right.

Iain: … and stay with the feelings as you were saying.

Jessica: Basically, it really helps if you've got a strong, strong curiosity that won't be stopped.

Iain: There's one thing you put in your notes, I also wanted to bring up briefly, that I thought was interesting, was that in the early days you tried meditation and it didn't work for you. It took the discovery of the body and the broadening of who you really are until meditation was something important in your life.

Jessica: Yes, you know it was really interesting for me, contemplating my journey to be here with you today, and I suddenly saw so many people whose path really has been through the classic meditation path and I'm struck by so many of them having really good parenting – not everybody, of course. I was already in such aloneness, for me to go sit on a pillow alone, there was too much congestion and suffering in this location [*gestures to her body*] I couldn't do it. It was like I needed to 'un-congest' myself to even have enough room.

I can remember when I was on this two-week meditation retreat – I'd already started working with Hameed – I was in so much pain and suffering and I felt like a total failure. And I went and saw Hameed and went, "Phew!" And he said, "Jessica, you know, kindness, kindness."

Just going from the body cast ... to be sitting in that posture. "Phew!" So, I needed – this is my location [*pointing to her body*] – I needed to open up some space where I could even begin to sit. You know, I love the Dalai Lama. He's one of my inspirations. He talks about how loved he was, so he's sitting learning meditation surrounded by love, right? That wasn't my beginning. So when I sat on the zafu, I still was feeling like an empty shell with no love around and the zafu just felt like, basically being in prison and I didn't have enough inner resources yet to understand the nature of the prison.

Iain: How long did it take you from first working with Hameed Ali and starting the Diamond Approach work 'til you really started to feel that you had a ground that was supporting you and you were really on your way, so to speak?

Jessica: Good question. Let's see ... I started with Dick and Chris probably in '74, met Hameed in '76. I would say by the time – probably by '84, '85 – I started feeling some kind of palpable inner ground. And as I say that, I'm also recognising one of the wonders of being graced with living in Big Sur for ten years, was literally all the movement work I did. It started giving me legs, the walking I did, the hiking. So I started feeling an internal ground and I started feeling connected to the literal earth, the ground, and it all worked in harmony.

Iain: Were there any particular breakthroughs you remember that were really important? Things you did or realisations you had?

Jessica: Ah, there's so many. Do you have a particular level?

Iain: I'm just very interested in when you had the early adventures. You were going through the different therapies and then you stayed with the Diamond Approach for thirty years or something, now...

Jessica: Which is beyond a therapy.

Iain: Yes, absolutely, it's almost a way of life, isn't it? You talked about one of your first sessions with Hameed. What were your other really impactful times or some, just one or two as examples?

Jessica: Well, it's interesting this comes up. I can remember my being in dialogue with Hameed and before I had the conversation with him – I think I must have been driving to go see him, or something – and I was doing my practice of sensing my arms and legs and I started going through and said, "Okay, I feel my feelings, I feel my body, I even feel my awareness." And I suddenly realised I had no idea *who* or *what* I was. It was the strangest thing. And so I went into this session or conversation – I don't remember the context – "Hameed!" I said, "Hameed! I feel my body, I feel my emotions, I know what I'm thinking, I feel my awareness, I feel the 'I' that's aware of all these things and I don't know who I am!" [*laughs*] It was this innocence, right. And I remember him saying, "I was wondering when you would notice." [*laughs*]

Iain: [*laughs*]

Jessica: I was in a group meeting. He said those words and all of a sudden the whole room started spinning. And I fell into a huge black space. Many, people write about this. It was like the black night and the stars and I suddenly really felt myself as a point of light. As this was happening, I remembered that point of light from when I did that anger piece I told you about earlier and I started feeling – and I get chills – that point of light as 'I'. It was an 'I' that was so beyond history and then, over time, that point of light became like an anchor and then it started changing. And I can remember going, "Where's the point? Where's my point of light?" Because, it was just space. And then, *it* started opening up. So the thing just keeps opening. In the Diamond Approach, we call it, 'open, open-ended enquiry'. No place is the final resting place. Anyway, I could just … it just keeps opening.

Iain: This interests me. So, who you are is constantly changing and yet you don't lose your ground of support even though who you are is changing, or who you feel you are, or your experience of who you are is changing, the ground, the being shall we say, is still supporting you. Is that the case?

Jessica: Yes, but it's even more mysterious than that.

Iain: Yes, go on.

Jessica: The ground sometimes feels like just dense holding and sometimes it feels like nothing is ground, kind of like the night sky that holds the planets. From when I was a little girl, feeling the emptiness as totally deficient and void, the emptiness or the spaciousness becomes an openness that creates the space for everything to arise and the openness itself, paradoxically, becomes ground.

Iain: So what does being awake mean to you?

Jessica: What is being awake? It means a love affair with reality. It means a sense of the grace and luminous that's at the core of everything that manifests, even hatred. Even hatred.

Iain: So, explain that. When we think of being awake we think, "Well, that's someone that's beyond hatred." I use the word 'we' but that would be my understanding – that it's moved beyond hatred.

Jessica: I don't know … first of all, I don't believe anything in 'anything is final'…

Iain: Okay.

Jessica: … when I said, "even hatred" – just very quickly – I had been doing a group of people with abuse histories and it was a particularly intense group, particularly intense feelings. Big compassion came into the room … and I was furious, about reality. This was, maybe, fifteen years ago. And I went to a session with Hameed and I was stomping, I was just furious. I was furious with a God that would allow …

Iain: Well, we all go through that sometimes, being furious with God.

Jessica: Yes, yes, and I had never really fully let myself feel the depth of my fury and Hameed really created the space. He even went to Gestalt, had me put God on the pillow and as I was in this full thing, my concept of God got revealed as just cardboard, it just dissolved. It was like 'Whoa!' and the room was full of this kind of light of love. So I went from being totally pissed-off to, "Oh, my God, God is just a concept in my mind." My concept of God, it dissolved and what's here is just incredible love.

So I left that session. I'm in this grace and love and it was perfect and I'm driving down the highway in Berkeley, the sun was setting, the colours were pink and golden. I remembered I had to make a phone call. In those days there were no cell phones so I stopped, got on a pay phone and there was a parade. I'm telling my friend, "Life is incredible! My God it's like, my God is beyond God and not only that, there's a parade happening!" And the parade – it was Berkeley – was a Ku Klux Klan anti everything parade with people with the white things. I was shocked!

And I looked into the eyes of the man leading the parade. He was saying terrible anti-human being things and his eyes were black points of hatred. And I just looked and then I saw it was as if that black point of hatred was like the most contracted point of love turned in on itself. And I thought, "What kind of childhood does that boy have?" And so the recognition was, that love is more primary than hatred and hatred is, in a certain way, the result of being so cut off from love even in the human form. Whether you're feeling it at the cosmic level or not ... I should stop here [*laughs*] ... I'm on a roll. Anyway, that's all I want to say about that.

Iain: What do you feel is most helpful for you these days in, let's call it, your journey? You mention it's an on-going process that, who you are is changing, does change from time to time. Do you have a practice that you do regularly that is particularly helpful?

Jessica: My main practice is being present, being aware of what I'm experiencing as intimately and as immediately as I can be, whether it's a positive state or a negative state and being curious. Even if it's a positive experience, like, "Ah, what's really here?" If it's a negative state, "What triggered it? What's really here? What am I taking myself to be right now? How am I really seeing the other? Am I really seeing the other?"

So, it's a certain kind of lived awareness and wonderment about the whole evolution. Truthfully. Like my working question right now is – I love these working questions – So, my working question right now is, looking at the whole arc of evolution in time and space, "How does a star gain a heart?" Or, "What is the purpose and function of the human heart?" And if we look at the whole movement of evolution, *it feels* like the human heart is at the forefront of our evolution right now. Being personal.

We were talking about the transcendent – really living. I'm not called to just "be transcendent." In a certain way, what I'm experiencing is not up to me.

Iain: Talk more about that. It's not up to *you* what you're experiencing...

Jessica: Well, you know, in a certain way it's like radical openness. Radical openness, like right now, I'm feeling a lot of grace and really enjoying being here with you. This is probably the most contact you and I have had. I'm liking it, I'm feeling pleasure in it, I'm feeling love. I feel transparency and I feel the goodness with you. And I feel you're feeling the goodness with me. That feels really something evolutionary about that. It's my feeling about it. So, that's my question. All the stars are becoming hearts. And what will creation... what's the Absolute up to? What's the mystery up to? What's the...

Iain: There was one question that I hadn't written down, which I really wanted to ask you. We have this ... it's almost like a dilemma in that, we've done so many interviews on Conscious TV, Renate and I, and a lot of them have been on non-duality which has been, I won't say restricted the interview, but it's been a certain way of looking at things and there've been different opinions on how people 'wake up'. And a lot of people say, that whatever they do in terms of work and determination and what else, when they did feel they 'woke up', then it was a kind of grace of God and all that work they'd done, didn't really contribute directly to the work of 'waking up'. I just wonder what your experiences of you at the times, when you've had the breakthroughs. Is it because of the work? Did the work contribute? Or did it happen in spite of the work? Was it a combination?

Jessica: That's a great question. My lived experience is, there's no one answer. For some people, the waking up is just grace. I think that's true. For some people, it's hard work. I'm a hard worker. I needed "to follow the urge;" – that determination, that curiosity, that love of the truth – wherever it took me. Why did I have that in my soul? Not everybody has it. So we could say, that's grace. And, something that felt like a personal 'I', chose to engage it. So I could say, okay, I was in partnership with it and for a long time that is the felt experience. And other times, I can say that, that feeling of that young girl... she wasn't seeing herself objectively. She, herself, wasn't arising out of the whole. So, it depends on where you're located, how you answer that question.

I don't know if that's helpful or not. My personal experience is that it's the combination of both. Like it's the form working with the formlessness, it's the sense of the individual soul working with reality. It's true nature working through the individual soul. I mean we could talk about this in so many different ways. And they're all valid.

Iain: And the whole? There's also a debate about whether consciousness can evolve. There're some people who say, consciousness is consciousness and you become awake, you discover who you are and you're never changing, all these different ways that people talk about it, the phrases. And that's who you are and that's it. And there're other people – and I think you're in there, the other group – where you feel and you know for yourself, that there is a constant evolution of consciousness.

Jessica: I'm definitely in that group, but I would also allow both, you see, because the inner nature of the consciousness and the dynamism that's unfolding and I do ... my own felt sense is evolving. This conversation you and I are having right now and how we're experiencing each other and ourselves having it, is relatively new on the planet. Certainly, between a man and a woman... so, there is within that changing, the unchangeable. That's part of the mystery, you see. That's part of the openness that the ego mind, the usual mind, can't think, "How can I have evolution of the unchanging?"

One way we could say it, is that the forms coming out of the unchanging are evolving in their capacity to express and reveal the full potential of the unchanging in all of this manifestation. One way we could say it.

Iain: Well, I think the important thing – I know for myself – the important thing is, it's following the potential in whatever I feel is me ...

Jessica: Right

Iain: ... and that, like you, it changes over time. And I think that's probably the message – not the message so much – but what we try and do at Conscious TV. It's about presenting all these different ideas and something, somewhere, it's moving forward. Whether it's moving forward to discover itself or whether it's moving forward ...

Jessica: ... I totally agree with you ...

Iain: ... because the universe is always expanding. We know that scientifically. So, why shouldn't consciousness always expand?

Jessica: That's my orientation with the unchanging, there. I mean, I love what you're doing on Conscious TV. Having all these different voices, I think it's just a great service for people.

Iain: Well, it's a great adventure.

Jessica: It is a great adventure.

Iain: We have about three minutes left. Is there anything that I haven't asked you, hasn't come up and you'd like to just quickly talk about, in the last three minutes?

Jessica: Well, I think the one *sense* I'd like to say because I'm feeling it right now, that came up while we were chatting earlier is, back to the body. I'm really aware of my experience right now, which continues to be very light, transparent, mischievous, that this question of form-formlessness and the mystery of that, from my location, is more completely understood if we include the body because it's the form we are most intimate with. That's what I'd like to say.

Iain: So we're born with a body and the body grows and eventually it seems to be that we, hopefully, grow in terms of understanding and our feeling of who we are grows and everything else, and in the end ...

Jessica: As you say that, the image of this death ... I was with a friend when she died and we had the great privilege of having her body for three, four days. And you know, what I see is, the soul, the consciousness expands. The body is a living cocoon that's not separate, for a long time, with the consciousness it nourishes and feeds and is a part of. And then in death, it does appear the consciousness expands beyond the body. So, is the body then an object? Or does the body become a part of the universal soul and the soul and consciousness of the earth? So, I'll leave you with that.

Iain: You leave us with more questions than we started [*both laugh*]. It's good.

Jessica: It's good, I'm very glad. Questions are the way.

Iain: Jessica Britt, thank you very much for coming along to Conscious TV. Appreciate that.

Jessica: You're welcome. It was a pleasure.

Sheikh Burhanuddin –
The Journey of a Modern Sufi Mystic
Interview by **Iain McNay**

*Y*ou can't be in peace on your own with everything, you can't be
happy with everything. So as long as there is suffering, as long
as there is our planet exploited and mistreated, our Mother,
let's say, we can't be in a complete peace. In myself, in my own personal
story, in my own cosmos it is possible, but in the moment we blend to
each other, we have to find our hands together [opens his arms], we share
always a common aim. So the final destination would be that everyone
comes home into himself and we see together with one eye, with one
heart, with one thought how everything is.

Iain: My guest today is Sheikh Burhanuddin. Welcome, Sheikh. I'd like
to start when you were very young because you were telling me that
when you were very young you were very drawn to nature and you had
to get your mother's permission to spend a lot of time in nature. So,
what was going on at that time; what do you remember from that time?

Sheikh Burhanuddin: When I was very young I always felt a very strong calling to nature and it was the place where I felt most peaceful and most connected somehow. I loved to watch the animals, I tried always to come close to the deer in the forest; it was a forest close by to our home and finally it came to a point that I asked my mother if I could stay in the forest overnight. I was also very interested in plants, which plants you could eat, which plants you couldn't. With one plant I ate I was not so lucky, but I managed (laughs). And I felt very integrated into the forest. I was watching the forest keeper, the one that professionally looks after the forest, and their team, and it was always my joy to watch them. But they never found me. Even so I made little tents because when I slept I liked to sleep in it or I had to try to protect it and I always slept in the wintertime in the forest which is not as bad as it sounds because the snow keeps you warm in a way so I did my homework at home but the rest of the time I basically spent in the forest.

Iain: And were any of the other children interested in that?

Sheikh Burhanuddin: When I became ten I had a great need of a friend and so I asked God somehow to have a friend and, in fact, then he came we spent every day from then on together in the forest as well; not sleeping there because his parents did not want that. But we shared almost everything.

Iain: When you say you asked God what did that mean, practically?.

Sheikh Burhanuddin: Well, you know, it's very difficult to speak about God. I use it as a word. I could call it also Existence or I could call it the Supreme Intelligence or whatever you like, you know, what is easier, but I use the word because in a way it's the word which tells the most. But it always caused conflicts the most. So that's not my intention but if I had to write a book, the first sentence would be: God exists.

Iain: Because there's so much confusion in the world about God when people say they act in the name of God.

Sheikh Burhanuddin: Well, if you have a confusion on that, and I meet people who have that sometimes, then I say you don't need to call it anything, you don't need to give it a name. You call it Love, call it Truth. You can say, 'God is Truth' but you can also turn it around:

Truth is God. Or God is Love, you can turn it around: Love is God. So if you just keep to Truth and Love you can never go wrong. If you go just with God it can happen that you go wrong as we see in so many movements. There is a danger.

Iain: And then when you were ten you found a photograph in a book, didn't you, that really drew you?

Sheikh Burhanuddin: Yes, I was coming into a library and I was looking and somehow a book fell in my hand. It was from, oh I forgot it, it was an Englishman, I think, or an American, who wrote about his travel experiences through India. Pleitner, I think, was his name. And I opened the book and there was a photograph of Ramana Maharshi inside which I didn't know that it was him. But it touched me so strongly that I thought I have to have it. But I didn't have the money to buy the book. So I came back the next day with a blade and I cut it out and I went home! And later, when I was eighteen, I came back to the book shop and paid the book. (both laughing)

Iain: Wonderful. And I think a little bit later you also say you met the Bible, when you were very young.

Sheikh Burhanuddin: Yes.

Iain: And you met Carlos Castaneda.

Sheikh Burhanuddin: Yes, that was very important and that corresponded very much with my nature interests, you know. And so I started to practise a lot of things which he described in his books, for example, walking in the nights in the forests, using the technique he described in one of his books, you know, bringing your legs up high (lifts one of his hands).

Iain: So, describe that – this was from Carlos Castaneda?

Sheikh Burhanuddin: Yes, I tried that out.

Iain: So you were walking in the forest at night and you say it was big steps, high steps.

Sheikh Burhanuddin: Yes.

Iain: And what did you feel that did for you?

Sheikh Burhanuddin: Hm. Not too much really, not too much. Somehow, I understood of course, if you make higher steps you will stumble less in the forest

Iain: Yes.

Sheikh Burhanuddin: So that's a practical and an advisable thing to do.

Iain: Did you ever have any fear?

Sheikh Burhanuddin: No, no.

Iain: Did you hear strange noises?

Sheikh Burhanuddin: No, there is not one noise in nature that makes me to fear.

Iain: Where do you think this attraction to nature came from to start with. Were your parents drawn to nature?

Sheikh Burhanuddin: Not at all. My mother, she sometimes walked with me, but she was not exactly a nature-oriented woman. So, I really can't tell you. It just happened.

Iain: And then when you were around fourteen – which is incredibly young for what you wanted to do – you wanted to find a master.

Sheikh Burhanuddin: In fact, I wanted to find a master much earlier but when I was fourteen it became a strong pressure. And I felt a need, a very urgent need, to find a man who is like Jesus, for example. That was one of the orientations. And then at fourteen Osho Bhagvan also appeared on the scene. Very attractive. And when I saw him I always thought that my master should have a beard, you know, and it was somehow always clear to me: A master must have a beard!

Iain: Did you ever spend time with Bhagvan?

Sheikh Burhanuddin: I had been in India in the years nineteen eighty, eighty-one.

Iain: And it was in Poona.

Sheikh Burhanuddin: Yeah, I was in Poona and I lived literally twenty meters away from his home but when I came he had made a pause and so I didn't really meet him face to face. But I lived very close to him and I saw him two times in his bathroom.

Iain: Ok. (smiles) so, because I was a Sannyasin of his for three years. Yeah, many years ago. And then, I was looking at notes here, at eighteen you went to India.

Sheikh Burhanuddin: Yes, for the same reason. To find a master.

Iain: Did you find a master there?

Sheikh Burhanuddin: No. Not at that time. It was in a way also very frustrating because I thought, you know, I hadn't read anything about India before. The only information I had was in a book from Hermann Hesse: *Siddhartha*. There was the picture of India for me and as it was not the time of the internet so you had go to libraries and this and that and I wasn't somehow interested having information in advance. So, I didn't buy a travel book, like *Lonely Planet* or this kind of thing. We actually escaped from Germany because my friend was still a minor, so we had to go by surprise in a way and we were not prepared at all what is going be there and our first contact with India was Calcutta, which, in the eighties, was still a town of poverty and overpopulation. People died in the street and they were collected in the morning by lorries. Very, very strong impressions for us.

Iain: What was pulling you, did you just remember what the energy was that was pulling you to follow this path?

Sheikh Burhanuddin: Well, I always had India on my mind, you know. And, it is difficult to say if you have not an external trigger that actually makes you move. So I had very little external trigger. Everything was triggered somehow as there has been a plan settled down a long time ago and I just had to follow it. And in a way in my view it is like this; that there is a history laid down a long time ago for every one of us already. But it is not in all dimensions developed, let's say two-dimensional. It is where you are born, it is what will be your name, what will be your shape. Certain things, your outer movements are basically defined, but how you are in your inside, that's up to you.

Iain: So would you say then when people go through difficult periods somehow they've lost their way in their plan?

Sheikh Burhanuddin: No, you have to fall to develop, that is a principle. You cannot develop yourself if you don't have crises, if you don't have breakdowns. That's not possible.

Iain: So often people say, especially on their spiritual journey, that something goes terribly wrong, maybe with a teacher or with their health or something, they tend to say: well, I went off course and I did not follow my path. But you are saying that that helps to build up their strength, their character somehow.

Sheikh Burhanuddin: There is a saying in Sufism that says: where the Dervish falls down is the place where he stands up

Iain: Yes, I can connect with that personally.

Sheikh Burhanuddin: Yeah, I think everyone can.

Iain: So when you were in India you decided to spend three months in solitude and just wrote notes.

Sheikh Burhanuddin: Right, yes.

Iain: So how did that take place, were you living in a cellar at the time or ... ?

Sheikh Burhanuddin: No, I was in a place which was called Dharamkot, that's near Dharamsala, McLeod Ganj, that's quite a popular place nowadays. A Tibetan place with Tibetan Buddhists mainly, and in Dharamsala was the head quarter of the Dalai Lama, I think it still is. And because before I came to India, I came at age fourteen in contact with Buddhism, somehow I entered India as a Buddhist. But I could not find a Buddhist master, really. I wasn't really feeling much with them, you know. I always thought they are monks, what can they possibly really know about life, about relationships, about daily life issues? So, I was always thinking: The master I know, I want, or I am looking for must be a master who lives in this world, who shares what I am experiencing somehow.

Iain: So you were in this period of three months when you were silent. Was that easy for you to do? It must have brought up a lot of things because you were having no dialogue.

Sheikh Burhanuddin: When you go into silence it is maybe in the beginning a little odd but very, very quickly it develops as a very peaceful thing, not to have to speak. It is an incredible relief.

Iain: I can imagine that.

Sheikh Burhanuddin: And also the effect it has on people is very nice. They are much more tender, much more present in a way and much more sensitive towards you. So it was a very happy time. The difficulty in fact was to return as I had an agreement with my friend to do it for only three months which was already a lot, so he had to do all the shopping, you know, and all these kinds of things. And I think it was in some way more of a challenge for him than for me. So I agreed with him that three months is it and then I'll come back. When it came to the end it was very difficult for me to come back. I actually did like it, if it was up to me I would have stayed silent.

Iain: It's such an alien thing to our modern world, isn't it ? In the west anyway, it is. Everything with social media, everything is action, action, action all the time. It's as if it's something that is forgotten really.

Sheikh Burhanuddin: Right.

Iain: We'll come on later because now you've been on what you call seclusion, which was also very important to you. In the end of this period of three months you had a very dramatic experience, didn't you?

Sheikh Burhanuddin: Yes, where I lived there was a waterfall nearby and I was always very drawn to that waterfall. So, finally, I made my way towards it and when I sat down there I had a very strong experience which drew me out of my body and I started to travel and I had a very strong light experience. The light was kind of a conscious being and I was determined to stay there, so I was asking it if I could stay there. And the answer was: No, you can't stay here. And I was asking: Why, why can I not stay here? And he said – it was a male voice – there are people that need you. And I said: Who needs me? There is only my mother, and she would be fine, I was saying (laughing). And there is no other. I have only one friend, he would be fine also. So there is no one who needs me. And he said: There is and there will be. And so you can't stay. You have to go back. And then I was sent back somehow and this was sad, actually. It was a sad moment. I felt repelled in a way, because I thought this would have been the ideal life, you know, just leave, stay there and be happy.

Iain: When you say you were repelled, what was it that you repelled you about coming back to the world?

Sheikh Burhanuddin: Well: living. Living in this existence has a certain struggle, has a certain effort, right? And I did not have any idea what I could do in the world. Even though I had been a musician from a very young age and I was very active with music. But I was very, very drawn to music and I spent a lot of time practicing my instrument, I played guitar, and so my idea was actually to become a musician but that is not really an easy career, you know. Let's say it like this.

Iain: So, you came back into the world and then, I think it was a couple of years later, you met Krishnamurti in Switzerland.

Sheikh Burhanuddin: I met Krishnamurti when I was nineteen in Salem, Switzerland, in his tent and it was a perfect day, really a perfect day. The sky was blue and it was pleasant weather, pleasant temperature, sun shining and it was really extraordinary. And the place where they put the tent is a beautiful place – there is mountains around and it is really beautiful. So I could get a good place in the tent, near his seat. He was already in his nineties I think, and very strong affected by the Parkinsons he had. So when he came he was trembling, he could hardly make the way to the chair, but even so his presence was enormous. And then he did a thing which is ...I came only later to know it ...that is actually really an impossible thing. He tried somehow to fix the microphone and as he was having such a strong tremor he couldn't really make it. Then came an assistant but he didn't like the assistant to do it for him. So, he closed his eyes and he concentrated and the tremor stopped and he fixed it and then he started again and what he used to do then is to put his hands under his legs.

Iain: Yes, yes I understand, so to ...

Sheikh Burhanuddin: To control it somehow, not to make it visible also and I will never forget the silence before he spoke, it was incredibly dense and when he started his first sentence it was almost like a bullet hits you. Very, very strong.

Iain: There is something I did not mention but which you told me, that when you were young you also used to go to sit in a church because the silence was very important to you.

Sheikh Burhanuddin: I did that when I was starting in elementary school. On my way was a church, a Protestant church, and it was always open. And my habit was to go after school to sit there and to enjoy the silence there.

Iain: I might guess that was always in the background when you were wanting to be in the forest in nature, there was always this pull to silence somehow?

Sheikh Burhanuddin: Now that you say it actually it looks like, but it wasn't a conscious thing for me at that time. It was more of an instinctive need that I felt it is good for me.

Iain: But you were able to trust your instincts.

Sheikh Burhanuddin: Yeah.

Iain: But other people can't, especially kids.

Sheikh Burhanuddin: Well, I think it was something I always relied on it very much.

Iain: So just to continue the sequence of your story, you then again saw a photograph of someone: Sheikh Nazim.

Sheikh Burhanuddin: Yeah.

Iain: Nazim. And again, you were pulled by a photograph and then he became your teacher, your master.

Sheikh Burhanuddin: I was sitting in an esoteric bookshop in Freiburg and there was a similar chair like this (pointing to a chair next to him) and a woman passed by it which was a little bit out of herself, let's say. She already had somehow made a scene in the shop, and so the shopkeeper said, 'Please leave the shop!'. She had a book in her hand and the book was about Sheikh Nazim and before she left she threw the book in my lap and said: 'This is for you!' And then she went out. So, I took it and I turned it around and there was a little picture of Sheikh Nazim and when I saw his picture I was very, very attracted. I mean he was an outstanding beauty. The most beautiful man I have ever met, really. And that was very well captured in that picture.

Iain: And you became his, what do you call it, disciple? He became your master?

Sheikh Burhanuddin: Yeah, yeah.

Iain: So that was the person that you thought you were looking for.

Sheikh Burhanuddin: Yes. Yes.

Iain: So how was that, now you had found your master?

Sheikh Burhanuddin: He was and is the Love of my Life.

Iain: This is so interesting, because I know you are married and I presume you have a beautiful marriage, but you talk about your master being the love of your life.

Sheikh Burhanuddin: Yes, yes. Well, if you meet a real one which is not that easy, if you meet beyond that a king, a king among the real ones, Meher Baba, Ramana Maharshi, I call them Kings. Kings of Saints, Kings of Masters.

Iain: What were the qualities he had that were so special to you?

Sheikh Burhanuddin: Well, it was first of all his incredible love which he emanated which was just pouring out of him. And if you came in his field, in his presence, you felt utterly safe, utterly recognised, utterly embraced, utterly loved and protected. You were so secure and it was so absolutely evident, obvious, that he is just living in God, living in Love, every single moment. It was magic, really magic.

Iain: And one of the things he encouraged you to do is to go on what you call seclusions, what we might call retreats in the west.

Sheikh Burhanuddin: That was later, the first thing actually he wanted me to do is to stop playing music. That was the first thing.

Iain: How was that?

Sheikh Burhanuddin: That was really, really hard. Because my whole emotional life was somehow going through the instrument and to take that out, to take that away from me left me very fragile in a way.

Iain: And why did he ask you to do that?

Sheikh Burhanuddin: I can only speculate, because he never explained anything. He was just saying: If you want to go forward you have to stop. All that. You don't listen to music, you don't play music. When you hear a radio playing somewhere you leave. You don't watch films, you don't watch movies. Nothing. And somehow, if you do that, first of all it makes you aware how much we are addicted to sound, permanent sound and how much sound is in the world all the time, that's another thing. And nowadays it's factor one and so I think he wanted to make me sober in a way. So that you experience yourself without any kind of crutches.

Iain: Experience yourself without any kind of crutches ... So it's just a raw "you" there whatever that is.

Sheikh Burhanuddin: Exactly.

Iain: It's tough, that's right, very tough.

Sheikh Burhanuddin: For a young man it was tough.

49

Iain: But your devotion to him and your commitment to him was enough, strong enough to go with it. Did you have doubts at the time?

Sheikh Burhanuddin: No, no. I was so crazy in love, that if he would have forced me to run naked through the city I would have done that.

Iain: (laughing)

Sheikh Burhanuddin: I can say my trust towards him was total.

Iain: And so I am interested in the seclusions as you call them because you were telling me you had forty days in a small cell just having a light soup every day. You didn't leave the cell for forty days.

Sheikh Burhanuddin: No.

Iain: That's incredible commitment with the sitting, does it mean you were just sitting there for forty days?

Sheikh Burhanuddin: Well, you know the ego is very clever and if you do a thing with a limited time you can sit it out, if you are not ready. You just somehow can avoid yourself. To be watched to be seen. Maybe not one hundred percent but if you are really willing to know yourself I think every method can be bypassed. So it sounds like a strong thing or a great thing and of course the solitude in itself has a certain effect. The eating just the same soup every day has a certain effect but those things were always easy for me. Fasting, any kind of discipline or ascetic thing, was easy for me. But to know yourself you have to be ready. You must really want it. Because whatever you watch will be against the image you created.

Iain: Explain that again: 'Whatever you watch will be against the image created.' What exactly do you mean by that?

Sheikh Burhanuddin: Well, we all create images about ourselves. We create roles and it's easy to understand that if we watch how we interact differently with people. We have an interaction with our wife, we have interactions with working people around us, we have a different interaction with the teacher in school or the boss. We usually have different roles into which we slip very fast and most of it is unconscious.

And we create a role first of all about ourselves. How we want to appear, how we would like to be seen. And if someone doesn't agree with that image we feel attacked. And so when you start to observe yourself you will see for example – I'll give you a very easy example – for example in the system we work first with complaint. Then you watch complaint and ...

Iain: This is when you are complaining about something or somebody on the outside.

Sheikh Burhanuddin: It can be any kind of complaints. Let's start with little complaints. Little complaints are: "The coffee is not hot enough. It's raining again. The bus is not punctual." All kinds of obstacles which we meet and we continually complain about. Then the next step would be: People don't understand me, don't respect me, don't value me. A higher degree of that would be to feel like a victim in your life. Then with your wife or with your husband. A wife may say: "My husband never listens to me, he doesn't give me real attention, he is there but he is not there and so on and so on. Then we would go to the very big complaints: The government is useless. The ecological situation is disastrous. Humans are not worthy, they are horrible."

Iain: We'll discuss more on this at the end because this is a whole process that you have developed, but what you are basically saying it's about clearing the mind of all our programmeming – is this correct? And coming back to something more essential that's not so much the "us" but the real "us" in terms of our human form.

Sheikh Burhanuddin: The mind of course has a purpose, but on the emotional side the mind is the one entity which conflicts us and which filters us also towards reality. I mean, every person who says that he has a spiritual interest has to ask one question and this is, "What is the purpose of life for me here? What is my purpose in life?" Many people want to find a mission, or they think they have a special mission and you find once they think they should become a healer and you have many Reiki masters in every country and you have all kinds of healers and whatever. But in my view we have a common mission and this is to reach reality. Because in that everyone will start to see and to understand what we should stop.

51

Iain: But you say: Reach reality. But that in itself is controversial what reality is.

Sheikh Burhanuddin: That's correct. But in the unconscious situation you always have a feeling that you need to reach, you need to fulfil, you need to conquer, you need to strive. In your mind. And this is what you find very much in the Advaita scene. If you have a clever mind and you can put words cleverly together you can talk yourself into, thinking that you understand and thinking that you are present. But that's not the case, it's just another image you create of yourself as an enlightened person who can function and who can maintain that role as long as he has a certain setup. You always find a certain setup.

Iain: You used the word feeling. So it comes back to the feeling that you must improve, or you must follow. So it's coming to a place – you know I am just trying to find the right words in more layman's terms – but would it be right to say you were in neutral? So it is a neutrality there, where you don't need anything.

Sheikh Burhanuddin: Neutrality is something I like very much.

Iain: OK.

Sheikh Burhanuddin: It is the neutral force which holds our world together, in physics as well. So in Sufism neutrality is the divine force. If you have trouble you have to bring the neutral force inside.

Iain: Ok – I am looking at the clock, we have about fifteen minutes left – so I do want to talk about healers – you also mention them, so I know there is an English healer called Stephen Turoff who is somehow quite influential for you. Do you want to talk us through what happened with him?

Sheikh Burhanuddin: He was very influential to me and we are still connected. We don't see each other very often but we have a kind of soul connection, let's say. Stephen Turoff is a very controversial person but he is one of the true healers I met. I met others, not much because there aren't many. But he is a real healer, shall we say. In his early years especially, he could almost heal any kind of thing in any state. I came in contact with him through my master because he sent his wife to him and he healed her. She had cancer in the uterus and he took it away from her. And it never came back. So from then on many of us went to him. And then I came in a situation that my mother should have had a heart operation because they found a hole a valve.

Iain: So she had a heart condition?

Sheikh Burhanuddin: Exactly. So I said to my mother, "You know what, Mama, why we don't go there and we try first this before we make this very serious heart operation." And my mother, thank God , was a very easy person, a very special person really and she said, "Ok, we go there." So we went there and he cut her womb open from left to right.

Iain: This is with a knife?

Sheikh Burhanuddin: With a knife, yeah.

Iain: Wow. Without anaesthetic – just boom (makes a cutting across hand gesture)?

Sheikh Burhanuddin: It was actually not a surgical instrument, it was not a scalpel, you know, it was more a knife like you would use for meat, but small, small, like a kitchen knife I mean. So he went into the belly of my mother, like this, [shows a hitting movement] with full power, like this, not subtle. It looked rather more as if he were going to kill her than to heal her, right? So when I saw that, you know, I was really medium sized worried we can say. But he had a very strong emanation also, you know. So when he came in he was around sixty and he had a – how do you say this when you have a [bends forward] ... ?

Iain: A hunch?

Sheikh Burhanuddin: Yes, a hunch and he limped also, he was limping and he was an old man, you know in a way. Or elder. And then he did that thing and he was looking at me, smiling sometimes, you know, because he understood I was pretty impressed by what was going on [laughing] with my mother. And my mother couldn't see because she was laying down, so she did not really notice and she looked at me because he asked her something so I had to translate for her. And that was really strong, it was really strong. Then he asked me for my prayer beads and

I gave them to him, he put them into the womb of my mother and he bathed them, he soaked them [shows with hand movements] in her belly, you know, and then he threw it to me and then he says, "Smell!" And I smelled, it was rose! Rose! Imagine. So I don't know what he did but he opened a rose garden in the womb of my mother, you know, literally. And then he threw things out and then he closed the thing and then you could see a scar, you know [makes a hand movement].

And then he operated on me. Yeah, that was really strong as well. He also cut me open but not at the belly down but here, like more this field [shows the solar plexus area] near the solar plexus, just under the rib cage, and he went with his hand inside and he took my heart in his hand, you know. Literally, from inside. And that feeling, I mean, you can't forget that, I mean that was really blowing my mind. And on top of that – he was somehow searching, you know, he came with the fingers and he started to search on my heart, but that was a really, really strange feeling. And then he grabbed something and pulled it out [laughing]. Yes, he pulled it out. And I was saying, "Stephen, what did you pull out of my heart?" And he said, "Something which was not good there." And then he also asked me to bend forward and he started to hammer my neck with a chisel and a hammer. Imagine! And I felt that blood came out and that it was running down my back and I was thinking, "God, what he is hammering on my neck?" It was a little frightening, I can say, but it was not painful. Then he closed it and at the end he embraced me and he was said to me, "Why don't you believe in the love of the Father?" That was very strong.

Iain: Why don't you believe in the love of the Father ...

Sheikh Burhanuddin: That's what he said. And it hit me very strong. And so we came in a kind of contact and you know, he is doing all these magic things somehow. The strange thing is that he does real things but he also does things which are not real. And that gives a very weird factor. And in his personality, he has a kind of naivety, let's say, or innocence. I don't know how to say it. For example, he got a lot of these photographs. He is photographed in very extraordinary images. Like there are rays of light coming on him or coming out of him, you know. There are things appearing in pictures like vases or things like this [making a round shape with his hands]. He is not very skilled, let's say, at presenting himself.

Iain: Yes. And the thing was that that had encouraged a very dramatic effect on you, that's what I am interested in and you were in darkness for a time and then you awoke and didn't feel the same at all, did you?

Sheikh Burhanuddin: No.

Iain: Just talk us through that briefly.

Sheikh Burhanuddin: Well, we had a seminar with Stephen, the first one he ever gave. It was in Como and it was intense, very intense. He explained things about physics and this and that, and during the seminar I already felt something happening with me. But I couldn't really grab it, you know, I just felt internally the need to clear out everything in my life situation, just to clarify everything. And then, as a next step came, somehow detached from my personality somehow, I don't know, from my personal role of perfect image. And I was somehow moving, moving inside and I fell in a kind of dark hole darkness, blackness, not just dark but blackness.

Iain: Like a void? Could you say it was a void?

Sheikh Burhanuddin: Yes, probably, where there was nothing than this blackness. But the blackness wasn't giving me fear, it was more that it was embracing me. It was more like coming into the womb of your mother somehow. But it was very, very black; velvety somehow. And something purified it. Let us say it like this. And I came into a very deep silence, very, very deep silence and I felt then after some hours, I fell unconscious, I fell asleep and in the morning I woke up and I noticed that everything was very shiny, very intense, very colourfully bright, very communicative. When I came out of the house – I had a view over the lake, Lake Como. It was a beautiful day and it was overwhelming, really overwhelming and the beauty of what I saw was so immense, the connection to the sky, everything was embracing me, you know, and I was part of a symphonic happening. It was incredible. And I came into a kind of ecstasy.

Iain: And that stayed for a time, didn't it? Sheikh Nazim I think got a little concerned about you and ...

Sheikh Burhanuddin: No, no, Sheikh Nazim didn't get concerned, but some of the people around me got concerned and then there was one Brother who also was a friend of mine, who called Sheikh Nazim. He was saying that I appeared to be different And Maulana (Sheikh Nazim) said, "Tell him to come and tell him also that he can't do it alone. He is now in Maqaam Fadani, that's what he said. I wanted him to see me, so I arrived in Cyprus, I entered and as I stood in front of him then and he said, "Is it Burhanuddin or does he just look like him?" He looked at me and he took his hand over my face and said, "I accept your light." Then we prayed and in the coming days I had very strong experiences with him because I understood that he was the only one who could hear me. And also I could hear him.

Iain: And that's a true master, isn't it? Someone that can really hear you.

Sheikh Burhanuddin: Yes.

Iain: After this experience it took you I think three years, didn't it, to get back to really be able to function in the world.

Sheikh Burhanuddin: Yeah.

Iain: So what happened through that three-year period?

Sheikh Burhanuddin: Well, I was first of all very blessed with a loving wife. Even so she was definitely scared. The easiest were my children in fact, they took it very nice and very sweet, and I was basically looked after, by people. Because I was not able to really take care of myself at that time.

Iain: So it's like your character had been blown away. I am just trying to summarise here so we can understand it.

Sheikh Burhanuddin: Yes, you could say that.

Iain: So your human functioning was compromised somehow.

Sheikh Burhanuddin: Yes, I was overwhelmed about the intensity in which I lived and also the perception – how I see people. So sometimes I could hear their mind and I always felt very, very clearly what is happening to them. But I couldn't speak about anything at length, so I was only using few words. And sometimes I was maybe too cryptic or not understandable. I slept very little or not at all. I rested but I didn't sleep, I wasn't going into sleep any more. In fact my nights were busier than my days. I was doing things let's say in the spirit world. And I lived very much in between the worlds. Somehow more on the other side than here.

Iain: And so was it a gradual process to come back?

Sheikh Burhanuddin: Well, it was a very gradual process, but it was initiated by the command of Maulana who said, "You are not useful in that state for others and you have to come back and you have to learn to live with it in a social way." And I don't know how he helped me, but he helped me. I think one of the magic parts of Sheikh Nazim was that he was really the master of the invisible. And he arranged things for you in the invisible. He could manipulate the matrix in any degree which you can imagine. So he somehow arranged my life.

Iain: So I wanted to come on just to talk a little bit more about what you call seclusions what we might call retreats. Did you still do those sometimes?

Sheikh Burhanuddin: I have short kind of seclusions.

Iain: Yeah. So, just tell me more about what happens, I'm interested for myself in what happens in a short seclusion.

Sheikh Burhanuddin: Well, it depends very much on your will, how much you want to know yourself. You may have noticed that if you start looking, if you start watching yourself, very quickly you come to your fears. We can say that basically our common prison is our fears. All our personalities are surrounded by our fears. All our images at the end of the day have the root in fears. And to pass through fears is very necessary and in the system which I received from my Sheikh the steps that bring you to a point that you allow everything to be whatever you observe. You don't try to transform it or to push it away or anything like that. You start to accept as a first step to allow everything to be there, with you. Whatever it is. And you should have a neutral friendly, slightly friendly, attitude and watch yourself. But that means you don't judge, you don't say that this is good, this is bad, this is this, this is that. No. And you do

57

that from the position of what we call the single player part, which means there is no other. There are helpers, this could be a wife for example. Helpers are people who hurt us and we hurt them. And in the unconscious mode we can say that everyone who comes close to us will be hurt Si or Si. Yes or yes.

Iain: So again: Everyone that comes close to us will be heard.

Sheikh Burhanuddin: Whoever came close and whoever comes close, unless, unless we are not really deeply conscious, will get hurt. That's what happened.

Iain: Ok, hurt

Sheikh Burhanuddin: Will get hurt. And you will get hurt by that person. This is a law. That's one of the things we have to accept.

Iain: Yes.

Sheikh Burhanuddin: So if there is still that mechanism happening that you hurt and that you get heard, that means there is still work, right? So that also has to do very much with fears. So to pass through one fear the possibility that you allow yourself to go beyond fear is really enlightening experiences.

Iain: So when you are in seclusion and probably this happened to you more in the past, and now your fear comes up, you are staying with the fear and you are saying you have a slight friendship with it? I think that was your word.

Sheikh Burhanuddin: The first is to accept. The second thing is to agree. That's already completely different.

Iain: What is agreement?

Sheikh Burhanuddin: Agreement means that you really, from the depth of your being, you allow things to be.

Iain: Ok.

Sheikh Burhanuddin: Because acceptance is: You start on the surface. You say, "Ok, ok. I let it be." But agreement is that it sinks down that you really don't want to move it any more, you don't want to touch it, you don't want to change it.

Iain: It's just that's the hardest thing not wanting to change something when you don't like it. That is the biggest human challenge I think.

Sheikh Burhanuddin: Well, that is, whatever you want to change, it's always because you want to recreate a role. But you have to look to the image which is beyond, behind the mirror. And if you want to reach presence you can't come with an image there. You can't come with a role into presence. That doesn't work. You have to forget yourself somehow, you have to be you without you. There is the moment you are in, if not: No. Whatever you wish, whatever you try to calm down, it is not working like that.

Iain: Because you talk about the single player mode and the multi-player mode.

Sheikh Burhanuddin: Exactly.

Iain: So just explain a little about that

Sheikh Burhanuddin: Well, the multi-player mode is the usual mode in which we live. That means we accuse people, we accuse circumstances, we make others responsible for how we feel. We want to criticise, we want to punish, we feel disappointed, we feel frustrated. We think to the past, we think to the future. Everything becomes a player, our car, our apartment, age, time, everything is a player. And in that play you try to sell yourself, to appear and you want the other players to confirm you. That's not going to happen, really. Not stabilised. So in the single player mode you understand that there is no other so you imitate the divine position. Let's assume for a moment God would exist. There is a creator, right? Now to whom he can complain? On which shoulder can he lean? What can he say? He did it all. He just has to see, right? How can he be in bliss how can you be in bliss seeing everything?

Iain: You see, I think for most of us in the west I can understand what you are saying and I can see the possibility of just the single player

59

mode. In a way in my term it's almost like you take responsibility for whatever is happening.

Sheikh Burhanuddin: There's one side effect of it.

Iain: But let's say you are in a prison cell in Syria or something, where you're not really a tourist, you haven't done anything wrong particularly, but you are there and you are getting beaten up and it's terrible food and it's just dreadful. To not kind of stay in single player mode then and not blame the outside when you are in so much probably physical and also emotional pain is a huge, huge challenge.

Sheikh Burhanuddin: It's both. You see, whenever you come in a very extreme situation you have very strong forces and there is one which may drive you crazy and there is one exactly the opposite. A very strong situation is not a situation which is necessarily worse than a good situation. Don't misunderstand me, you know. I am not saying this is what is good to do to people or – we don't go there. But let's say it will happen to you, you get kidnapped, for example, and you end up in a prison in Syria. But whatever it is the process is always the same. You look to yourself, you are there. And now, in such a situation in fact it's much easier, you know, to go into your single player mode. It does not matter whom you make responsible – what does it help you? You are there, you are pressed into yourself. Because in my understanding every obstacle which happens to you is an invitation to make you realise that the answer is not outside, it wants to press you inside. All our existence finally presses us inside. Age presses us inside. When we get older we don't have any more the sexual attraction as we had when we were young. So already that is again something which wants to invite us inside. So, an accident, a sickness, whatever it is which stops your planning towards the earth, towards the outer existence is an invitation towards the inner.

Iain: Yes. This reminds me – as a kind of example – I was talking to someone a little while ago. My wife Renate and I were involved with a charitable Prison Phoenix Trust and they do good work, they basically send people into prisons to teach yoga meditation. I was talking to a guy, he is out of prison now, he was in for twenty years, for he murdered two different people and for other crimes. And when he first went to prison he was put in solitary confinement for a year. This is someone with no spiritual training. And I said to him: Wasn't that incredibly hard? And he said: No. It was the best thing that could have happened to me, because I was able to take the time and realise what I had done and start looking inside. It turned out he was uneducated but actually a very bright, smart guy. But yes, to have that time if you are able to do that, I can see great value in that. I just want to finish off by one thing you have said to me or I picked up from the notes that were sent to me was that true enlightenment is collective. Can you just talk about that?

Sheikh Burhanuddin: Did I say that?

Iain: Well, it was either you said it on the phone to me or [laughing] it was in the note sent to me.

Sheikh Burhanuddin: You can't be in peace on your own with everything, you can't be happy with everything. So as long as there is suffering, as long as there is our planet exploited and mistreated, our Mother, let's say, we can't be in a complete peace. In myself, in my own personal story, in my own cosmos it is possible, but in the moment we blend to each other we have to find our hands together [opens his arms], we share always a common aim. So the final destination would be that everyone comes home into himself and we see together with one eye, with one heart, with one thought how everything is.

Iain: So this single player mode cannot be the final destination, because there it's still focussed on oneself to some extent.

Sheikh Burhanuddin: Well, the single player mode is somehow imitating a kind of reality but it is not an egoistic just-looking-after-yourself-thing. That must be really understood. It is not that I don't take care of others anymore. But, you know, a helper can be a very egoistic person.

Iain: Absolutely.

Sheikh Burhanuddin: While, let's say in the single player mode you don't become a helper but you become more a servant.

Iain: Yes. Ok Sheikh. I've enjoyed the interview very much, I find it very interesting.

Sheikh Burhanuddin: Thank you.

Iain: I love your story as well. I know it's only a story but it's a great story.

Sheikh Burhanuddin: Thank you.

Linda Clair – I am Enlightened
Interview by **Renate McNay**

*P*eople think, 'Well, without your emotions you must be a robot.'
*That's not true at all. Without your emotions the selfishness goes
because I can see now that emotions are just very selfish feelings,
"It's all about me." That's why I really started this whole journey, because
I was sick of everything being about me – everything revolved around me.
I couldn't feel real compassion. I couldn't really feel sorry for someone
because it was always to do with how I felt about it. I wanted to feel
real love. I wanted to feel compassion at times, but I just couldn't do
it because I was so obsessed with myself, incredibly obsessed. So, the
opposite happens. Rather than becoming a robot, you become truly
authentic, really authentic. The self-consciousness goes. The fear goes.*

Renate: Linda comes all the way from Australia, and we're happy that
you're here with us. This is Linda's book. It's, *What Do you Want? –
Conversations about Enlightenment*. And, Linda is also featured on
this lovely DVD which is called, *Meetings with Remarkable Women*.

I really enjoyed this book, by the way. One thing, Linda I took from your web site was this sentence which was very sweet – you said, "Getting enlightened was like a fairy tale come true." We all want this fairy tale to come true. [*both laugh*] I want to start with talking a little bit about -how did this fairy tale come true for you? I know you had a happy childhood, and you had a happy life, so you weren't looking for anything. You had children and a husband. Everything was working fine. Normally if we're happy, we're not looking for something.

Linda: I think everyone is unconsciously looking for something, and some people are actively looking for something, but no, I wasn't consciously looking for something. My partner at the time was very much into meditation, and enlightenment, and the spiritual quest. He's the one who actually introduced me to my future teacher. We were on holiday one time, and he had been to see this teacher, and he wanted me to come and meet him and do a meditation evening with him. I was very reluctant, I was saying, "No, we're on holiday. I don't want to go and see this teacher. It feels like work." [*laughs*] But, eventually I said, "Yes, I'll go and see him." We went, and it was good. There must have been something there because I was interested in seeing him again, but it didn't happen straight away. So, I met him a couple more times, and we became a bit closer. We went around to his place one night for dinner, and we went outside after dinner – it was dark – and, Peter – the teacher's name was Peter Jones...

Renate: I tried to do a search for him, but I couldn't find him.

Linda: He calls himself PeterJi now, so it's very difficult. And, he's not teaching at the moment. He's quite sick, so he's not teaching. But, I still remember that moment. There are a lot of things I forget now, but I do remember that moment. I just looked at him, and suddenly something clicked. It felt like I had never really looked at someone before – like really looked at them, even my children, my partner, my parents, everyone I'd been intimately connected with, I hadn't actually felt such a closeness with everyone. The light went on. Something happened. And, like I said, I wasn't actively looking for anything, but something happened.

Renate: But, okay, so you said you didn't look like that before, but what were you seeing?

Linda: I was seeing myself. I was seeing my potential. I was seeing something that I'd never seen before. In everything else, I had seen myself, but it was my ego self, whereas this was something beyond the ego that I saw. So, I saw the potential to be without an ego, and I saw it in him. I just never realised that that existed.

Renate: But, did you know at that time there was something beyond the ego, or was it just something you felt? Did you have the concept already – okay, there is an ego, and there is a non-ego place?

Linda: I was aware of it in myself to a degree that there was an ego there, but I had done very, very little really. I hadn't really been interested in meditation or spiritual matters. There wasn't this searching, so I didn't really know all the theoretical story about the ego, the mind, and all that. It was just something I simply felt. Like I said, "The light went on," and I was like, "Ah, that's what I'm looking for," even though I wasn't consciously looking for something, it was like, "That's it. That's what I'm looking for."

Renate: And what was it exactly you were looking for?

Linda: Well, I didn't know. Eventually I realised that it was something that I couldn't put my finger on. That's what I saw in him. It was something that I didn't know. That's what I was looking for, because I was sick of trying to know everything, and trying to know what was going to happen. Thinking was just a repetition. So, I suppose, in a way, I was starting to get a little bit bored with my life, because it did feel like a repetition – this would happen, and I'd react a certain way, and I'd have a nice experience, but the experiences would always end. And, there were times when I really wanted to stop thinking, like doing things that I really enjoyed, having a massage, something like that, and I couldn't lie there and really be there and enjoy what I was doing. When I was with my children, my partner, there was still this thinking going on. So, I was aware that I didn't want it to be like that, but I had no idea that it was possible to be free of that. I thought, 'Oh, that's just part of life.'

Renate: And, what happened then, after this first experience?

Linda: Well, not long after that we invited Peter down to do a weekend in the city that we were living in, in Adelaide, in South Australia, and

65

he accepted. And, I felt it even more strongly while he was there. As I said, I'd never really been a spiritual person, and I'd always been quite logical, so it was quite a surprise to me, but I felt this almost magnetic pull towards him. So, he stayed with us for about a week, and it just became stronger, and in that week we thought, 'Ah, we need to move to be close to him.' So, we moved up to Northern New South Wales, Northern Australia, where he lived, and lived about five minutes away. My partner and I both started going to meditation sessions with him. After about a year, I was doing a retreat with him and something happened. I'd call it an awakening.

Renate: When you started meditating, did it come easily to you?

Linda: Relatively. I didn't feel it was easy, but it was more natural. It didn't feel easy, but I felt at home doing it. So, in that way, I was a natural meditator. I did realise that I had been, in a way, meditating – not formally – but really watching my mind for a lot of my life. I thought that was just normal. I thought everyone did that.

Renate: Which kind of meditation did you do with Peter?

Linda: He was doing Vipassana meditation. He had done a lot of practice with Burmese Sayadaws. It was called Insight Meditation. It was basic Vipassana meditation; just sitting, feeling your body, sitting still for periods, sometimes long periods. That was basically it.

Renate: And, watching your thoughts?

Linda: Watching the thoughts, watching the breath. Really being very aware of the breath, and sitting as still as possible, and seeing the mind – coming back to the body. So, coming back to where you are. Rather than using the mind, it was more like using the body – becoming more and more grounded in the body.

Renate: Feeling the body from inside?

Linda: Yes. Really feeling the body. Being very aware of sensations. Not ignoring anything. Being very aware of sensations. Looking at the difference between pain and pleasure, and whether there was any difference, and why there was an avoidance of pain and this reaction

66

to pain as, 'Ah, that's bad. It shouldn't be there,' and pleasure, 'That's good. I want more of it.' So, it was trying to watch that from this neutral point of watching, non-reaction.

Renate: And, you had a lot of pain in your body.

Linda: Yes.

Renate: How was that for you?

Linda: It was hard. It was terrible. [*laughs*]

Renate: And, you still were okay sitting in the pain, or did you have some tricks?

Linda: I had lots of tricks. [*laughs*] I found it difficult when I first started to even sit for even half an hour – it felt like a long time for me. And, I started off sitting on a chair, and then gradually went down and sat on the floor by the end. That took about six/eight months for me to really graduate down to the floor, because I'd never really sat on the floor much before. But, it was really difficult. A lot of people don't talk about the pain that everyone who goes deeply into it feels in meditation. A lot of people have got the wrong idea about meditation, and what it involves, and what it is.

Renate: Are you talking about physical or emotional pain? Both of them?

Linda: Well, you feel both. There's an emotional reaction to feeling that pain, because it's facing the pain that you've been avoiding for most of your life. So, sitting there, keeping the body very still is an incredibly …

Renate: Challenging …

Linda: Yes … challenging thing to do. It's much more challenging than moving around trying to relieve things. Sitting still for long periods is incredibly challenging. It's like you're challenging your mind, and your mind starts to react and says, 'No, you're not going to do this. You're not going to sit through this.' And, it does its best to stop you.

Renate: 'Come here. I need you for this problem. It's much more important to put your attention there.' Yes.

Linda: But, when Peter explained this method, it just sounded incredibly logical and simple to me. I wasn't attracted to rituals. I wasn't attracted to religion. I'd never been religious. I'd never been attracted to spiritual groups – I thought I wasn't really spiritual enough, compared to my partner. I thought he was the spiritual one, and I wasn't.

Renate: Did it become easier, sitting?

Linda: No. [*laughs*]

Renate: So, you have a lot of determination.

Linda: You have to. It's part of it. You have to be very …

Renate: There was a goal there.

Linda: Well, I thought there was a goal. The only reason I kept going was because of my teacher. And, as I kept going more deeply into it, my connection with my teacher became closer. That's what spurred me on. And, my love for him became deeper, and that's what spurred me on. Yes, there was a lot of determination required and involved, but a lot of love that was involved as well. That's what kept me going. And, it was often at times like he was holding up this carrot saying, "Come on. Just keep going a bit more, a bit more." And, sometimes it was ecstatic, and other times it was just awful. It was really, really difficult at times.

And, like I said, people just don't talk about that, whereas he was very honest about it, about what was involved. And, he was very honest about how much it took, and how a lot of people could have an awakening, and I could see when that happened to me, it was very tempting to just stay there and go, "Okay, I don't want to do any more," but it was because of him that I knew that that wasn't it, and I needed to keep going.

Renate: So, what I'm hearing from you is also the importance of having a teacher.

Linda: For me it was essential. And, I'd say for most people it's essential. The habits of the mind are so deep-seated, so strong, so habitual that you actually need this body sitting in front of you who has realized that reality is possible, that freedom is possible. You need it in human form, or at least I did, in front of me to keep reminding me, and also to challenge my mind that this is possible.

Renate: Yeah, and we also need the pointers, you know – what can come up, what to do if something comes up. I know I read once in one of the Dalai Lama's books, and he said, "There are hundreds of monks sitting in caves, all over Tibet and India." He said, "If they do not get pointers – they can sit there for ten-twenty years – but if they do not get pointers they never break through the mind. They always stay underneath."

Linda: I agree totally with that – you need someone. I could become deluded within a few days. I used to go and sit with my teacher two or three times a week, and then do retreats with him. I would go on a Tuesday night, a Thursday night, and sometimes on the weekend – and, between Tuesday night and Thursday night I could become deluded, and suddenly feel I was somewhere where I was not. So, the teacher was necessary in so many ways. Energetically, it really intensifies the energy. When I was sitting with him, I did feel more pain often.

Renate: What did you do with emotional pain when it came up – with belief structures, or delusions?

Linda: Watch them, came back to the body, watch. Of course, sometimes I'd get involved in the emotional stuff that was going on, and I cried quite a bit. I think you need to cry at times, but not feel too sorry for yourself. At times I felt very sorry for myself, and then I'd come out of it, and it would be okay. [*laughs*] But, the emotional pain – there's no easy way through it – just sitting with it, sitting still. After a while I started to crave doing retreats. So, I would almost live for retreats. In between retreats of course I'd meditate, but it felt like I was just waiting for the next retreat because I knew doing seven days, ten days of intensive sitting would really make a big dent in my ego.

Renate: So, how many hours did you sit in intensive retreats?

Linda: In intensive retreats, probably about seven or eight hours a day, which isn't all that much ...

Renate: It's not? [*both laugh*]

69

Linda: In Japan, in some places they sit more ...

Renate: They don't even lie down at night. They even sit in a box ...

Linda: In some retreats in Japan, they do ...

Renate: Okay, so you had your first awakening in one of the retreats with Peter. What was the awakening? What did you realise?

Linda: I realised that I was not my mind. It wasn't just that I intellectually understood it. It was that I realized that I wasn't my mind. To realise something, you can only do it through your body, through the body, through this body. That's what I realised.

Renate: You take a lot of emphasis on being grounded in the body. You say that only through the body you realise we are not the body.

Linda: Yes. Meditation is really preparing the body for the shock of realisation, which is realising I'm not my body.

Renate: Right. And, what else is involved in this shock? What happens to the body in the moment of the realisation or waking up?

Linda: Fear. It's partly the realisation that it's nothing like anything you felt before. It's the shock of living with no fear. So, suddenly all this fear – well not all the fear, because even at that point which you call enlightenment, all the fear doesn't go – 99.9% of it goes – there's still a bit later on, and that's a whole different journey. But, the shock is that there's suddenly no fear there. So, the whole body ...

Renate: is free ...

Linda: ... is free. Not the whole body, but most of the body, and that's a huge shock. And, it's also because, I think in everyone, before realisation there is a part of you that really doesn't believe that it is possible for you. And, like I said, it was like a fairy tale coming true, and that's a shock. It's a huge shock.

Renate: A surprise, I guess.

Linda: Yes, and the shock was that it was felt so ordinary and so simple, whereas I felt it was going to be more special, more of something.

Renate: With fireworks, and …

Linda: And, it wasn't like that. It was like something just clicked into place, and everything that I thought was real became unreal, and everything that seemed impossible was suddenly real. I said it was like this fairy tale coming true – it was almost tangible, like I could touch this reality.

Renate: Yes, so you saw reality in this moment in a different way, when you say everything you thought …

Linda: Well, I had no idea before that what reality was, and you can't because it's not an experience – it's not something that you go in and out of. Reality is something that you're in, and that's it. That's what enlightenment is. So, you can't go back. Maybe that's part of the shock too, that you can't go back.

Renate: Well, some people seem to go in and out.

Linda: Well, I would say that's not reality and that's not enlightenment.

Renate: I guess that you would call it an awakening.

Linda: I'd call that an awakening …

Renate: And then they remember the awakening, and then they try to integrate this awakening experience. Into their life.

Linda: [*agrees*]

Renate: So, I guess, if I look at it, it's the ego which is actually then doing the job without realising it, that needs to die. How would this "integration" work? You know what I mean? Your awakening or enlightenment was an abiding enlightenment. It did not leave you.

Linda: [*agrees*]

Renate: You had two different awakenings before this.

Linda: Two? Did I say ... ? [*laughs*]

Renate: Did you say ... ? [*both laugh*]

Linda: Actually, yes, well, I would have called it ... And, I was talking with a friend yesterday about when I actually met Peter and the light went on, that was an awakening. So, around a year and a half later there was another, deeper awakening. I feel like when you have an awakening the best thing to do is forget about it – just forget about it and keep going, keep working. And, it's the same with enlightenment, which is really realising you're not the body. What you need to do is – but, you can't help doing that then is – just forget about it. Don't try and remember it. Don't try and repeat anything.

Renate: But, isn't part of the remembering important to integrate it more into your daily experience in life?

Linda: I can only speak from my experience. What happened during my practice is that I forgot more and more. My memory really changed. When it first started happening it was a bit disconcerting because I would just forget things. Then Peter said – and, I've read it with other teachers too – that that was part of the whole thing because thinking is just remembering. When the mind starts breaking down you just naturally stop remembering things, trying to remember. It doesn't mean that you can't function because the body has got its own memory, and it will do things that it needs to do. But really, we don't need our memory nearly as much as we think we do. The big thing about enlightenment was that the desire to remember went. And, I realised that I don't need my memory. The trust is that everything will happen without trying to remember things. So, after enlightenment, no I didn't need to remember anything. Everything just started happening without me involved.

Renate: So that 'the me' was gone.

Linda: Almost gone. There was still a bit there.

Renate: You said, which I like, "I was free of myself."

Linda: Yes. I was free, but then I became free-*er*. I know some people say there are no degrees of enlightenment, but I would disagree, in my experience there are. I'm in a very different state now to the state I was in ten years ago.

Renate: How can you become free-*er*?

Linda: After enlightenment it happens naturally. But, one of the main things I feel is – humility. And, that's another reason for a teacher – humility.

[*long pause*]

Renate: I realised we were jumping away from your fairy tale story, [*both laugh*] because I know you went to Japan then, and you meditated …

Linda: I spent around six years with Peter, and then he wasn't teaching quite as much then, and I wanted to do – I felt like I needed to do some more intensive retreats. So, I started doing some Zen retreats with a master who lived in the area. I still had contact with Peter. I really enjoyed the whole Zen practice. I felt like I needed a little bit more discipline. Then he mentioned that they took western students into this monastery where he spent time with his master. As soon as he said that I was like, "Ah, I'm going to go!" So, not long after that I went over and spent six weeks there. That's really when it happened – when it really finished me off. [*both laugh*]

Renate: Yes … The human story ended then.

Linda: It did. It was the start of something else.

Renate: You had children at the same time. How was that for you to do all this meditation, taking care of children, and all the change or awakening? How did you deal with all that, with the simplicity of your life, of having a family and having to go shopping, and so forth, cooking, and what have you … ?

Linda: It was a great thing. I started my practice with Peter when my son was thirteen, and my daughter was twelve. So, they were becoming a bit more independent by then. And, sure it was hard doing retreats and things, and organising child care, and that sort of thing, and maybe going and doing a day's intensive meditation, and then coming back, and having to help them with math homework, or something like that. But, I can see now, it was a great thing. Of course it was difficult, but bringing up children is difficult. It was a great thing because it grounded me. It really stopped me from getting too obsessive about the whole thing. It was like this anchor in the world. It was great. It just kept me really earthed – down to earth. It was really good.

Renate: So, would you say Linda that you've reached enlightenment through your dedication and meditation, and [that] everybody else can do that?

Linda: Well that's just a small part. I would say I'm enlightened because of my teachers – that's why – because of their compassion, their love. It's because of them. It's the only reason I kept going. [*laughs*] I wouldn't have kept going without them. Of course, yes, I'm determined and all that, but it was just …

Renate: I like the way you say, "I am enlightened." My teacher said once, "This is such a rare occasion that somebody gets enlightened." Well, he said that a few years ago, "Maybe in the moment on this planet are just a handful." How do you feel about that? What is your experience with people you're working with, or you're meeting?

Linda: I haven't met many. I've met a few, but not many. What I feel is, 'Why shouldn't it be possible for more people.' But, it is rare, and it's incredibly hard. It's the hardest thing I've ever done in my life. It just was so difficult. It's the most valuable thing you can do in your life.

Renate: What was the most difficult thing?

Linda: Everything. I can't pinpoint one thing. It was different at different times. Sometimes it was sitting there in a retreat with this incredible pain in my head that was just blowing my head apart. And other times, it was just not being able to see my teacher when I wanted to see my teacher. Other times it was – it was different at different times, so I wouldn't pinpoint. I know the time in Japan was incredibly difficult for me because I was out of my comfort zone. The practice there was just intense, really intense. It was so cold. I'd never been in such cold.

Most people there got frostbite. I got frostbite being there. They don't have heating. You sit in this ...

Renate: Minus twenty degrees. [*laughs*]

Linda: I don't think it was that cold, but it was snowing. We weren't supposed to wear socks – not in the Zendo, not when we were meditating. So, it was a real shock, but it was the most amazing time as well. And, I needed it. I needed it at that time. Not everyone does, but I know I needed to do that. And, I needed to meet this master there, who's incredible. But, I needed to also get away from my comfort zone – my partner, my children, my house, running hot water, everything. [*laughs*].

Renate: We don't like to leave our comfort zone.

Linda: No, no. And, I was still into my comfort zone. So, it was a good thing for me to do at the time. And, by that time I was desperate. I would have done anything – I really would have.

Renate: So, you're a meditation teacher now, and you do retreats and seminars. How do you bring your students out of their comfort zone? [*both laugh*]

Linda: Depends on the student. It's different for each student.

Renate: Can you see where each student needs to be thrown out?

Linda: Yes ...

Renate: What intrigues me when you said, "I am free of myself," and your relationship to your body – you said you experience your body in a different way. You also talked about how all your senses changed. Your vision changed after enlightenment, your hearing, your memory changed, you mentioned. So, what happened to your vision and your hearing? Why does that change?

Linda: Because you stop focusing on something. It becomes much less fixed. So, the vision actually widens – you're very aware. When there's not all this stuff going on in the head, and you're not using the mind as a reference point, then you start to use the senses in a very different way. It's more as a survival instinct which is what they're meant for predominantly. I mean, it's good to have pleasure, but you become more like an animal. So, the vision becomes much more ... I'm very aware of things to the side as well as the front. Even when I'm looking at you, and mainly looking at you and looking into your eyes, I'm also very aware of the plant and things all the way around. So, it's almost impossible to focus exclusively on something. With the hearing, it's the same. If someone is sitting nearby ... If I'm talking to someone and then there's someone talking not very far away, and I can hear that conversation as well, it's very hard to actually separate it – I just can't separate anything. So, I'm very aware of all the sounds around as well.

Renate: Is it the same with the feelings? Do you feel the feelings of people around you, their pain, their emotions?

Linda: No, no.

Renate: So, I guess there is nothing in you anymore which is kind of a reflection – no, reflection is not the right word – where something from the outside can get stuck.

Linda: No, I can't remember what it's like to suffer. I can't actually remember what that's like.

Renate: And, do you still have feelings of being sad?

Linda: Sometimes, yes – a bit sad. They go through very quickly. It's very different. People think, 'Well, without your emotions you must be a robot.' That's not true at all. Without your emotions the selfishness goes because I can see now that emotions are just very selfish feelings, "It's all about me." That's why I really started this whole journey, because I was sick of everything being about me – everything revolved around me. I couldn't feel real compassion. I couldn't really feel sorry for someone because it was always to do with how I felt about it. I wanted to feel real love. I wanted to feel compassion at times, but I just couldn't do it because I was so obsessed with myself, incredibly obsessed. So, the opposite happens. Rather than becoming a robot, you become truly authentic, really authentic. The self-consciousness goes. The fear goes.

Renate: So, what is your reference? Is there still a reference point in you? How do you know, if there is no self? How do you know it's you if somebody says, "Linda," if there is no reference point anymore?

Linda: I don't know. [*laughs*] Someone says, "Linda" – I go, "Yes?" [*laughs*] I don't know.

Renate: So there might be still some memory.

Linda: There's memory – there's still memory in the brain. There's just not emotional memories. So, when there's no – well almost no – I can never say that there's none at all, but when there are almost no emotional memories. For example, I can meet someone who I've known for a long time and it can be like the first time we've met. Of course I know who they are – I recognise who they are – but, there's not all this stuff going on around, "Ah, he said this to me last week" – that sort of thing. It's just fresh, and new, and open.

Renate: Isn't that nice in a marriage? [*laughs*] You see your partner everyday fresh.

Linda: Well, I'm not married at the moment. [*both laugh*] But yes, that's how it feels. It's like everything is new, is fresh.

Renate: Everything is created in this moment, fresh. And, this is actually your experience?

Linda: Yes.

Renate: As I'm looking at you, I keep spacing out. [*both laugh*] So, I have to read my notes. I'm also very interested in this body – how the body becomes free, because there is so much, belief structures, paranoias and what have you is stored in our body, like every cell has a memory – an unpleasant or pleasant memory. It's fascinating when you said, in the moment of your awakening it's like the body became free, or was there a process of alignment?

Linda: There was definitely a process. What I feel is happening with meditation, and what was happening with me, and anyone who gets deeply into this, is that the cells of my body were purifying, being purified of the emotional memory. That's what meditation is – seeing and cutting that thinking process. It's not about stopping thinking, but just seeing, realising what thinking is, understanding the mind, and realising that thinking is just a movement away from now. It's just this movement. We put a lot of importance on what we're thinking. The subject of our thoughts is not really important at all – it's that movement away – that's just the bait, what we're drawn towards. So, it's breaking that habitual movement away from here, and coming in. Each time you do that, you're purifying your body, maybe just a small degree. That accumulates. And, enlightenment is that point, that critical point where so many cells in your body have been purified that it tips you over the edge.

Renate: So, I guess, what the tip is, as more cells become free, the current, or the vibration, or the light, or however you call it, can pass more strongly through your system, or your nervous system?

Linda: Yes. I think it actually happened when I was in Japan, and I didn't realise it. About nine months later, after I left Japan, I did a retreat with my Zen teacher in Australia, a Japanese man. We were sitting there one morning, and he came around – he used to adjust people, adjust posture every now and again. He adjusted my posture – he hardly ever did that – and I suddenly let out this strange noise when he did it, and it was really embarrassing, and I felt really self-conscious about it. Something in me suddenly went, "You've done all this practice, everything, and you can still feel embarrassed and so incredibly self-conscious about something like this." Rather than feeling sorry for myself, something else just clicked in. It was almost like a turbo-boost, like, "Okay, this is it. I'm not going to put up with this anymore."

So, from that moment on, during that retreat, I decided to sit through all the bells. So, rather than getting up and doing the walking meditation, I would just sit there. I'd sit in the mornings about three hours. I'd hear the bell and my body would start vibrating and there was this incredible fear. It was like … my heartbeat seemed so loud that I was sure someone could hear it, and I felt a great fear. This went on for a few days, off and on, until it gradually started to subside. It seemed as though the final bit of fear was just coming out of my body.

Renate: Was it fear about something, or was it just fear … ?

Linda: It was just fear. It felt like pure fear, pure fear.

Renate: You mentioned in the beginning of our interview – fear, but there's a whole other level of fear.

Linda: After enlightenment?

Renate: Yes. Do you want to say something about it?

Linda: So much has happened since then. When it first happens I would definitely describe it as enlightenment. There was no question about it. There were no more questions. And, the way I expressed it was quite final like, "This is it. This is enlightenment." Then after a while, I realised there was still a degree of fear there. There was still a bit of fear. But, when it first happens to you, the contrast between how it was and how it feels now, is so great that it does feel like the total opposite. But, after a while, like I said, I realised that there was still fear there. You have to admit that to yourself, and it's very difficult when you're teaching to actually admit to yourself, "Okay, there is still a bit of fear there." But, that just naturally starts to go, to dissolve those bits of fear. But, you still need to respect your teacher, to feel deep gratitude to your teacher, and to be very open to the fact that there's more that needs to happen in you. That can be difficult when you're teaching – and teaching implies there's authority there. You can feel, and I'm sure some teachers probably feel that if they admit that there's still something there it's going to affect their authority. But actually, the opposite is true. Once you start to admit that there is more to do, you automatically become more humble, and that gives you this deeper, much deeper authority, because people can sense when there's fear there, and they can sense the authority in humility.

Renate: I sometimes look at teachers and I can sense they're not completely clear.

Linda: No. Well, I would say I'm not completely clear, but who is? Maybe that only happens at the point of death. I don't know. I went to India a few months ago and sat with a teacher there. He's been in this state for maybe thirty or forty years. It was obvious to me he was more deeply here than me. A few years ago there might have been a bit of reaction to that, "I don't really want to know about that," but at this time it just felt quite beautiful, and an incredible opportunity for me to go more deeply into this. That's the excitement about the whole thing – that it does keep going. It can't be finite. You can't say, "This is the end," because in eternity, there's no end. That's the most beautiful and exciting thing about it.

Renate: In what do you go further into? How do you experience more freedom? Where do you go? Where do you expand into? I think I read in your notes that you said, "I go deeper and deeper into the moment."

Linda: Into the unknown.

Renate: Into the unknown. So, the moment, the now …

Linda: The now is totally unknown. When you're completely – I still say completely, but – when you are completely here, it's unknown – you can't know anything. Before, the unknown to me was scary, "I don't know what's going to happen." Now, it's incredibly exciting and beautiful – this unknown. What also happens after enlightenment is that you do have to – well, it happens gradually – it took me seven years to really integrate the relative and the absolute. I'm still living in this body. I'm still living in this world. To really feel completely one with it, for me, it took seven years to feel that union, so there wasn't that abrasive quality of the world, of everyday life – it just all became one.

Renate: So, when everything is one, how can one person get enlightened? How does that work? If the experience is, there is only one, how can you say then, "I am enlightened?"

Linda: Well, of course, using that language, you can say, "Nobody can be enlightened." But, you need to use language to communicate with people. The only reason I said, "I am enlightened," was because I know during my practice, that's what I was interested in. I know not everyone is consciously interested in becoming enlightened. But for me, that was the thing. And, if I saw a teacher who said, "I am enlightened," I wanted to find out whether they were or not. That's what got me going. I didn't want someone to say, "No, I'm not enlightened," – I wanted to know it was possible. And, I know when I started saying it – I don't really say it as much now – I just don't feel to, but it's true – I am.

Renate: And, I am intrigued by that, that you can say that. [*laughs*]

Linda: Yes, and that's why I say it. When you do say it though, you get a lot of people saying, "How can you say that? And, you can't be enlightened because you say that. And, what an arrogant thing to say." The only reason I can say it, is because there's no arrogance there, and I really don't care what people think of me. What I care about now – the only thing that really gets me going is the fact that it's possible for others to be free. And, it is possible.

Renate: One of the beliefs we have, a lot of people have, is that it only can happen through grace. But, listening to you I get the feeling if you put in enough effort, and dedication, and make it the highest priority in our life, we can get it.

Linda: Well, that's what you need to do. You need to put it first, before anything. That's what happened with me. I didn't make myself do it. It just happened. You can say that grace was meeting my teacher – that was the grace. Then after that, it was up to me to use that grace, and to appreciate that grace, and to work because I had the good fortune to meet this deeply enlightened being, and to connect with him. So, it was up to me to fulfil my potential, which I saw in him.

Renate: And when you work now with students – you have students mainly in Australia – or you also have students in England?

Linda: I haven't got many in England. [*both laugh*] I've got a lot in America. I'd be happy to do some things in England, but I haven't actually worked at it. I've been travelling quite a bit lately.

Renate: You go to Denmark afterwards.

Linda: Yes, I'm going to Denmark to do a retreat at the end of May. I can't remember the date.

Renate: It's all on your website.

Linda: Yes, it's all on the website ...

Renate: But, what is the biggest obstacle? What's in the way with people?

Linda: Fear. It's all about fear.

Renate: Fear of?

Linda: Well, what it comes down to is fear of death of the body. So, it's fear of death. All our fear comes from that basic fear, that primal fear.

Renate: So, it's basically deep identification with the body. How can you break that?

Linda: How can you break that. Through seeing again, and again, and again that I am not my thoughts. Breaking that momentum of the thinking process, and coming back to the body. It's really the practice that I teach. It's just basic Zen practice. It's all about the body. It's using the body to realise that I am not the body. Which sounds like a paradox ...

Renate: I like that, yes, I like that.

Linda: It's through the body, and even after enlightenment, it's all about the body.

Renate: Well, I just realized I have to stop. [*both laugh*]

Linda: That was quick.

Renate: I know. I just wanted to go more into the body, but maybe next time when you come to England.

Linda: Okay.

John Butler –
Discovering Stillness – Parts 1 and 2
Interview by **Iain McNay**

I think one of the impediments, one of the things that stops us setting out on the spiritual life is that we are not sufficiently unhappy. We are too content with this sort of compromise with life, with all the little sandwich bars and baubles that life offers to us; that comfort of a teddy bear and you know for some people that's not good enough, you want more, you want the real thing. And I guess I was one of those people.

Iain: Today my guest is John Butler and we are not in London in our usual studios, we're up in Bakewell in Derbyshire. John wasn't able to come to London. So, we are actually, in a very special location; we are in All Saints Church in Bakewell and we are here because John comes to meditate and pray here at five o'clock every morning for two hours and also later on in the afternoon for two or three hours. So, we heard about John because someone wrote in and told us about him and he's written two books; *Wonders of Spiritual Unfoldment* which is four hundred pages and it is a very interesting read and *Mystic Approaches* and he also has two books of poetry, which he has just given me and I have not looked at yet, *Destined to Joy: Mystic Verses Part One* and *Do You Pray For Me: Mystic Verses Part Two*. So, if you want to read more about John there's plenty out there to read. So, John, welcome to Conscious TV, and I am going to ask you first of all about your father because he taught you some great things in life, didn't he?

John: Yes, he was a quiet man, an artist, a craftsman. Very conscious of his surroundings. A landscape artist mostly at that time. He taught me to observe nature, to see the beauty of what was in front of me. Nothing elaborate, just the hedges, the trees, the grass, to notice the sky. He was also very conscious of good work. He loved carpentry, he taught me how to use tools and I remember so well him saying "pay attention, keep your eye on what you are doing. When you are sewing a piece of wood, listen to and watch the movement of the saw, watch the hammer so that you hit the nail straight. And these two lessons of one hundred percent giving attention and observing what was around me have stood me in good stead all my life.

Iain: They're wonderful qualities which are probably quite rare these days which is sad but that is the way the world is… and what did you get from your mother?

John: Mum was Russian. Well, she was also an artist in her way. She was a housewife of course, which is what women were then they called themselves that and were proud of it. When Women's Liberation came in she said there is nothing wrong with being a mother and a housewife. Anyway, what I got from mum was primarily a Russian heart and Russian hearts they just spill out all over the place. And I was always told as a child that I wear my heart on my sleeve, well, people laughed at me but it is one of the best things, to have a great heart. To work from the heart, to ealizez the existence of the heart and the whole household shone with that tender loving care that emanates from someone that loves their work and gives themselves to it; the way the table was laid, the way she knitted our clothes for us, did the mending, did the washing up, everything was a work of art and done with love.

Iain: And I know at seven years of age you were sent to boarding school and that was a little bit of a shock but you escaped to the chapel and prayed when you needed didn't you, to find your solitude and balance again.

John: [Laughs] It was a shock because up till then we had lived in the deep country and I hardly knew what another little boy was. My former companions were nature and animals. And I was suddenly thrown into this world of other little boys and I was completely lost and for the first time in my life I knew what it was to feel isolated and lonely. Thank God the school was in a rural setting so there were big gardens where I could go and, also in my little childish way I remember so well just burying my little head in my hands and closing my eyes and saying, "God bless mummy and daddy and my sister and our dog." What a haven of home and security that was for me!

Iain: It seems even at an early age you had a way of going inside and finding somewhere you could rest, as you used the word haven just now.

John: Yes, I think that probably was so, if not inside, at least to stillness and quietness. In nature, it is outside, isn't it? You look at a tree and put your arms around a tree and you're held in stillness, in quietness, in that reassurance of simply being itself. And what a contrast it is to the noise and the agitation that you get from most people.

Iain: At the beginning of this book [*Wonders of Spiritual Unfoldment*] you talk about being committed to discovering stillness.

John: Well I wouldn't say that, no, it is really a book committed to discovering ... well, I don't really know what really... if I use clever words like the Infinite, or even God, I still don't know really what they are, who does know what God is [laughs]? Nobody knows what God is, but there's, how can I put it ... ? Perhaps one longs for the unlimited, for freedom and for love and any worldly experience, all these things are finite; they have an end. You go out, you discover freedom, go out and climb a mountain but then you have to come home again. Love is wonderful in its flowering but then sooner or later it says "no", it has an end. All the things you love, the happiness, it all comes and goes, doesn't it? I think that perhaps I was just greedy, I wanted that which didn't end.

85

Iain: But sometimes we need that, you call it greed, that commitment to find, otherwise we never find it.

John: Well, absolutely, that's the motivation, isn't it?

Iain: We will come on to that a bit later, I just want to go through your story sequentially and just discover these important pointers in your life. So, there's so much we could do because you are now seventy-nine years old, there's so much we could talk about but I'm going to summarise it to some extent: You were an army officer, which I guess was National Service, involved with the family business and then in 1963 you went to South America ...

John: Yes.

Iain: What took you to South America?

John: Oh, I wanted to make the world a better place [laughs].

Iain: What was your vision of making the world a better place?

John: Well, I was a farmer, I'd loved farming since my first breath, I was soaked in farming. I wanted to be a farmer, it was my overriding dream really. And I had studied the subject and it was the time when these charities like OXFAM were just beginning, so it was the fashionable thing really, I suppose. I had another mate and we were going out to Bolivia They were giving grants of a thousand hectares to new settlers who would go out and grow food for the hungry, so we thought we would go out and do that. We were young and strong but my mate didn't come, he met a girl who stayed in England and I met a Peruvian girl and her father invited me to go and work for him in Peru, so I did that on a big sheep hacienda. But that was my Socialist time of life and I wanted to do good so I ended up working as a volunteer agriculturalist in the mountains of Peru.

Iain: Which must have been beautiful, actually.

John: Well I wouldn't say it was easy but there was plenty of space up there and I loved that, I loved the donkeys and the oxen. And yes, it was a good year but I think like most people who had done voluntary

86

service it gave me much more than I gave to it really and I learnt probably the greatest lesson of my life: I remember sitting on a mountainside one day, I had done a lot of work and a little bit of work planting trees on eroded mountainsides and of course the local sheep and goats had come and eaten them all off, so I was sitting there a bit depressed. And it seemed, a little voice said to me, "Make whole, be whole."

Iain: Make whole, be whole.

John: To make whole, be whole. Well I hardly understood what that was then but I had read a little bit about meditation, not that I really understood it. But I saw myself as a mixed-up young man trying to help people, the local Indians, who were older and wiser than myself and more able to live. And I ealize I had to do something about sorting out myself before I could be much use to others. So, having read a bit about meditation, when I came home to England, I looked for and I found a school of meditation.

Iain: I wanted to just point out one more thing that I thought was important in your book. There was a situation, you were in the mountains, in the jungle I think in Peru and you felt the only way was to surrender.

John: Ah, yes [laughs].

Iain: Do you remember that? That was quite important I think.

John: Yes, I had a pal and we'd found an Indian who would take us, and we had several days in the jungle, just walking through the jungle which was ...

Iain: ... it must have been an incredible experience.

John: It was an incredible experience, it was absolutely wonderful. The jungle is very thick, it is quite difficult to walk through, with great trees above us, very little sunlight comes down to the forest floor, you creep along over the fallen leaves, huge lizards, snails and snakes, you see monkeys up in the trees and at one point we came to a little creek with sandy banks and there was a great sort of furrow gouged out of the sand as though someone had dragged a big oil barrow through it. We looked at the guide and it was a huge snake, an anaconda and I wanted to follow up and find it but he wouldn't let me, he said it would be lying curled up ready to grab us. Then it started to rain and we camped just near there, just beside it and we made a little fire, just sleeping on the ground there and I didn't sleep very well, I think maybe I woke up in the middle of the night and the rain had cleared, and you know the jungle's full of shrieks and funny sounds, rustlings at night, all the animals come out and move around and I sat there by the campfire, in this little circle of light and I thought of this great snake, I could reach out and touch it probably for all I knew. And I began to feel fear and we were alone in this jungle and if the Indian deserted us God knows what we would have done. And then quite inexplicably I just, perhaps I had stopped fighting, I gave up the struggle, I surrendered. I just relaxed into the situation as it was, into the unknown and I suddenly felt peace, such as that I'd never felt before. Just total peace, in which all the threats that surrounded us were contained and alright. And I look back on that as one of my first great spiritual experiences.

Iain: Yes, you say in the book "I put my trust in forces greater than me."

John: Yes.

Iain: Yes, which we all have to do, don't we sometimes, if not all the time?

John: Yes, in a way, I've been doing it all my life. That is the essence.

Iain: [Reading from the book] "putting your trust in forces greater than you."

John: That's right.

Iain: Yes. Do you feel that peace now?

John: Absolutely.

Iain: Yes

John: Of course. I am nervous before an interview but what do I do? I find that stillness and I feel confident, it's like an invisible hand to hold, a rock.

Iain: So how do you find the stillness?

John: How do I find it? Well it can't be described.

Iain: Yes, and you said you were nervous before the interview and you find that stillness ...

John: ... yes, how do I find it? I've had many years of practice, it is second nature to me now. Probably my first nature. It is so obvious, we are sitting in it like fishes in the sea. You can never not be still but the trouble is we just don't see it. We look down and we just live in this cocoon of mental agitation [covers his eyes with his hands], lost in thought; that's the human condition. At least what we call the human condition, but actually it's lost, it is not reality at all, what we are, and that is the cause of all of our problems. We are absent from the presence of God.

Iain: And this in a way, the groundwork is what your father was teaching you, about watching the now...

John: yes, to be present, to be present. The present is such an important word, now, the present moment here and now. The present moment ... [the church bells begin to chime] ... you can hear the church clock chiming, can't you?

Iain: I can.

John: It is sounding in stillness, isn't it?

Iain: It's one o'clock ...

John: ... in stillness and in timelessness. Time goes round, round and round in eternal presence, the peace of God that passeth understanding, right here and now, you can never be closer to God than right here and now.

Iain: Okay, so I am going to keep going with your story. You were starting to say that when you got back from South America you were twenty-seven and you discovered this school of mediation.

John: Yes.

Iain: Tell us about that, about how you discovered it, not so much how you discovered it but how it was important to you.

John: Well, it certainly was very important. Yes, I had to go to London to be taught. My first farm was at Bakewell then, so I had to get the late night train back from London to look after my animals the next morning. I was sitting in St Pancreas station waiting room, among all the rubbish and the unfortunate drunks and homeless that used it and I sat and closed my eyes and meditated as I had been told and there and then in that seemingly uncongenial situation it opened up, like that [raises his arms high] and I ealize that all the space, the freedom that I had longed for and that I had been travelling the world to find, the deserts and the mountains of this world were within me, and that discovery, that discovery, well it has been going on ever since. Bigger and bigger, greater and greater, better and better.

Iain: So the discovery was the beginning of something in a way.

John: It was the beginning of ealizezed. Of course, I had the theory, I was brought up in a Christian school, I had ten years of compulsory chapel and scripture lessons, I knew a lot of the Bible by heart and the old prayer book; "The kingdom of God is within you," you know I'd learnt that but what did it mean? I didn't really know but very soon in those first few periods of meditation I had ealize there was this dimension that was not of this ... not what we call ... this world. There was a further dimension that could be ealize. That's the word ealizezed. The Biblical phrase comes alive ;The Kingdom of God, what does that mean? I don't know it's difficult to say even now but it's within you, it really is within. And the peace of God that passes understanding, it is beyond the thinking mind. You don't get it by substituting one thought for another but by opening-up to this dimension of spirit really, that's what it is. Invisible. You can't describe it. Everybody knows what silence is but no one can describe it. Who knows what silence is?

Iain: I'm not sure that everyone knows what silence is actually. They think it's just not hearing any noise.

John: Well, exactly.

Iain: We will go into more detail later but I think there is almost an art to silence somehow. I know you had some, again, important experiences which helped deepen your ealizezed. There was one time when you were on the London Underground train and you saw everyone as Jesus, is that right?

John: Well I know I used the word when I described it, but I'm not sure really what I meant by it. I think the words Jesus and Christ so often get used with very nebulous meanings and different people of course mean it in different ways but I think how I would describe it now as far as I remember, it was this ealizezed of this stillness, that this underground train carriage was full of this stillness and within this stillness the bodies, the sounds, the personalities took place and actually pervaded everybody.

Iain: Whether they ealize it or not.

John: Oh absolutely, I mean if you look at people's eyes, everybody every eye shines with more or less light even if the eye is very dull. It is the same light isn't it, how many lights are there? There is only one light isn't there? And so, it is, there is only one stillness, there's only one stillness. And I think these first experiences of mine were like that.

Iain: You had another time when I think you were also in London where even you saw the garbage as beautiful, everything was shining.

John: Yes, well again it depends what you're ealize on. There are levels of consciousness, if your heart is light, if your heart is full of light, you see light. And everything that is in it is light, you know beauty is in the eye of the beholder isn't it, if your eye is full of beauty that's what you see.

Iain: Yes but I think it was also important from what you explained in the book about that ealizezed, I am just trying to find the words here [from the book] that forced you to review some deeply negative attitudes towards ealizezed's city life.

John: Absolutely, yes, well I think I said, being a country boy I was at that time very negative about city life as a sort of worst of the worst [laughs]. You know we used words like Townies to describe those not fortunate enough to live in the country and ealizezed was the very antithesis of nature. Unnatural wasn't it, and so these were some of the great lessons I had to overcome and certainly meditation did help to clear-out some of those negative thoughts from my mind but unfortunately there were many, many more of them deeply buried inside. It is a long process.

Iain: It is a long process and I think that one of the things that comes across, certainly in your book and your story, is this motivation, this determination to keep going somehow, you didn't give up. Let's go through the story and we'll come to some examples of this: so in your thirties you actually thought of becoming a monk at one point, you were in and out of monasteries, you were searching still in the Christian tradition I guess there.

John: Yes, I don't remember too clearly what my motivation was, I think perhaps it was a reaction, I didn't want to be what most of my contemporaries were; I didn't want to go into business, I didn't want to go into the professions. Monastic life seemed to offer an alternative but that was about the same time as I learned to meditate and it certainly raised the question, do I follow this way or that way of meditation? I don't see any conflict now but then I did and it seemed an either/or situation. At that time – things have changed a lot in that last fifty or sixty years – the Church was really, quite suspicious of meditation, it regarded it as something Eastern which is very odd. But, anyway, it did and I guess I was caught up in that but I decided to stay with meditation, because even in those early months I ealize, or I felt it was, for me a more effective way of spiritual work.

Iain: You say more than once in the book that your two loves at that point were meditation and farming and animals and there's a lovely example you gave, one point you had to sell your farm and you were quite sad about that and you were just sitting, feeling it and this ram came over to you. Just talk us through what happened there.

John: Excuse me, may I just jump back for a moment to make a little comment about that decision about meditation?

Iain: Of course.

John: The accusation is often made that meditation is a withdrawal from this world but absolutely on the contrary, the key principle of the method that I taught was that you practice it while living in the world. A monk's life may possibly be considered a withdrawal from worldly life but meditation, absolutely not. It is the art of finding the eternal, in the midst of the marketplace, the stillness in the movement.

Iain: To be, I forget the exact phrase, but to be in the world but not of the world.

John: Absolutely, that's the good phrase in the world but not of the world. Yes.

Iain: I understand that.

John: Yes, and it is utterly practical. It is absolutely not a withdrawal, an opting out, it is a completely different understanding.

Iain: I have read many things over the years about monks that have spent years meditating in very confined places, like a cave or a monastery and they come to the city and they are lost.

John: Yes.

Iain: And what you're saying is that, that stillness, that presence it's right in the marketplace, in the city.

John: Yes, in the most chaotic imaginable situation. Yes.

Iain: Yes.

John: God is with us.

Iain: Yes. I am going to insist on the story about the ram because I love the story.

John: Yes, so do I [laughs]. I think it is one of those wonderful things that I have got no explanation for but at that time ... one of the great loves of my life are sheep ... I can tell you a lot about my understanding of the lamb of God [laughs] anyway, at that time I had quite a considerable flock of sheep; about one hundred and fifty sheep, and five rams I think and one of these rams was an old warrior, where through much fighting he'd split his skull and was ... an old soldier [laughs]. And just before things happened; I had to move on from my first farm. I was sitting on one side of the field, I'm not sure if I'd been crying, but I was very unhappy about it all, losing my beloved animals and these rams were lying under a hedge at the other side of the field about a hundred yards or so away. And, to my amazement, one of these rams; this old warrior, he stood up, he left the others, slowly and deliberately he walked across the field, he laid his head in my lap and just stood there for a minute or two, or three. And he turned away and went back and laid back with his companions. It brings tears to my eyes to tell you. Well, what do you make of that?

Iain: That extraordinary connection that you have had with nature, which is everyone's potential in a way.

John: Well, maybe that was it. I did consider that [to be] one of the greatest honours of my life. I couldn't ask for more.

Iain: One of the greatest honours of your life [nodding]. Yes, wonderful.

John: See, this Russian heart brings tears to my eyes [wipes his eyes dry] even in front of a camera, I'm sorry.

Iain: Well, you have had a bit of an up-and-down story in some ways and I'm going to now move on because in your late forties, your life fell apart and you had quite bad depression. How did that start?

John: Well, I had a second farm then, it was a lovely little farm and that is really another little story. I was happy as a farmer, I was married by then and had a good wife ... but we had many meditation students at that time who used to come to the farm. I was quite well known, as one of the first organic farmers. There was a woman that came to meditate and on one occasion – we meditate with closed eyes, by the way – we were sitting together and we'd just come to stillness and I saw our two souls rise from our bodies and merge as one. She was a woman with very open clear eyes and when I looked at her, I saw right through to the infinite beyond.

Iain: So, what does that mean?

John: What does that mean?

Iain: The "infinite beyond." What did you actually see?

John: Well you have got to ealize there are two sorts of sight; there are the eyes of flesh and there's what's called insight ... seeing with the eyes of the heart, [smiles]. Flesh sight is always limited; it has a boundary, flesh sees flesh. But we all have to some extent a sense of indescribable beauty, or indescribable peace ... something like that. What did I see? I saw the indescribable, right there. I saw the infinite indescribable. But it is the realest of the real when you see it. And what really tipped me back, tipped me into depression was that I was still a young man, a hot-blooded young man, still very much living in my physical body and my human emotion. How do you reconcile the two? There was that spiritual union, if you like, the mystical marriage, contrasted with two people living lives both with their own marriages, their homes, their jobs that were separate. How do you reconcile unity with separation? Well, I couldn't at that time. It was beyond my ability, my experience. I couldn't go back into that old life. Of course, I couldn't escape it either, really, I was sort of, imprisoned in it.

Iain: So it was an experience that took you out [raises arms in a wide arc above his head] of your world.

John: Yes, that's right. I suppose in modern jargon, it blew my mind. I'm not sure if that is accurate or not. It's not a phrase I normally use.

Iain: Sounds very accurate! It blew your mind [laughs].

John: But, I went back home and there was my dear wife but somehow it was all too small, I couldn't ... I had been shown something ... well anyway, the gist of it was it threw me into a turmoil of emotions and I left. I had to really break away.

Iain: You had to leave your marriage.

John: I left my farm, I left my home.

Iain: Wow.

John: I had one of the little motor caravans of that time and I drifted around for some years homeless, jobless, loveless and alone. And it was a wretched time of life. I just picked through it, I did what I could.

Iain: But you'd had that experience. So, had that given you a reference point, had it given you an opening?

John: Yes it did because how can one access it? Well, meditation of course does just that. Because in meditation you ... if I can give you a demonstration, the beautiful demonstration of meditation, I hope the camera can see my hands, is just that; [unfolds clenched fingers into open palms].

Iain: It's just an opening.

John: It's letting go.

Iain: letting go.

John: Now this is how we live [tightens fingers again], forgetting, forgetful of the One.

Iain: Trying to hold on ...

John: ... trying to hold on. We hold on to our personal life and so we are imprisoned with our ego, which is our sense of separation. And in meditation, it starts very gently at first, so it is not frightening or anything, but very gently it helps you to do that [unfolds fingers to open palms again]. Now when you let go, you discover that you are not actually separate at all. You are united. You are in that which is undivided. Indescribable but undivided. There's not two at all, there's just One. One love. One person. Singular. Adam in the paradise was singular, one I Am. Now that's what I had been shown in this dramatic episode with this woman; the Oneness. Well, you could say, that then the work, the real work began because the two polarities had been clearly identified to me. I was too muddled really to put it as clearly as I am saying to you now but that's what gradually dawned on me. At one time in the motor caravan I went to spend a winter in Spain, alone of course and I spent hour after hour after hour just meditating. I moved from doing the standard half-hour morning and night and meditation became salvation because in salvation you are taken out of this imprisonment and [unfolds arms] you are shown what's real. You're saved from drowning in this world, just as when Saint Peter was walking on water; he was drowning in the world, and there was Jesus free beside him. Peter was drowning, he reached, he said, "help me." Jesus said "what were you frightened about? What were you drowning for? Have faith!"

Iain: Have faith.

John: That's what it's all about.

Iain: And you never stopped having faith even though it was a difficult time?

John: I don't think I ever did because I had this wonderful practice and this practice [meditation] is such a wonderful way of putting it into practice. So twice every day without fail and for increasing lengths of time. I was just surrendering to that total presence and to that love that has no end. That love that never says no. To pure, total love which is, which I'd seen in her eyes you see? And yet the body of course said no ...

Iain: ... in a way it wasn't to do with her ...

John: ... well ...

Iain: ... she was a portal somehow ...

John: well the body was a portal because that isn't really what we are. And this is the great discovery; that man is not limited to the flesh, the flesh as the Bible tells us is prophet of nothing.

Iain: Yes.

John: The flesh is just ... look, anything that dies, mortality, the whole world [that] comes to pass is not what we are. Man, is eternal being.

Iain: Okay. I am going to go back to your story a little bit because I think it is important for people to see that your path wasn't always smooth, it had ups and downs, and how you dealt with the downs I think is so important and people somehow, they get stuck in having the highs, as they see them; the experiences but these practicalities.

John: Yes of course, well, it's discipline that pulls you through. You have just got to keep on ealizeze. Practise, practise, practise.

Iain: This discipline, in the motor-home, you kept the discipline of meditation.

John: Yes, but in a way, it isn't difficult because it is a way, in a way it is like, well it is being described as a trail of grains of sugar, you know? You follow it because it's always leading you from better, to better, to better.

Iain: From better, to better, to better.

John: Yes, it's described as a trail of sugar, you see, leading to the sugar mountain, which is of course the Kingdom of God.

Iain: Yes but unfortunately in our society there's so many false trails, trying to take you from better, to better, to better and all you end up with is an unhealthy body and an overdraft and credit card bills [laughs] and ...

John: Well I think one of the impediments, one of the things that stops us setting out on the spiritual life is that we are not sufficiently unhappy. We are too content with this sort of compromise with life, with all the little sandwich bars and baubles that life offers to us; that comfort of a teddy bear and you know for some people that's not good enough, you want more, you want the real thing. And I guess I was one of those people.

Iain: Yes but you also had what I would call, the taste, not the taste, as it is not a strong enough word but you had visions, in one way, you had big, big, clues and not everyone has that.

John: Well yes, that's also true and am I not blessed?

Iain: There is a blessing in that, you are absolutely right.

John: Absolutely. You know the Bible tells us we are saved by grace. What is grace? It is something that comes unseen, unknown, you know, it is like memory, where does memory come from? It just comes, doesn't it?

Iain: So, what happened next was in 1998, you went to Africa for a time.

John: Yes, I was offered a job out in Africa, South Africa. I went out there, the job didn't work out, so after some time I hired a little car and I just drove off. I didn't really have a plan, I didn't really have a proper map but I just followed the road and it all unfolded in front of me. I slept in the back of the car or out on the ground under the stars; I actually loved it. The space, the glorious space! And I never went to any big towns only little ones, I just bought what I had to and got out into the open again [laughs]. I just found the big empty spaces on the map and I went there.

Iain: It comes across in the book that you are always drawn to wide-open, preferably wild places.

John: Yes.

Iain: And, but for the wind, there were utter silences that you'd never known before.

John: Yes.

Iain: There was no place for your depression anymore.

John: No, I suppose, out there... I was so thrilled by it, so ...

Iain: Utter silence.

John: Yes, so I just couldn't get enough of space and silence. I have always loved space and silence, they're just natural to me, I belong there. That's where I feel at home.

Iain: But it seems to me that it is kind of, what you've told us so far about your life, it's almost like there is this dance of space and you are drawn to this space on the outside whilst you ealizez the real space is primarily on the inside. And you are in Africa and of course you are completely attracted to the stillness of the space, nothing around for miles and miles.

John: Yes, I actually loved that. When I was a boy at school, my favourite picture was of a cowboy riding up to the crest of a hill with the caption,

"Don't fence me in". I loved that phrase; I was in the Kalahari and the Namibian desert and that ... oh I just loved it. It always seemed obvious to me why the early Christians, why men of prayer, went to the desert. I experienced it for myself and it is just all so obvious there, it is all just before you; the Infinite. You are nothing. You are taken into the immensity of what's there.

Iain: Because you talk in the book about when you are in Africa you sense the absence of subject/object relationships. It's not you and the other, it's just the One.

John: No, that's right. All that dies away. All the personality is, is nothing.

Iain: Yes.

John: The 'me', the John Butler is just ... you forget about it ... it's just nothing.

Iain: Yes, and of course you came back from Africa to England ...

John: Yes, [laughs] where you can imagine that is the opposite, getting back to England ... well I'd get back into John Butler again [laughs]. Or what the world considered that to be.

Iain: And you found it tough again, didn't you?

John: Well, I, you know, I had lost my job as a farmer. I was desperate to find some sort of work and what on earth could I do? I wrote a CV [curriculum vitae] at that time and I remember more-or-less what I wrote. I wrote I knew something about freedom and therefore I could help others to freedom. And of course, freedom is love. Love is freedom. The two are really the same thing, spiritually speaking. And if someone could give me a channel for my love, I would give my all. That was what I was looking for. And of course, who answered my CV? Nobody [laughs]! I was looking for freedom in the world of bondage.

Iain: But you'd also had the ealizezed before when you were in London and you saw the garbage as beautiful in the London Underground station and somehow, you'd had those experiences but something ... it is hard isn't it? I'm just pointing out that you had had these reference points but you had this openness in Africa, this stillness. John Butler has almost disappeared and you get back to England, and the reality of day-to-day life hits you again.

John: Well, I suppose, I hadn't ... I was still ... we are such spiritual infants, you know, even now as an old man I am still a spiritual child. It's a long journey and one is learning all the time. You learn something every day. And at that time, I was still grappling with questions that I, that now, I no longer have these problems. But at that time, I did.

Iain: I just wanted people to understand where you really were. You said again that you fell into personal desire. You had to deal with what you call the cancerous root of egoism by exposing it bit-by-bit. How did you expose it bit-by-bit? The cancerous root of egoism.

John: Yes, that's a good phrase [laughs]. How did I deal with it? Well, how indeed. I'm not sure that we can deal with it because you see we/I am the ego, so it is the ego trying to deal with the ego. It's the pot calling the kettle black. The blind leading the blind. We are saved by grace. Well, I meditated. At that time, I met a teacher, a young man and I looked into his eyes and I had that same experience of seeing the infinite beyond.

Iain: That you'd had with that woman.

John: Freedom, yes. And I followed him out to America, to San Francisco. I was that desperate. I knew that's what I wanted, I didn't want anything else. So, as it were, I jumped off the precipice to him and while I was in America after I had been with him a few days ... I remember it was a big meeting, and he looked at me and he pointed out my pride, my arrogance and my egoism, which completely crushed me. I was exposed in this room of, I suppose, a couple of hundred people. I'd been called in the room and I felt within me a monstrous, almost like a worm and I didn't know what to do with it at all. I was absolutely terrified, and I fled.

Where did I flee to? I fled into the wilderness. I got a car and I just drove into the desert. And I thought I was going mad at that time. I had such a sense of evil within me and I didn't know how to deal with it at all. I meditated but somehow even meditation didn't deal with it and fearing I was really going to lose my wits.

I took a job as a cook in a funny little motel/gas station, I worked in the kitchen there, frying eggs and things in the Mohave desert, which is just on the border of Arizona, surrounded by desert-country.

One day after work, I walked up the side of the valley, there was a little motel, this little spot at the side of the valley, I sat on a rock and I think I put my head in my hands and I think I just was finished then. And someone came and stood beside me. I didn't see anybody, I didn't hear anybody, no man was involved at all but I felt there was a presence beside me. I suppose it was Jesus. I never doubted it. It was nothing to do with the church, nothing to do with religion at all. And I didn't really notice any difference, the depression didn't end but I wrote a poem, that's right "depression didn't end but from then on I had a friend." I certainly didn't have any human friend at that time. And then a few more months passed and I ended this job with a pocket full of money, so once more I hired a car and had a wonderful time exploring the western states, the cowboy country and more animals and more beloved prairie, then I came home and once again in this awful abyss of not knowing what to do.

Iain: So what the breakthrough was for you was the appearance of what you felt might have been, could be, Jesus. It was about having a companion, a friend, a support, a guide ... am I using the right words?

John: I think you are making too much of it. I wouldn't use any of those words, it was less defined. It was very undefined. Soon after I got back, I had some friends then that did healing and I remember they prayed over me and it was extraordinary, I felt like I found myself screaming, I was thrown into the ground and something was expelled, some revolting thing came out of my mouth, it opened my mouth so wide that my mouth split but what came out? I never saw it. I suppose, one idea expelled by another. And just before that happened, I had gone into a Job Centre, I was invited to an open day and I was invited to go to Nottingham University to study Russian as a very mature student.

Iain: So, at the age of fifty-three you decided to study Russian; because you had a Russian mother?

John: Yes.

Iain: ... and you already talked earlier about this Russian heart.

John: Yes, well, what a thing to do. Why should I, a farmer, lover of open spaces, want to study Russian? Well, I was that desperate, I'd been homeless, jobless, loveless and alone for a long time and I was really desperate for direction and something worthwhile to do. Not just aimless wandering. So, I was only too grateful when I was given this opportunity.

Yes, Mum was Russian, from Siberia, born in 1904. When the Revolution broke out in 1917, the family was dispersed and she found herself a refugee, sent to England in her late teens. Speaking no English, she had a difficult life until she met and married Dad. Anyway, I'd always felt that I wasn't really English – but some sort of a misfit. I suppose that's why I was more at home with nature than with other people. School tried to make me into an Englishman and it didn't really work. I didn't fit that mode, I didn't think that way. And I didn't know why. I suppose it gave me a sense of guilt and failure throughout life as I just felt I was different, I didn't belong. And when I began to study Russian, in very little ways at first, something seemed to come together in me. Even the language books, particularly those with illustrations, seemed to go just straight to my heart. Something seemed to be happening ...

Mum never taught us Russian as children. She was so ealizezed by her own dreadful experiences as a young woman that she only wanted to protect us from it, she didn't want us to carry the weight of all those terrible events that happened in Russia, so she shielded us. But especially as I grew older I wanted to know more and more, and when I went to university I really was hungry to discover all I could about where I came from.

Iain: And you actually ended up teaching in Russian schools.

John: I went to Russia ... and that is another long story. Yes, I went there at the end of Perestroika, in Spring 1991. The Iron Curtain had just come down and I found myself in a small town in provincial Russia. Being the only Englishman there, the first most of them had ever met, I soon became a novelty. The children wanted to learn English and so naturally I found myself drawn into schools and teaching. I had never taught before. I had no experience of children but it wasn't difficult. I loved it. All I had to do basically was speak English.

Iain: And what was happening with your meditation, at this point? Didn't it become more like prayer?

John: Yes, but not for a while. Not for several years.

Iain: Did learning Russian influence you in terms of your meditation?

John: That also came later but, to begin with, you may remember, I had gone through a long period of depression – a really awful period of depression until, thank God, being busy and having something else to think about at University pulled me out of it. When I went to Russia, again it was very difficult at first, for my ability to speak the language was abysmal. I was alone, with no reliable connections, nowhere to live. But eventually I found my feet and really loved it. I couldn't help loving it even when lost and lonely. I remember very soon after I went there, standing at a bus queue on a cold miserable day with a wretched cold myself, and people all huddled up in their overcoats and I felt such happiness. Again, I am going to cry, because I knew I was among my own people and these were people who thought and felt as I did.

Iain: Yes.

John: And I was no longer alone. I was among my own people. I can't tell you what that meant to me. It was a journey of such great discovery for me. Love is not really a big enough word to describe it.

Iain: Yes, I'm just thinking of how this can help people. So, you found your own people and it was to do, partly, with your genetics, your history with your mother. And that was a heart-full connection which you had never really found in England.

John: No, but again that was at the human level. So, it was important at that level, at the level of my personality but that's of minor consequence compared to the spiritual work. I suppose at that time, my spiritual work had rather gone into the background. I was absorbed in the discovery of Russia, but after several years in Russia it began to re-emerge. When I first went into Russian churches, and discovered Russian Orthodoxy, it seemed very strange to me and alien – quite different from the Church of England – at least in the way it's presented. And I had to learn another language, not even ordinary Russian but what's called Old Church Slavonic, to read the prayers and that. But I did it, I plodded on and figured it out and learned to read these simple children's books at first. It was like rediscovering Christianity for the first time, really, rediscovering it ... in a much deeper and more meaningful way.

Iain: Okay, so I understand now. So, it was almost like a letting go of everywhere you'd got to, even with your spiritual experiences and understanding and ... restarting.

John: No, it wasn't a restarting ... but extending. An extending and ... [pauses] ... an extending of the background, rather than the actual experience of Spirit. The spiritual work was not noticeably increased or improved.

I told you that when I started to meditate, the Church greeted it with suspicion and to some extent still does. I think for most Church people, meditation is something they don't understand ... they feel a bit uncomfortable with it really. Even here in Bakewell Church, I feel that it's something they can't quite understand. I sit there with eyes closed and feel them thinking 'What on earth is he doing? Why doesn't he do something?' But when I went to Russia and started studying Orthodoxy, I understood that what's called the Jesus Prayer, which is the Orthodox version of meditation, is very alive and part of the Orthodox tradition.

Through Communism, for three generations, Christianity was virtually abolished in Russia – they had three generations of persecution. Ninety-nine percent of Russian churches were closed, desecrated or destroyed. Millions of Christians were martyred for their faith. Then I saw with my own eyes the miraculous resurrection of faith in Russia and I was right there at the beginning of it. And my own discovery of this tradition of inner prayer meant so much to me because I was no longer an alien from the faith that I'd been brought up in. It brought Christianity and meditation together.

Iain: So, what is the Jesus Prayer?

John: Well, the Jesus Prayer uses – some people will be cross with me for saying this – but basically the Jesus Prayer uses the name of Jesus as a mantra.

Iain: Yes, okay.

John: Now, do you want me to explain what a mantra is?

Iain: I know what a mantra is, explain very briefly what it is.

John: Very briefly, I've explained how we live in this sort of bubble of thought. The human condition is basically ninety-nine percent of the time, lost in thought. You have your bubble of thought and I have my bubble of thought and so we think we are separate. And, to find freedom, or Spirit, we need to discover what is beyond thought. It's a bit like when, on a cloudy day we live under a blanket of cloud, and then what happens? You get in an aeroplane and go up through the cloud, and beyond the cloud you discover the beautiful open sky. Now, that's what meditation is. In meditation, a mantra is like an aeroplane. You get in, you sound a mantra, and this sound in your mind acts like a mental handrail which leads you through the world of thought, of subjective thought up to the open sky.

Iain: Yes.

John: Now, there are all sorts of mantras and methods of meditation, people have their choices but if you are brought up in the faith, if you have a love of Jesus, if you have any sort of connection with Jesus, it's a very comforting thing to use the name of Jesus. Of course, we all grow in faith, starting from what may be really very childish concepts of what it is all about, but we go on growing all our life, we never stop growing in faith and in understanding what it's all about, and what Jesus actually is. My understanding of Jesus has expanded enormously from what I understood when I was being taught in scripture lessons at school. So, anyway, at this time, for me, meditation and Christianity came together.

Iain: You see again, picking out some quotes from your book, which I think you did touch on but I'd like to maybe explore more. You say "Beyond our active mind lies another faculty; quiet and reflective and beyond that again, an indefinable heart or soul. This is the innermost essence of what we really are."

John: That's right.

Iain: "A quiet mind may have aspects of eternity but for fuller access to spirit it's necessary to discover and work with the heart."

John: That's right.

Iain: I suspect with the Jesus Prayer, you are talking about working with the heart?

John: The Jesus Prayer, like any other deeply effective meditation can also be described as prayer of the heart.

Iain: Okay.

John: Yes, that's another word for it and in Russia certainly, the phrase Prayer of the Heart is often used.

Iain: Yes, but you almost talk about three levels here, there's the active mind, beyond the active mind is the quiet and reflective ...

John: ... the reflective mind yes.

Iain: Which could perhaps be called the observer in some traditions?

John: Well ...

Iain: ... anyway, just to stick with what you are talking about here; and then beyond that again, there's the indefinable heart or soul. So, it seems to me that there are almost three levels of us before we get to the Influencer.

John: Well, there are many levels of consciousness, aren't there? There's unconsciousness, there's consciousness of the body, of appetites, of desires, there are states of dreaming, states of awaking, there's day-dreaming.
  Most of us go through the day half asleep. We are not awake at all. Occasionally, something, some noise disturbs you and you wake up and think' 'Good God, what was that?' And you wake up to a higher level of consciousness. Where was I before? Oh, I was half asleep. Now, we go up and down like a yoyo throughout our day, between these different levels of consciousness all the time, and spiritual development is really moving to higher levels of consciousness.
  Just like an aeroplane, it goes up, it starts on the ground and it goes up through thick clouds, then more wispy clouds to where there are no

clouds at all. It goes up through clouds of the mind. You can describe thoughts as clouds of the mind because they are limited, they all have a boundary and you can describe them and the practice of meditation takes you through to the Indescribable. To the Unlimited. Which is Spirit. From Spirit we may ask ... what is God? God is Spirit.

Iain: [laughs]

John: And it is all right here. All these states of consciousness are here ... here in you and me, sitting in bodies, talking and it's all within this [raises arms up in an arc] context here and now.

Iain: Okay, I'm just trying to look at my notes to try and use you while I have got you here and other things that I wrote down from your book ... there's so much in it. "In order to purify one's self, associated ideas of me need to be let go ..."

John: Yes.

Iain: "... left behind," and you call that repentance.

John: Yes, well, whether it is political correctness or what, I don't know, but for some reason the word sin has been largely missed out of common, modern life, but I'd like to give you a very simple understanding of sin. Now look, if I turn like that [faces left towards the daylight] and I look at the light, my face is lit, isn't it? I am in the light. Now, if I turn around like that [faces his right, which is dimly lit] my face is in shadow. I'm in darkness. And what I see is in shadow; the works of darkness. Now, there is the light and there is darkness. This is the Presence [turns to the light], the presence of the light, the presence of God and this [turns to the shade] is absence.

Our human condition is absence. Adam fell from the Garden of Eden, from paradise, he fell in consciousness, to a lower state of consciousness, of absence from the presence of God, and this is the human condition ... and this is what's called sin. This is where The blind lead the blind, so we think we need education. We turn away from the source of life so we get ill and, of course, the wages of sin is death. Everything that dies is sin. That's what sin is. Sin is death.

Now real life is what Jesus says "I am the light ... he who walks in light, does not walk in darkness but has the light of life." [Turns to face the daylight] This is eternal life, that's what man really is. In Spirit, enlightenment, he lives in light, he lives with God, he walks with God, [then turns to face the dark] and this is absence, and all human shortages, poverty, and desire, is because we are trying to make up for what we've lost. And so we try to fill ourselves up with other bits of darkness and, of course, nothing works, it all has an end. It comes to an end. And then we are disappointed. So, we look for more things but we are just playing with darkness, when all we've got to do is this [turns to the light]. And what is repentance? That's repentance, it's turning to the light. It's so simple.

Iain: But who is turning back to the light?

John: Well, man has a choice. In order to be what we are, we have to come out of what we are not. Now then, here, you and I are sitting in our bodies. But in a few years these bodies will die, go back to dust. Am I the body? Is this what I am? I live in it. If I raise my hand ... look, I raise my hand, but am I the body? What am I? Well, let's take it a bit further. I think these thoughts, but my thoughts change from day to day. There's nothing consistent about thoughts. My emotions are like a seesaw up and down, this way and that. The changing conditions of my life are here today and gone tomorrow. So, what's left? If I eliminate what I'm not, what's left? Now you are looking at me and deep in your eyes is some sort of recognition, I can call it light. Well, the trouble is if we put a name to it we limit it, but there is that Unlimited and that is what I am. What is the name of God? I Am that I Am. How did Jesus describe himself when Pilate said "Who are you?" Before Abraham was, I Am. Timeless, spaceless, indescribable, pure being, being oneself, I Am. That's what it's all about, discovering one's self. Discovering what we are and when we discover what we are then we can begin to be of use.

Iain: And your journey through its ups and downs, through life, your human journey has been taking you towards I Am.

John: Towards that, yes.

Iain: Yes, and in a way, all our journeys are taking us towards I Am.

John: Of course. That's right.

Iain: But it's not always easy to see as there are so many distractions.

John: Well, at the beginning of course, we don't see it. We may read it in the Bible but we don't really know what it means.

Iain: And you describe yourself now as a quiet old man of regular habits, going up and down the hill to church everyday, and you sit just there [points to his left] from five o'clock in the morning for two or three hours – you were there at five o'clock this morning. When it's warm you sit on a bench outside – you don't speak much, except in interviews with Conscious TV. And your adventures are on the inside. What adventures do you have on the inside?

John: Oh, my dear, it never ends [laughs]. Well, I suppose that could bring me on to the great subject of prayer. Would you like me to go on to that?

Iain: Yes, absolutely.

John: Can I take you back to that sitting on a mountainside in South America, when I felt I received a message, To make whole, be whole?

Iain: Yes, when the voice – you felt a voice spoke to you, that we spoke about in Part One.

John: Yes, To make whole, be whole. If you laid a blanket on the ground and then took hold of the centre and lifted it up, it pulls up the rest of the blanket with it, doesn't it? Now, whatever we do affects the world around us, doesn't it? Smile and the world smiles with you. And with the raising of consciousness, which is really what we are talking about ... though you may not see the effect, though other people around you may think you are just a silly old fool sitting there ... the raising of consciousness inevitably raises consciousness of what's around you. Just like when the sun comes out in spring, you can't help that every part, every blade of grass, every little bug responds. Well, really, effective prayer is the raising of consciousness to where, of course, in Spirit there's no problem. Nobody dies, nobody is ill, nobody's hungry.

Iain: But what's the primary difference for you between prayer and meditation, is there a difference?

John: Oh, there isn't any at all. But to begin with, like at the bottom of a mountain everything seems different, doesn't it, with lots of different paths. Prayer is generally taken to mean, at least in the Western Church, an appeal from someone who is separate, to God, who's over there as another separate entity. So, we say "Lord have mercy," or something like this; I'm the sinner and there's God. So, we start off from separation and we usually pray for some object, some other item of separation, "Make Mummy better," or something. So, we are playing with separation, we are still in the world of separation. Now, as long as we stay in these verbal expressions of separation, that's how it is. Wishful thinking, may or may not have an effect. Does it influence God? Well, how can I answer that? How do I know? But eventually, you may say fewer words and do a bit more listening, or just sitting there and feeling the presence of God, or maybe not.

Now, meditation starts from a slightly different place because instead of using words to express thought, or desires, or even faith, you don't use words, apart from a mantra word, which is really a symbolic word. You let go, which actually lets go of separation. The aim of meditation is union. So, both methods, prayer and meditation, pursued ... but when I say pursued, it takes much practice, time and faith ... will bring you to union, will bring you closer to God. So, really they merge, they become the same thing, but I know it's very confusing at the beginning because prayer ... well, people think of prayer and meditation as two different things. It's really just two different approaches to the same thing.

Iain: Just reading my notes again; "I used to consider myself rather unhappy, a sort of misfit exile in the wrong place, which I was not able to explain. Lately, though, I know what I am, and where I belong and even though outer circumstances sometimes pale, I often feel the happiest, most blessed man alive.

John: Amen.

Iain: Must be wonderful. You feel the "happiest, most blessed man alive."

John: And, best of all, I know now what to do ... the answer to that awful question, What should I do? I found the work. This is work, real WORK. Somebody dies, you know he doesn't die. Somebody's ill, you feel the wholeness. Someone's poor, they're not, for abundance is all around. Everything's made whole. Now, people may not believe you, well ... that's the human condition, isn't it. But this is what wise men have always said. It's all given to you. It's a gift! The Kingdom of God is total, there's no need at all, nothing dies, nothing's ill, nothing's unhappy ... it's all light.

Iain: And I think the wonderful thing is, for me, that you never gave up. You had your ups and downs, you are seventy-nine now, it wasn't always easy but there was a determination, a motivation, a discipline to your meditation and prayer.

John: And the wonderful thing is that all that I as man have failed to do, I now ealize, is done by God, by Spirit. You know, I write books and most people of course don't read them but Spirit penetrates everywhere. In a way, even more so than sunshine, the real Spirit enters every heart, you don't have to do anything, all you have to do is remove the obstacle of 'me', my own blindness. You just have to come out of this blot upon creation, which is John Butler, this darkness with which I infect the world and create the works of dark. When you let that go, which is full repentance and totally accept Thy will, not mine, abandon the ego, the demon within you, the devil within you ... then everything that we try inadequately to do as people, is done automatically by God.

Iain: Okay, I think that's ...

John: Perfection is achieved.

Iain: I think that's a wonderful place to finish.

Billy Doyle –
The Mirage of Separation
Interview by **Renate McNay**

*R*elaxation is our natural state. So what's important is not to try
to relax but just to be aware of what is not relaxed. To be aware
of the tensions. Not to fight them but to actually welcome them,
not to make them a problem that I want to get rid of because you can't.
The only thing to do is actually sit with them and allow them. Not to fix
them but to actually feel the tension and feel the tension in your brain for
example. The left hemisphere, the right hemisphere and if you just listen
to the brain the vibration of the hemisphere, it will begin to relax because
in just listening and just being aware of the feeling, the sensation you're
no longer actually creating the tension. You're no longer an accomplice,
you've stood back. You're just listening, you're just observing.

Renate: My guest today is Billy Doyle.

Thank you for coming. Billy is a spiritual teacher in the Non-Dual Tradition and he's also a yoga teacher in the Kashmir Tradition and he wrote a book called, *The Mirage of Separation*, and *Yoga in the Kashmir Tradition*.

I read fifteen pages and I think it's going to be fascinating. So, Billy, first of all let's clarify what is the Kashmir Tradition and what is the difference between Kashmir Yoga or Kashmir traditional yoga and normal Hatha Yoga.

Billy: Well, it's the yoga I learned from Jean Klein.

Renate: Yes, so let's say who Jean Klein was.

Billy: Jean Klein was an Advaita teacher, a master of Advaita and yoga which is perhaps a little unusual that somebody has gone deeply into the Advaita and also deeply into the yoga side of things, the more bodily aspect. In his approach the emphasis was not so much on the physical body but more on the energetic body, the subtle body, which he would say is the real body. We don't usually experience our body, the energetic body, because of contraction and defence, but through listening, through relaxation, the energy body can come alive and we experience a body that's completely different than the solid heavy body that we normally experience. So there was always the emphasis with working with the body as energy, vibration, as spaciousness, that was one aspect. The other aspect was from the very beginning it is stressed that there's nothing to attain, nothing to become. What we are is already totally present and what we need is only to listen and come to a feeling of openness. So, it's not the progressive approach where I'm refining or going through various levels but it's seeing in the moment, you could say what I'm not, understanding what I'm not and on understanding what I'm not, you open to what you are.

Renate: Yes, so the Kashmir tradition really came from Jean Klein?

Billy: He brought this approach back to Europe.

Renate: I understand.

Billy: He refined and developed it himself and taught it in the West. It just spoke very deeply to me from many sides.

Renate: It sounds really fascinating reading your manuscript of your book and we go a little bit later into the art of listening and deeper into what the Energy Body is and so forth. First, let's start with you as a child already having a strong sense of spirituality. How did that manifest?

Billy: I remember just sitting in the church praying to Jesus and having this very strong feeling of love there. I think that stayed with me through childhood. I even remember a dream that I didn't understand at the time but I remember that a steam roller would come across me and I would disappear and I remember in the dream, it was somewhat of a recurrent one, that I was very happy to disappear. I didn't know the meaning of the dream and I didn't understand why I should be happy but when I look back, I think the child had some understanding that for love to be, you had to disappear yourself.

Renate: That there was some kind of memory coming through?

Billy: Yes ... yes.

Renate: Yes, it's interesting that you would think that to disappear. It's incredibly frightening for us, incredibly frightening for our ego structure.

Billy: It is because the ego is a very insecure ...

Renate: Structure?

Billy: Yes, it's always looking for security, for solidity. It's always looking for an image. It's always holding onto something because ultimately it's unreal. The last thing we want to do is disappear. It is frightening.

Renate: Of course, yes.

Billy: For the identification we have but I think there's also something in us that wants to let go, that feels this image, this centre, as a burden as well. So there's another element in us that would like to let go.

Renate: So when you had this experience as a child and you said it was recurring, did you speak with anybody about it?

Billy: I don't remember speaking with anyone ... no ... no.

Renate: Okay, any other experiences as a child?

Billy: Nothing comes to mind directly.

Renate: So, in your twenties you went the first time to India to be with Mother Theresa in Calcutta. How was that for you?

Billy: Well, I had some fascination with the East during my adolescence and I saw slides of people who had been there.

Renate: You trained as a teacher?

Billy: Yes, I did train as a teacher. The first thing I did when I finished my training was to go to India. I was attracted by the orient, the mysticism, the simplicity of life there. I'd also seen a programmeme about Mother Theresa on the television. I thought it would be interesting to spend a summer working there. So that's what I did and I travelled a little bit in India and it was the first of what was to be later, several journeys with different purposes.

Renate: You were visiting there or did you work there as well in Calcutta?

Billy: I worked in a hospital with Mother Theresa. It was a hospital for dying destitutes. I helped out giving bandages, washing, giving out tablets. That kind of thing.

Renate: Did you have a kind of relationship with her as well? I heard she was quite difficult, quite a powerful woman.

Billy: Right … I only met her once when I arrived there. She struck me as somebody who was down to earth and good at organising. That's it. I didn't get to know her on any other level really.

Renate: Yes, and something was triggered there in India because you became a spiritual seeker, you started to read spiritual books.

Billy: Yes. I think looking back again I can find a thread even from childhood but it was in my mid-twenties that the questions came to dominate my life. Who am I? What is truth? It led me to get involved in meditation, in yoga, in returning to India again.

Renate: Yes, you started to get involved with transcendental meditation.

Billy: That was at the very first I think. At that stage it didn't have any radical change in me. I think it was more I learned it as a technique. The underlying understanding wasn't really there at the time. So it was some years later perhaps that something deeper took place.

Renate: And through what? What happened?

Billy: Through reading books by Alan Watts, Suzuki, Rajneesh, Krishnamurti and Ramana Maharshi. I think when I read those books I felt I already knew what they were talking about somehow. I didn't though, but there was part of me that said this must be the case, it had to be true that I was not simply this body, this mind, this personality. There was something beyond that and it resonated very, very deeply with me and I went back to India again. I went to visit Rajneesh and spent about four and a half months at his ashram and travelled again in India.

Renate: What did you do there? (Laughs)

Billy: What did I do there? I danced a lot.

Renate: I was wondering about that.

Billy: I love dance and I listened to the talks he gave. Beautiful talks and he told many stories. At that age he was just the teacher I needed, it helped to open me and to liberate me and I left a lot freer, not in need somehow and maybe it was that, which opened me to the possibility of meeting Jean Klein who I feel was my real teacher.

Renate: Yes, you were his student for fourteen years and he was your main teacher. What was the most important thing you learned from him? And how was your relationship with him?

Billy: Well, he was a very beautiful man. He was a very cultured man. He was a very warm person, a very welcoming person. It was just beautiful to be with him. I would sometimes meet him when he came to London or I visited him in Switzerland and other countries sometimes and attended his lectures and retreats. It was just very, very deeply moving to be with him. His presence, his words! His words seem to bypass the mind and speak to my heart. He explained that to know who we are, we must first know what we are not. It's by understanding that I'm not the body, not the mind, not a personality, not something that changes, that we become open to what we are. We can never know what we are in terms of the mind. We can never know in terms of the senses because what we are is beyond the mind. We can never know it. We can never grasp it. We only know it by being it. It's not an object, so we can't describe it, it's indescribable. We can use words like spaciousness. We can use words like awareness, consciousness or love to come close, to give us some indication but ... a mind would like to grasp what I am, who am I? It's not possible and when we deeply understand that, the mind stops. It stops running after trying to find truth. It begins to relax so there's a possibility that something beyond the mind can manifest.

Renate: That something ... my teacher also said once .... he wrote fifteen books and has a big school and he says, 'I'm writing all these books and telling you all these things, only for your mind to relax, because that's the only thing which needs to happen'.

Billy: Right, right. Yes it's the mind and the body because the mind and body are one.

Renate: So can you say a little bit more about the mind as I've never heard that the mind and the body are one. What does that mean?

Billy: Where is anxiety? Where is anger? It may be in the mind but it is also in the body. It's in the breathing and in the tension in our breaths. I would say it even goes down to the cellular level. In some way the patterns that we create in the mind come from the belief system that I am a separate entity, that I am a particular person, which brings up a certain defence and fear inevitably comes taking ourselves to be a fraction in a universe. Taking ourselves to be an individual inevitably brings up insecurity and fear. This is also in our body, in our breathing, in our cells, I would say it is a feeling of contraction, of heaviness, a feeling of being localised ... it's actually easier to relax your body than to relax your thought. So through relaxing the body, the muscles, the joints, the nervous system, the mind begins to relax as well. A relaxed body is already the beginning of a relaxed mind.

Renate: Did you in your own process find that easy to do, to relax the mind?

Billy: Yes, yes.

Renate: What did you do?

Billy: Well, relaxation it's our natural state. So what's important is not to try to relax but just to be aware of what is not relaxed. To be aware of the tensions. Not to fight them but to actually welcome them, not to make them a problem that I want to get rid of because you can't. The only thing to do is actually sit with them and allow them. Not to fix them but to actually feel the tension and feel the tension in your brain for example. The left hemisphere, the right hemisphere and if you just listen to the brain the vibration of the hemisphere, it will begin to relax because in just listening and just being aware of the feeling, the sensation you're no longer actually creating the tension. You're no longer an accomplice, you've stood back. You're just listening, you're just observing.

Renate: So what do you mean? Is this listening becoming aware? It's not an actual listening to the body?

Billy: It's just letting come up what's there, whatever there is. The vibration, the warmth, the feeling of something solid, crystallised, dense. Just letting whatever is your body speak to you but what's important is not to fix it but to let it unfold because there are many layers of tensions, between a very solid heavy body and the real body, which I would say is something like space, it's transparent. There are many layers to unfold and when we listen we can allow that unfolding. I'm not trying to push away my feelings. I think Jean Klein said, 'You have to love the tensions, you have to welcome them, not fight them.' Then they will inevitably, over time of course, as these things have built up over many, many years, they will free themselves when you learn how to listen to them.

Renate: One thing you told me Billy, over a period of twenty years you went every year for three weeks in a retreat place to be in silence. In one of those times and I'm quoting your words here, 'All identification with a separate identity dissolved. I knew myself as Silence.› I think

I asked you on the phone if this experience stayed. You said, yes. Did the ego structure never form itself back or what happened to the ego structure? Tell me a bit more about this. I am fascinated by this.

Billy: Of course in my case this understanding didn't happen out of the blue. There was a long process of self-inquiry I was very fortunate to meet a teacher like Jean Klein that helped me to understand what I was not ... and I think there came a deep relaxation, understanding that there was nothing to get, there was nothing to become.

Renate: Sorry to interrupt but the inquiry was that you learned the method of listening? And through the listening, out of listening, your body started to relax, your nervous system calmed down.

Billy: Yes that's true and also by questioning the beliefs I had about myself to question, am I really this body, this mind? Understanding that I can't be a perception. My hands are a perception, the glass (points to table) is a perception, the space, the carpet is a perception. I would also say my mind is a perception, these things are always changing. To understand that there's something that knows all these objects, that knows all the change, so there's a certain logic there as well, to understand that I'm behind the world of objects. I'm the subject, let us say the ultimate subject.

Renate: Would you not say, okay, we are changeless, we are the background but we are also the manifestation.

Billy: Absolutely, absolutely both are true, so the problem is we identify ourself with a particular manifestation.

Renate: So when you say, I am not the body but is it not that I am not only the body or how does the body come in?

Billy: Yes, it's a pedagogical aid to say to myself, I'm not the body. I'm not the mind. I'm not the thoughts. I'm not this changing world. It helps us to bring a space dimension from what we're so obviously identified with and so I'm able to stand back and not be so closely identified with a particular body/mind, with an I-image. You find yourself with a certain distancing. A certain freedom from what you have always taken yourself to be. When there's a deeper understanding you also discover that the expressions of consciousness are also in consciousness, that the expressions are nothing but consciousness. So everything is within you but I'm making a distinction between consciousness and the expressions of consciousness. I think that's important.

Renate: So what you are saying is, first of all it is important to realise who we are as the Absolute in order to get a certain distance from the manifestation and then as the Absolute come back in this world. Is that how you would say it?

Billy: I think it's important to understand that you cannot be an object. When that's deeply understood you begin to relax, you become open to the possibility there's something beyond the mind. Then all you can do is, in a sense, is live that openness and maybe one day that understanding will arise. It arises, not that you understand something, it's just that understanding is the disappearance of the illusion of being somebody. So when I say, I knew myself in Silence, I didn't understand anything in that moment. There was nothing new I understood. There was no intellectual understanding, there was nothing I was able to grasp or tell you I understood something. It was just in that moment I lost all sense of localisation, there wasn't any division anymore that's all. No longer identifying with a particular body/mind.

Renate: And this is still here?

Billy: It hasn't changed ... no ... no.

Renate: So if I say, does that mean that there is nothing going on inside because there is no localisation. Are there still feelings, sensations and emotions?

Billy: Yes, yes. All these things carry on but you're no longer saying, 'That's me!' You are no longer identifying with them. They just happen but the record player that goes round and round has finished. The one that is always going to the past, looking for security, looking to the future, daydreaming, fantasising, looking for security in the person, that aspect, which perhaps is more than half the usual thoughts that go on in our head, that becomes redundant. You no longer fuel that belief system, those belief systems are finished but life continues, feeling continues, everything else continues.

Renate: And what happened to all the structures, the ego structures in your physical body? Are they finished as well? Are they transformed or disappeared?

Billy: I think even to come to the understanding they dissipate because I would say that perhaps it's a very few rare human beings that come to this understanding out of the blue. I don't know. I would say that the vast majority of cases the understanding comes because you have let go of all those tensions. You have become a more open human being and after the understanding that process may continue. These residues of tensions belong to time and space. They've developed over many years and they don't necessarily just disappear overnight but because the belief system that fuels them is no longer there they do tend to dissipate but they are no longer a problem. You see them and they release themselves.

Renate: So when you look at a physical body or movement, a posture from this non-dual space, what is the body? What are movements? What are we doing? (laughs)

Billy: Yes ... (smiles), it's a kind of celebration of Life. To move, to be, to enjoy the elasticity, the flexibility, the movement of the body.

Renate: Like celebrating life?

Billy: But I think Life is celebration.

Renate: Yes, yes.

Billy: It's, it's this joy and it's beautiful to share that.

Renate: You said something in your notes or I think I read it in your book which really hit me, which was, 'Only in our absence are we truly present.'

Billy: Yes, that's the sentence from Jean Klein that reverberates through many of his books. It's also something that struck me when he was talking.

Renate: So, explain that when you say, 'only in our absence,' what is absent?

Billy: You don't have the slightest notion anymore of being anybody. There's just completely empty space. There's no man, there's no woman, there's no old person, there's no young person, there's no self image. There's just transparency. That absence is not any kind of negative or something lacking.

Renate: It's not the ego trying to be Absence?

Billy: It's a feeling of fullness because there's nothing lacking here, in this absence that we're talking about. It's an absence of all objectivity and all images. Actually, that's what we are in any case, silence. Who am I? What am I? It's only the mind that comes in and builds up this belief system with I'm Mary, I'm John, I'm a bank manager. In silence what we are, who we are, it's actually something incredibly simple this understanding. It's very paradoxical that we spend many years looking for what I always am. It's a strange paradox isn't it? (Renate agrees).

Renate: (Renate looks through her notes). That's what I was looking for, the sentence, 'We are free but we don't know ourselves in this freedom.' You know when I read that and it still brings up so much sadness in me because looking, there's something so close and if we look at humanity and see all this suffering.

Billy: Yes, our real nature of course is always free but we superimpose on top of it the images, a belief system that buries our real nature.

Renate: So, how do we go about it Billy because there's also something you said, 'When we proceed from the relative to the ultimate reality in stages, the ego remains engaged.' So where does that leave us, the searchers?

Billy: If we think that Me as the 'I' image is going to progress and become more spiritual, attain freedom, we're going to bring the 'I' image with us and we're going to perhaps even expand that 'I' image. You have to question at the beginning, who is this me? Who feels a lack? Who is trying to progress? You have to start really looking at who you are at the very beginning.

Renate: But it's our ego structure in the first place that starts the search.

Billy: But the real desire to know ourselves comes from what we desire, which comes from our real nature. It's looking for itself. So when we begin our search, it's actually our self speaking to us and at that moment we begin to open to our real nature. We all feel this when we are identified, we all feel this lack, some kind of lack of fulfilment. That's very important to recognise that and it's that lack that starts us questioning, starts us searching. If we didn't feel that lack perhaps we'd never bother or if we didn't recognise it or we often just cover it over with our endless activities and entertainment. When we stop, look at ourselves we look at that. It's an important thing to acknowledge that in myself and to discover what is that lack, where does it come from? Why is it there?

Renate: Do you feel that over time your personality changed?

Billy: Certainly! I think I would say I began to relax more and was able to live more in the moment, not running after things, not trying to accumulate things and I think that leaves your personality more spontaneous, more open. Actually, it's that when we don't identify with our personality, that we free the personality. it's nothing to do with denying our personality. This understanding gives freedom to our personality. Do you see what I mean?

Renate: Yes, well, the way I see it, is that somehow this constantly reflecting back on yourself, this mechanism stops. Would you agree? You just leave yourself running spontaneously. (She laughs).

Billy: Absolutely! You become I would say ...

Renate: You don't think I should do that or I should do this .... I should be nicer. I should be smarter.

Billy: No. I would say that life becomes much more spontaneous. There's no self image you're worried about or concerned about. You become really open to other human beings. (He laughs).

Renate: Do you have a poem in your little book which fits? (She laughs).

Billy: Which fits .... (laughs and puts his glasses on and picks up his book from the table).

That which you seek
is not to be found
it is much too close to touch
much too close to see
it is the touching
it is the seeing
there are not two
or some other
the necklace you thought was missing
is still around your neck

Renate: Beautiful.

Billy: Shall I read a second one?

Renate: Yes, read the second one and then I have another question.

Billy: Perfect.
a vigil for the Self
long into the night
waiting without expectation
what might I be
no answer was forthcoming
but the question was no more
nothing was missing
the silence was home

Renate: Thank you. That's beautiful. So, I'd like to talk a little bit about your work. You mentioned at the beginning the Energy Body is our real body. How can we learn to encounter the body? What do you do in your yoga?

Billy: To become in contact with the Energy Body ... I would say it's paralysed by muscular contraction. The first thing you have to do is relax, to recognise the tension. Some people don't even know that their shoulders are up here. (He pulls his shoulders up to his ears). It's become so normal, so deeply ingrained.

Renate: And to relax? What you said earlier, is it just to become aware that you're not relaxed, that you have tension?

Billy: To actually feel and welcome the tensions. To really be in contact with them, not to fix them, to listen to them and let them unfold. They will, if we let them, if we listen in this way without trying to change them or try to get rid of them. We are in a kind of neutral territory. The body will release because the natural state of the body is a relaxed body. The tensions we create will dissolve and when we come to the relaxed body, the more subtle energies in the body begin to free themselves, to manifest and we can begin to experience them. I think it's perhaps in the hands that it's easiest to experience them and later in the whole body. It helps to free the body of the feeling of solidity or heaviness and that's also very important because it's quite difficult, I would say, very difficult to really understand our real nature when our body is just a mass of self-defence and solidity. How can truths cross those barriers? So, opening of the body for me, has always been very important. It leaves us more vulnerable to reality. The feeling of the energy body eats up the feelings of solidity and we feel ourselves becoming more transparent, more open and it frees us on many levels.

Renate: You even mention that this energy feeling is actually the healing factor of the body.

Billy: Yes, it's the healing factor, yes. It's what gives the body life, the real body. It permeates the whole body, it surrounds the physical body and it gives life to the body. The more we experience it, the more there is harmony and health on all levels including our eyes and ears and how we sense the world.

Renate: I know from my own experience when I take the time and just sit quietly, just see what I feel in the body, the body starts talking to me.

Billy: Absolutely …

Renate: And if I let it talk and do what it wants to do, go through what it wants to go through, then it starts releasing. It's really fascinating. You are so different from all the other non-duality teachers I have met over the years because you include the body, you talk about the importance of freeing the body as well.

Billy: I'll just continue the story to the end about releasing the body and say, ultimately in that listening to the body we don't emphasise what we listen to but just listening itself. It's the object that brings us back to the ultimate, so called ultimate subject. So everything is a reminder of who we are. And the body, once it's unfolded and dissolved, we let it go and we find ourselves simply in listening, simply in being. So the body is a way to bring us to ourselves.

Renate: I just feel I entered your silence. (They laugh).

Billy: There's no 'my silence'. There's only silence.

Renate: There's only silence, yes.

Billy: It's not mine. It's not yours. It's just Silence. That's all there is mm ....

Renate: Mm ... so we have one or two minutes left. Is there anything you would like to say?

Billy: Just this word Silence. We tend to think of it as an absence of thought but Silence itself doesn't matter whether there's thinking or there's no thinking. Everything is part of that silence. It doesn't matter, everything is silence. So we shouldn't try to make our mind silent, that's a kind of violence. The mind may be silent and it can be very beautiful. But silence itself can be there when you're walking down Oxford Street or wherever. It simply is. We mustn't confuse silence itself with simply the silence of the mind. It simply is!

Renate: I experience that in a funny way when you mentioned Oxford Street. Sometimes when I walk down Oxford Street there are thousands and thousands of people, you bump into people and when I'm not present or not in the silence, I experience myself bumping into these people and then I become aware. Then I go into presence, or into silence or connect with silence and it's so interesting, you go through it and you don't touch anything. It's like the way opens. (Billy agrees and nods his head). Do we have time for another short poem?

Billy: Okay, let's have a look. One more poem.

Go by way of negation.
Take the empty road.

before proclaiming I am all
be yourself nought
leave aside assertion
before knowing what you are
know well what you're not
body, senses mind, explore the landscape well
discover its transparency, lest you carry it along
go by way of negation, be yourself nought.

Renate: Beautiful. Thank you for coming and being with us.

Georgi Y. Johnson – I Am Here

Interview by **Renate McNay**

~

*B*eing born here is a bit like working, in a way for IBM. You know you work for IBM and at the end of the day you give back your equipment and you're free of IBM and IBM goes on. It's not really our problem but we are here and we're here because it's absolutely right for us to be here, right here in whatever position we are. The most damaging thing we can do to ourselves is to believe we're not free in being here. And with every judgment that we make on ourselves, that it's not okay to be as we are, we are taking away that freedom which is always here regardless of what form we're taking and it's very deeply programmed and this, this goes back to the deeper layers of liberation in a way. It's in the Bible, the throwing out of Eden that happened because we're guilty, this condemnation.

Renate: Georgi is a spiritual teacher and she offers non-dual therapy with her partner Bart ten Berge around the globe. Georgi wrote a wonderful book called, *'I Am Here: Opening the Windows of Life and Beauty.'* I must say, this is one of my favourite books. It gives such a clear window into consciousness and what it means to be a human being. I've just heard the follow up of this book is in the pipeline and it's going to be called, *'Stillness of the Wind'* – a very interesting title, and the book will be about the dance of duality.

Georgi was born in the UK, she presently lives in Israel with Bart and they have ten children. We're going to hear about the process which led her to writing this book and we'll start chronologically with your first awakening experience or your first memory, which was even further back.

Georgi: When first we open the windows of feeling we have feeling-memory and we also have our memory of what has happened – a story-memory. Feeling-memory is based on our experience and so, there are plenty of feeling-memories of the first atmospheres before conception and in the womb, those places that we call home, which feel like the reality here.

But then there's conscious memory. I must have been around two years old, just learning to talk when one day my mother had put me to bed, to take a little rest I imagine. I was told to go to sleep now for a while, she went downstairs, and I lay there and I looked at my little legs. It was a big full-length bed and I looked at these little legs and I noticed that they'd grown longer than they were before and it was a kind of mystery that these legs would grow longer too. As I lay there, looking at these legs, I needed to sleep, so I closed my eyes.

It was the late sixties, so I imagine the word guitar was very much in our vocabulary. My father was a record producer, so the house was alive with that culture. I started thinking about guitars and saying the word "guitar" in my mind. It must have been that I'd just learned the word and had been appreciated for knowing the word. So I started thinking the word guitar and started saying, "Guitar, guitar, guitar, guitar, guitar, guitar, guitar, guitar ... " chanting it. Then I kind of woke up again and it was a realisation that the words, had nothing to do with the object. It was just syllables in space of guitar, guitar, guitar in my thought...no connection. It's kind of tricky when you're learning to talk as a baby to have this disconnection happen ...

Renate: It didn't have a connection to what?

Georgi: To the object – to the guitar that it was supposed to signify.

Renate: Oh right, yes, yes.

Georgi: It's just sounds. So I tried it with my own name … and so I began Georgi, Georgi, Georgi, Georgi, again there's no connection and then it was, "So who am I?" This was the question … "So who am I?"

Renate: You realized that you were not the name.

Georgi: Not Georgi and not a guitar. [Laughs]

Renate: Yeah...

Georgi: Not this thought, not this label and so this question came, "Who am I? What then? What am I then?" There was a kind of sense of consciousness and then a leap of consciousness becoming conscious of consciousness. It was overwhelming … conscious of conscious of consciousness, this expanding existence. I was lying on the bed looking towards the window where the sunlight was coming through and there was a leap to a point of not being able to contain this pure consciousness of who I am. I kind of retracted from it to "Where's my mummy?" I could hear her downstairs in the kitchen, hear the pots and pans being washed up and I began thinking. "Mummy, it's not mummy." These sounds have no connection, but the feeling was of incredible wholeness to it. It was almost like I was climbing the ladder back again. It was like reconnecting to a source, and it was so clear that it was where I'd arrived from.

Renate: Did you know exactly what happened? Or is it just something you felt?

Georgi: Something that I very much experienced and what's amazing is that this memory is like a deep notch in my mind, in my mind. I never forgot this memory.

Renate: But you didn't have the word consciousness at two years.

Georgi: No ... no.

Renate: So what was it? How could you define the experience at that age?

Georgi: Yes. So Georgi was gone. There was no Georgi. Georgi was just Georgi. It was just Georgi, Georgi, Georgi. So it was this seeing, the seeing of the curtain and of the light of the little body on the bed. But I wasn't this little body either and then it was the seeing of the seeing and then it was the seeing of the seeing, of the seeing but without leaving the body ... expanding in a kind of light of perception. But you know we try to give words to it because we don't have words.

I didn't have words then for sure ... it was a very, very vital home, which was more home than the home I was physically in. It's not that the home I was physically in was a bad home, it was just much more familiar but also in this kind of conscious of conscious of conscious, not containable either. After that I went to sleep, which is also home, gone!

Renate: So, you didn't run down to mummy and told her what you experienced? [They both laugh].

Georgi: No, well mummy wasn't mummy ... no and I wasn't afraid. I really wasn't afraid. Maybe I was more afraid when I was put down to bed to sleep and began thinking about guitars.

Renate: And did something change after this experience for you and the way you related?

Georgi: It's so early, it's such an early one, that in a way a link that normally would be cemented between thought and language and words and identity and the world was broken very early on, so I never really trusted it. I never really believed a word was what it said it is. I never really believed I was Georgi. Never really believed in this calling of identity. So, in a way it was a tremendous gift, like you're here and human but remember. Remember who you really are. I don't mean who you really are in a personal private perspective at all. It's a benevolent breakage between word and what it's supposed to mean. Since then it became like a natural escape door in a way, so when I was suffering I could come to this place of pure consciousness, in the Now and step... not step out of it but contain it much more easily, be free of it within it.

Renate: So what did you have to do to step back into that?

Georgi: Go into the felt sense of the body and really allow it. Really be as real as we can be, the Real Reality and that's not the reality which stops here. We can't find a reality but we can allow reality to come to life in a way. So it's moving into the now. It's connected with the body, the miracle of the body and letting it be and then consciousness is free in a way.

Renate: So you mean with letting it be, whatever feelings are coming up, whatever emotions coming up it's free to be. Is this what you mean?

Georgi: Yes, you know when you're able to let something be, there's two. There's you that is able to allow and there's that which is experienced.

Renate: Yes.

Georgi: So the moment that you can allow something to be, that which can allow comes much more to life.

Renate: Yes, I understand that.

Georgi: There's a space that opens up.

Renate: It's so interesting after doing so many interviews over the last years, we only started, recently realizing the importance in the awakening of the body.

Georgi: Yes.

Renate: Awakening happening through the body. There's so much out there, so much talk about the awakening of the mind, but somehow the body doesn't play any role and that is more and more coming to the foreground as if it is an evolutionary move into the body. That is how it appears for me.

Georgi: Yes. You know there is an evolution happening also in terms of our basic attitudes towards life, towards creation, towards this world of duality. Many people, myself included, are no different, so we, in a way are often motivated in a spiritual search by an aversion to the physical, to all of this suffering. We have a body but it's not going to last. It's dying, it's aging. You can't trust it, we have a certain amount of time, but we don't know how long.

Renate: It fails, yes.

Georgi: It's full of loss, all the time … loss, pain, nothing is stable. We try to make it stable, it breaks in our hands, there's love but we can't hold it, we can't keep it. So, many spiritual motivators of development come from this rejection of creation, and by creation I mean the physical world that we are seeing here now. Very quickly we move to this letting go. You're not your feeling body, you're not your feelings, you're not your pain, you're not your emotions. But what we are really moving with then, is the energy of rejection, which is a big duality. "It's not me. I'm enlightened! This is not me I'm awakened now, so I'm not my body," and that energy becomes dominant, so we launch into another spiral of illusion. It's based on fear. Nothing needs to get left out if we are not afraid. Nothing! Not one aspect, not one particle of our experience needs to be rejected. It's not even ours [arms extended], but it's not even personal.

Renate: Yes, but it's the failure. It is as you say there's suffering but I am not suffering, there's pain but I don't have pain and it's allowed to be there because it's shared.

Georgi: Yes, it's tricky, because when you drop all form, you move beyond everything that you can perceive, everything that you can think, everything you can feel, even a sense of being, you just let it go completely. What emerges of itself is a natural care. We care. Life cares. It really deeply cares and so we care about the suffering. We care so deeply about the pain, which is here, that by choice we would be reincarnated again and give up our enlightenment to be back here to be of service. It's unstoppable this care at the core of creation. The problem is that we have these minds that want to avoid suffering and in this kind of either-or thinking of the way we are programmed as little children, we believe that if we don't suffer it, it's not there. Or if I pretend I'm never going to die it's not going to happen. If I don't let this cruelty into my feeling of cruelty, if I don't acknowledge this feeling it won't exist.

And this is, in a way, the Achilles heel of the healer. It's the trap of the healer because every doctor knows that you cannot heal any ailment unless you are prepared to go there, to look at it, to go into it, to receive it. The same way every doctor knows that, you're not really healing anything, you are creating the conditions in which healing can happen through the natural wisdom of life. Life is the healer. We make the conditions by removing the obstacles for life to do what it, of itself does with this supreme intelligence. So, sometimes we (Bart and I) find that it's important to really allow suffering in our lives and in our teaching. It doesn't matter if it's our suffering or not, it doesn't matter if it's on our bill or on the other's bill. To really, really, really allow it completely, to allow it to transform through you, or to allow it to be is enough. This is where the depth of karma is created when we reject the pain, the things we don't want to feel. There's such an agenda there and the agenda is to get back again into the light, "I'm enlightened that means I'm free of suffering, free of fear, free of jealousy, free of anger." It's not true! Not with me, not at all. I'm free within it. Anger is free here, suffering is free here, jealousy is free here. It's free to move, it's free to tell its story. Fear is free and often... I'm afraid, often utterly and totally terrified but it's just terror moving through me. I don't even know any more if it's mine or not, it doesn't matter. It's not a problem because the freedoms also here. Does that make sense?

Renate: Completely. Our normal reaction is to run away.

Georgi: Yes.

Renate: And we don't want to feel it. It's too awful this feeling.

Georgi: ... to run away or to freeze or just to try and hold things as they are...which is totally fine but then it's important to relax in the running away and to stay present to the running away and to relax in the freezing. If you relax in the freezing it can be quite beautiful.

Renate: What I experienced several times in the midst of the worst suffering is ... is beauty.

Georgi: Yes.

Renate: If it's allowed to be ... it just moves into beauty.

Georgi: Yes, because if it's allowed to be, it has such depth of truth in it.

Renate: So, let's move a little bit back to your story, [laughs]. So you had continuous awakenings of similar kinds through your childhood and at one point you were puzzled how this awakened consciousness couldn't stay. In the interim you would disappear ... so in retrospect do you know where you went? Do you know what happens when we lose awareness?

Georgi: No! I remember one when I was walking to school in the morning and suddenly I was there. I am here. Totally conscious with this strangeness, a strangeness like when you revisit yourself in your life.

Renate: It recognizes itself.

Georgi: ... then I'm walking, vowing to myself, 'I'm going to stay here. I'm going to stay here ... grrrrr ... [*Renate and Georgi laughing*].

I was saying to Bart last night that it's a little bit like we are all drugged. There's this opiate but like a dolphin you pop above water and, "Ahh this is truth!" And then whumph! into the drugged state again ... you come up again, "Remind me of this, remind me of this, keep me there," then down again ... so that's the question; What's with this ocean of non-awareness, non-heightened consciousness, what's in that ocean?

So, if we take the body as a landscape in a way, the ocean is here, the horizon of the ocean [hands horizontal to the shoulders]. Here is the air and the sun [hands pointing above the head], some seagulls and a lot of thoughts and here's the horizon and the ocean is feeling, feeling energy and the feeling isn't a thought. How do we know feeling's not a thought? Because if you feel a feeling, immediately you're out of time, you're in the now. You can't feel your anger or your love for tomorrow or for yesterday or as part of a story. You can as a mental activity and kind of rip up a bit of love and put it in but fundamentally if we agree to feel how it is, how it feels to be here, we are immediately in the now. So we move beyond time, just like that, power of the now, just by feeling a feeling, even a sense perception in the feeling body but also in feeling a feeling emotion and we are in real time we are in the now. We are in the now and it's not stable, but here in the level of feeling and that is what we call awareness as opposed to consciousness, there is still space, there's bounded space so we have a feeling, for the first feeling could be, "This is where I am and this is where I end".

Or the grief can be here but I don't want to feel the grief now so I'll go to the joy which I can get in the crack between the grief and next day's dinner. [laughs] So we move into a dimension of space and it's important to realize that there are two kinds of experiences going on when people talk about awakening and enlightenment. One is the freedom from the mind, freedom from time, the freedom from the story and then there's another kind of description where people talk about the sense of infinity and boundlessness. Those ones talk very much about love, these ones talk very much about peace, peacefulness from being free from the mind, the peace of mind ... which very much comes as a backdrop to conscious freedom of consciousness. The second one's experience. This opening of the heart unconditionally, nothing confines them anymore. Their free of some kind of energetic restrictions in what they are allowed to feel and how they are allowed to feel. Their being becomes one with the kind of one being.

Renate: You talk about this, your own process, your first awakening was from the head and then you say your heart was still held prisoner and then later the heart was opened to unconditional love and yet the body was still held prisoner. So what were the different stages? I think we covered your awakening from the head. So how did you awaken your heart?

Georgi: A few decades later. [Laughs].
You know, conscious awakening was great for me. It got me into Oxford. The conceptual mind was open. I could theorize an incredible amount of freedom in a way to a kind of universal mind and all of this but, like we said, if the heart was ...

Renate: You studied Literature?

Georgi: English Literature ... the theory of literature, how we approach it from a Marxist perspective or from a feminist perspective. I went deeply into the Jungian perspective at that stage. But as children we get shaped in how to be here in a way which is different from our real identity, it's how we are allowed to be. So are we allowed, is our love allowed to be unconditional? Are we allowed to feel our emotions? Or do we get rejected? So, for a child when they are rejected for crying too much or being too angry or being natural in a way, there is a kind of deepening of separation, and a kind of separate self at the energy level of feeling, of what they are allowed to feel. It's a contraction: contractions of form, are created. It's not even personal. Whole families carry contractions. Whole nations carry them, whole cultures carry contractions of form, for instance that we will not be afraid of or we will not talk about death, and sexuality is huge too. There were two dirty words for me when I was a child, one was sex and the other was God. Not because my mother wasn't spiritual, but I felt so ashamed to say these words. So, here there was no freedom and the best response for me was to fix that with the mind and so I moved very much like other interviewees who were talking, in a way to...to fix that with the mind and so I moved very much to fixing the outside, saving the world from this conscious, awakening perspective. So I went deeply into journalism and exposing all kinds of horrors that were going to happen to the world. I was right but

Renate: Just to mention that Georgi worked for the BBC.

Georgi: A little bit at the beginning and later as an independent investigative journalist about the threat of global terrorism but before there was before September 2001.

Renate: You were already ahead!

Georgi: ... or it wouldn't have been a secret would it?

But what was really driving me was the threat of the collapse of my own separate self, the fear of this ego needed to die and at a certain stage it became so obsessive that the identity broke down under the pressure of this thinking, thinking. I went into a period of panic attacks and anxiety, which of course, at the time was a living hell. It really is a living hell to be suffering from panic states, with three little children to care for. The professional authorities of course come in with medications, which I'm so grateful I didn't take and all kind of diagnoses, which I'm so grateful I didn't believe.

Renate: Were you afraid of something, or was it just panic, just fear?

Georgi: The focus of my attention was on the threat of non-conventional terrorism and exposing it. The work of an investigative journalist is very much imagining what could happen, so it's very fear-based but I would empathically imagine, I would experience how it would be and this in the end had its incredible toll on the nervous system. I was trying to save children from that horror, so it was quite an obsessive spin, driven from this incredible difficulty to come to peace, beneath the level of the head.

Renate: Did you understand at that time what had happened that this is connected?

Georgi: No, I was saving the world. I was on a campaign to bring the truth and to save lives … especially living in Israel. The threat that Jews could be gassed by terrorists and thousands could die and that they weren't being told of the threat and being sent to gas mask stations to get equipped and all of this, and a lot of this felt for me an incredible outrage. So it was also the sense of justice and a history behind it. But I was running like hell away from myself. I was at the same time a mother of three children: the greatest miracle of life was giving birth. I tried to fix the world but I was terrified of myself.

Renate: And so what stopped you? What turned it around?

Georgi: I think I cracked! [Laughs].

Renate: What turned around?

Georgi: What turned around was I became dysfunctional. I couldn't function anymore and luckily we took a sabbatical in that time in England and I saw an NHS counsellor who was amazing, just listened, she just listened, no judgment. Then it stepped into a kind of apocalyptic depression and I felt like I was looking at the ruins of my own ego structure. There was no way I could pick up the stories again. I had many connections through the internet and they were kind of nagging for me to continue with the campaign. It was before September 11, the threat was coming but I was finished. It was like seeing myself as a destroyed city and hardly able to move through the day and … little by little life picked it up. I kind of surrendered to the depression but then magical things like once when I was just walking, because walking was the only thing that gave a moments mercy from the suffering while the children were at school, I went into a bookshop. I walked immediately to a shelf and there was the face of the Dalai Lama looking back from a book *The Way to Happiness*, and there was this moment of instant recognition. I took the book, like a lifeline and his writings about compassion as an antidote to fear and the practice of replacing yourself in the other. I would try anything at that moment and it really worked and so there were many little synchronicities that helped show the way forward, step by step. I began just massaging people's feet, not my own because that didn't somehow help me feel better but the feet of the children, the feet of my husband and then I moved into aromatherapy. This helped so much, the sense of smell. Now it makes sense to me because smell bypasses the control function and it's a sensory perception that directly awakens something from far beyond normal thinking mind and so that was a process of erasure.

Renate: And Georgi, all this time of suffering, did you ever remember the experience you had as a child?

Georgi: Yes but I was so nervous, so anxious it wasn't possible to have the nervous system activated like that. In a way I was always in an awakened, aroused state. It was a total imbalance. There was nowhere to sink down into. There was no way into the body. It was a kind of spiritual psychosis in that sense.

Renate: You could not sense into it?

Georgi: But then ... one time I lay down in total panic, my stomach totally contracted and in a way just surrendered to the horror of it. I hadn't quite fallen asleep and I had a vision. I wasn't in meditation or anything at that stage. I was on the hills near our house in Mount Carmel in Israel and I saw a nun and a woman coming from a distance. I was laughing because the man, who I knew so well, was dressed as a nun. They we walking towards me across a golden field and as they walked there were two spheres of intense white, white, white, white light expanding out of them. As they moved towards me, it was like I was going to dissolve – I was going to disappear inside the blessing of this white light. My son Adidya, my first born was next to me as a young boy and he looked at me, I looked at him and we both turned towards a rock. I held the rock and that brought me back ... it was as if I almost died, it was almost as if they came to take me and I made this choice to stay by moving towards the rock with my children. Because

I was kind of in a psychotic state I began collecting rocks and moving rocks around our garden as it really made me feel better and created a picture.

Renate: Trying to ground you.

Georgi: Very much trying to ground myself, yes. I would cling to the rock, cling to the rock.

Renate: And that was, I assume the third stage when you said yet was the body was prisoner, still held. How did you open?

Georgi: Well, first there was the stage of liberating the feelings which was very much through studying with my partner, he was my teacher in spiritual psychology. This is an education which is really about ... when we say let's get free of mind, that's a thought. So this beautiful exercise is given by my partner's teacher, Bob Moore, who taught in Denmark, through feeling perception, the felt sense on the chakras on certain energy points to allow the energy to move by itself without a story. He also taught in Israel.

Georgi: Little by little ... but of itself without even the story, (the stories would come later) but the energy itself would kind of present itself. The blockages and this spaciousness began to open up into first of all a permission to just feel what you feel, just feel it and not just feel it and okay, been there, done that, but really collapse into it to be curious about it, even if it is an unpleasant feeling. It's a switch where experience becomes yummy, even if it's negative or positive. And it's like we said, the moment you move towards experience like that, towards feeling like that, you're already not the experience, there's a greater spaciousness opening up. So there was this *satori* stage when the heart could just burst open. This unconditional love went on for a few months and I was more functional than ever. This now wasn't a psychosis. It was years after the anxiety but this incredible release of holding, holding the heart, always holding, always afraid, always with conditions. It all felt like dominoes, it fell and it fell and it fell for a few months. More expansion, more expansion and I'd reach a border and go through it ...and such a stillness and such a love, such an opening to energies and felt presences around as well, otherworldly in a way. Then the last ... I was hanging out the washing outside, because at the same time I was still a functioning mother and all that and I noticed it was like hitting a brick wall. I was really hitting a wall with this. There was one place where this unconditional love wasn't going to go and then I realized it was toward myself. I would love Bin Laden. I would love George Bush, [*Georgi and Renate laughing as she speaks*]. I would love ... but this, [holding her hands to her heart], this was still a resistance and that's the bridge to where the block was, being in a physical body at all in a way.

Renate: How did you overcome that?

Georgi: We jump forward another ten years. [they both laugh]. So, this left me extremely happy. These words have hooks, so this *satori* or enlightenment, this experience of liberated awareness, boundless awareness, left me in a very, very good space with a lot of freedom. But it's like being in a place then of almost happy, almost, almost free. It wasn't quite ... totally relaxed and peaceful and okay yet. It was okay up here [arms raised to head] and it was okay in meditation but in terms of living it wasn't quite there yet and at a certain stage I was in the middle ... I was giving a meditation in where we live and I came up against 'this not quite there yet,' feeling and there was such a spiritual tiredness in it. Such a ... almost boredom of being in this place where there are layers. It's almost like states of subtle despair, states of subtle boredom or subtle resistance like ... like smog.

Renate: I call that the itch of the ego ... [They both laugh].

Georgi: Maybe it's the breath of the ego ... the smell of it. [Laughing].

Renate: I know what you mean ... [Laughing].

Georgi: There was such a tiredness with it and then I could feel beneath it. I'd really had enough, really had enough of this. I could feel lifetimes behind me of going through the same cycle and I had such a passion come forward. I want to get this now! I don't care if I die in it! I don't care if the worst nightmares happen! I don't care what happens, this is it! I totally give myself now to go all the way. There was a choice and there was a choice really from the bases. It's enough now. Now I get it. There isn't a tomorrow. I'm not waiting any more even if I burn in it, even if I suffer.

Of course, the conditions begin to come forward in meditation and there was a choice and then things began to move very, very fast.

So, already there was this open question of the difference between awakening of the mind, this consciousness and the opening of the heart. Between head and heart is the constant spiral and it seemed clear to me that the heart wasn't a resting point either and nor was the head and so there was a duality here. I wasn't using duality and non-duality as terms then I didn't even know about it. But there was clearly a spiral. It's got a peace between head and heart and then ... intuition really, really came to look down on the third level to look towards the body, and there was guidance there as well. In the healing education I'd done, we'd do all the chakras and of course I knew that it was important that there were chakras ... was like the root chakra...yeah, yeah, yeah you know, that's the baboons [*Georgi and Renate laughing and agreeing*]. Don't do a root chakra here! No need for that and, somehow, the invitation came to move more deeply into the body and what I did was move very deeply into the... just the feeling sense, the sense perception of the coccyx of the tailbone. How was it to like ... how was it to look at the world from there?

So we've got consciousness, this whumph! We've got awareness, this, this boundless space. So, what does it look like from the perspective of matter, from the body, from the bone, really from the base bone of the spine. What does it look like? Let this consciousness completely sink into the.... of course it brings also the atmospheres, so I was pondering that. Still I had to go to work at the university, so I packed up the kids to school and I was driving to the university.

They'd just built this great big tunnel, Mount Carmel tunnel. It was still fresh, a fresh tunnel underground and so I drove innocently inside this tunnel, all the time in my tailbone, eyes and ears, in a way sensing through the tailbone and something flipped inside the tunnel where, all separation physical, with the physical began to dissolve. I went in the tunnel in one form and I came out in another form ... it's really weird. In a car it's very easy to move into altered states in a way. The mind is occupied with the driving, so that's taken care of, the automatic pilot is busy but also you've got sense perceptions happening all the time there's the rumble of the car. There's the music playing, there's the wind, there's lights changing all the time. It's very hard to grab hold of anything and you don't push it away either. So the sense of the engine of the car coming and going, passing physical sensations and feelings would come forward, but they come and they go, and thoughts would come but thoughts were much less at that stage as they weren't that relevant because feelings are more what cause thoughts. Thoughts would come

143

forward like a field, so it's like it's bounded in space. I'm not bounded in space, the one that can feel the feeling, the sense perceptions, so, the body like now ... we don't really know we're alive except through our sense perceptions. So, we feel our body on the chair. You see me. I see you. We don't see ourselves. We see each other and it's changing all the time. We feel the air on the face but it's not stable. These are the only way that we even know we are here. So ...

Renate: Through our senses ...

Georgi: Through our senses and if you really allow the senses to be here, they're changing all the time. They're channels, channels into the physical. They are the windows of the five senses and there are more senses which are the windows of the physical and what's being channelled through the physical into consciousness and from consciousness through the physical. Its content is changing all the time and it really doesn't matter. Because the one which is moving, the one which is really here, which is here wherever we go, that never moves isn't that which is bound in time or bound in space. So this one gets stronger and stronger and stronger and expands in a way, into a kind of unity.

And I arrived at work and it begins the technology transfer. The discussion and everything is fluid but I'm absolutely going through the motions but everything is fluid and she's talking and I'm looking at myself talking in a way. I don't mean any personality, it's like empty, this emptiness.

Renate: So Georgi was gone?

Georgi: Georgi was gone and Georgi arrived at the same time.

This was the *here* from the, I am here. This is a kind of arrival point at the other end of the tunnel, like arriving into a *here*, which is not local to sitting on this chair. It's a *here* which is here, also when Georgi was two years old and closed her eyes and thought how, I'm supposed to go to sleep, the darkness inside. It's the same here tonight when I close my eyes, this timeless unconfined here. That's the entry point. It's beyond space and beyond time and we're programmed to not trust it. It's beyond...it's prior to consciousness. It doesn't need to see anything or to be conscious at all in order to be here. It's not separate.

144

Renate: Is it existence, existing itself? Or experience, experiencing itself? There's no gap, no somebody who experiences it?

Georgi: There's a somebody but a somebody is a kind of channel to the source of experience, the source of consciousness, the source of existence.

Renate: Do you call it the Absolute or is it prior to the Absolute?

Georgi: You know absolute is a tricky word because absolute suggests it can be seen, it suggests a form, an absolute form and it's really not a form. You know, it's also not possible in any way to hold it. Just as you can't...you can be conscious of the effects of consciousness, you can even be conscious of consciousness but the real source of it, it doesn't see itself. The moment it sees itself it's made a loop and the real source of it is. ... it doesn't need to be conscious, that's a condition. It doesn't need to perceive. It's not dependent on perception. It's not dependent on form to be formless. It's the other way around. Form depends on the formless in order to be in form. It's the source.

I'll give an example: We all want to be loved. We all talk about love. We all know what love is but when you really go into the feeling of love. How do we know what love is? How do we feel love?

Renate: Are you asking me? [Laughs].

Georgi: Yes.

Renate: It's just ... I guess it's just a knowingness. It's ... I just cannot say in the moment. It's ...

Georgi: Yes.

Renate: It's just ... an interesting question ... [she laughs softly].

Georgi: I asked the wrong person because you...that knowingness is really, has got absolute quality to it, for many, me included, love would be described as a warmth, an opening, a pleasant sensation, a nostalgia, an expectation.

Renate: But not if you are inside the love ... if you are inside the love you cannot name it.

Georgi: Yes ... exactly. So, all those feelings, like this feeling of heart opening, of expansion, the feeling of warmth, the feeling of pleasure, the feeling of happiness to which we associate with love. These are the effects of love. This is what happens when what you could call the Absolute is moving through this dimension and this great unknown, imperceivable absolute is moving through this form. So this effect is an opening, an opening of the form but the effect is not the cause, the cause is something we can dive into and be at peace in. If that same pure life is moving through the head, it's much more likely to be experienced as peace because the effect is a quietening of the mind, an expansion, a resting, a release of stress but it's the same one moving, that one is us. It's the source of who we are and it's not bound in time. It's the same one that was there as a little girl. Nothing moved, nothing happened, nothing changed. It's the same one that was there when we were most in illusion, most lost, most ignorant. Same one. Nothing moved. It will be the same one without anything happening at the moment we die. It doesn't go anywhere also when we die, it doesn't, but here can be trusted.

What I didn't expect was is that it is at the core of matter ... but then when you begin to look at the science of it, and this is where my day job helped. I interview a lot of scientists in my day job. You get down to the individual cells and all the intelligence of life, which is from the stem cells through to the cells expressing itself in form, in harmony, in duality, left hand, the right hand, in this remarkable beauty. But you go deeper down, you go down into the fundamental particles that make up the cells and look into the fundamental particle and it's 99.99999999999% empty. All of that is imperceivable. That bit that can be perceived which is our whole life, our whole experience, all the love, all the longings, all the yearnings, all the fear, all the dramas, that's .0000001%. That means that the only restriction on our pure freedom, on our pure infinite spaciousness, on our indestructible strength and creativity to be here, is our minds!

In saying that it's the other way round, all this stuff is ninety-nine percent and we are the one percent that's God, that's the source of ourselves, a little tiny bit, it's misprogramming. Matter dissolves when you get to the core into pure energy, and that pure energy, I would gamble, is consciousness, it's perceptions, where we are perceiving ... and in perceiving creating we're co-creating.

Renate: So can we say freedom is in our body or through our body?

Georgi: There is no freedom, which excludes anything, certainly not the body. And the body is ...who are we trying to kid that freedom wouldn't be through the miracle of the physical for as long as we are here? That the opportunity is not here in this miraculously strange thing which we're in, this fluid living life. Everything is here and that's where there is a kind of time restriction because this is our chance while we're physical, while we're manifesting physically, there's an opportunity to do something, to let something move through us. It's really okay, it's really okay. Being born here is a bit like working, in a way for IBM. You know you work for IBM and at the end of the day you give back your equipment and you're free of IBM and IBM goes on. It's not really our problem but we are here and we're here because it's absolutely right for us to be here, right here in whatever position we are. The most damaging thing we can do to ourselves is to believe we're not free in being here. And with every judgment that we make on ourselves, that it's not okay to be as we are, we are taking away that freedom which is always here regardless of what form we're taking and it's very deeply programmed and this, this goes back to the deeper layers of liberation in a way. It's in the Bible, the throwing out of Eden that happened because we're guilty, this condemnation.

Renate: We are a sinner.

Georgi: We are condemned. It's not just religion that does this. It's also the healers. It's also us New Age people. We're trying to fix it. So in trying to make the world a better place, what are we saying, what are we feeding? Feeding a message that the world is not okay as it is. We don't accept it.

In a way, collectively we are perpetually condemning ourselves. Humanity puts itself in a state of condemnation and then begins this whole game of being okay. Is it okay for me to be here? Am I acceptable? Did I do good? It's very childish in a way, but inside the opium field of the collective awareness we need those leaps of freedom into conscious awakening, in order to release the condemnation. Maybe that's what they mean when they talk about redemption ... [laughs] ... and but it's not historic and it's not future, it's inside us.

Renate: Georgie, I'm afraid we have to stop [laughs]. We just covered a fraction of your story ... but maybe we will have another chance. Anyway, it was beautiful talking to you.

Georgi: It was beautiful talking to you too.

Renate: And so this was Georgi Y Johnson and I show her book again, *I Am Here: Opening the Windows of Life and Beauty.*

Cynthia Bourgeault –
Seeing With The Eyes Of The Heart
Interview by **Renate McNay**

We have our life to live and we either live it awake and consciously or we snooze through it. And if we live it awake and consciously, we touch other human beings who are trying that same way and we begin to touch a container and a shape of awakeness that's different from anything else on the planet. So that's where I work and, while I hold down the corner in Christianity, it really is a universal work. Each of the traditions participate in it in their own way. To reveal, I think, what divine love looks like in created form.

Renate: Cynthia is a modern-day mystic, episcopal priest, writer, and internationally-known retreat leader. Cynthia divides her time between solitude at her seaside hermitage in Maine and travelling globally to teach and spread the recovery of the Christian contemplative and wisdom path.

That sounds lovely to have a seaside hermitage!

Cynthia: Oh yes, you should try it in December though!

Renate: In December?

Cynthia: The sea is an angry mistress!

Renate: I would love to have a hermitage in the mountains. I'm more a mountain goat than a sea person.

Cynthia: Why doesn't that surprise me?

Renate: So I'm showing you some of Cynthia's books: *Centering Prayer*, and there is a follow-up to be published in December 2016 called *The Heart of Centering Prayer: Non-dual Christianity in Theory and Practice*.

There's a book on Mary Magdalene, *The Meaning of Mary Magdalene* and, of course, a book on Jesus, *The Wisdom Jesus*. And *Love is Stronger than Death* – this is a *very* beautiful book, my most favourite book, I've already read it twice. And *The Wisdom Way of Knowing*, and *Mystical Hope*. Do you write all these books in your hermitage?

Cynthia: Yes, actually I think they all got written there.

Renate: OK, Cynthia, I like to start with the question: How did your Christian life begin? How did you come to choose the Christian path?

Cynthia: Well, in a way it was what the Buddhists would call 'a choiceless choice'. I found myself growing up as a child in the 1950s in the area around Philadelphia, in the United States. Christianity was all there was, I mean our biggest choice was were you a Catholic or a Methodist? And what really began my journey was that my parents sent me to a Quaker school. That was easy to do back in the Philadelphia area because it's one of the natural homes of Quakers. We had this wonderful little school – about sixty children between the ages of five and twelve – and, as part of the Quaker heritage, we would all go in once a week for a silent meeting for worship. We would troop into this beautiful old eighteenth-century meeting-house with great clear lights pouring in from upper windows. And the whole programmeme in Quakerism is to sit and gather your heart in silence until the spirit might move you to speak.

Renate: What does that mean: Gather your heart?

Cynthia: Gather your heart in silence? Well, it means, to begin with: Shut up! So instead of going into a place where you start, like you do in a church, with people proclaiming words at you or singing songs, you come in and you sit in silence in what looks like, and really *is*, meditation. And the only real difference between a Quaker meeting for worship and silent meditation is that if the spirit moves you after a time, in Quaker meeting, you get up and speak the message that's been given in your heart.

And then it goes back into silence and then somebody else might stand and speak, moved by that message but not debating. So it kind of builds a teaching, which is almost downloaded from the cosmos and created by the listening hearts in the room. In that kind of environment, I first touched, in a very simple and direct way, what you might call the mystical field of love that surrounds us and binds our hearts together, and is the real presence of God.

Renate: You were only six years old.

Cynthia: I was only six years old.

Renate: And how did you figure out what it was?

Cynthia: Well, you just know it in the heart. I mean, with all theories of reincarnation aside for the moment, there is an ancient knowingness in the child. There is a knowingness that seeks for familiarity. And the things in the world that are true, that are powerful, that are unobstructed, unveiled, ring so clear in the heart of a child.

I was going off to Sunday school, too, at the Christian Scientists', which was my parents' denomination, and I didn't feel that clarity. I felt noise and words and theories and manipulation. And there was just this deep, *deep* profound *yes-ness* and connection that I knew in the Quaker meeting. So that, plus the natural world around me, was the start. Then, in the course of time, I began to become interested in music: choral music spoke to me deeply. And it was through that that the path of Christianity, that I'd formerly only known as doctrine and dogma shoved down my throat, began to come alive in that same way it had as a child – as the experience of love and beauty offered to the infinite.

So I always had those kinds of streaks already under my belt and I would say that there were a couple of reasons that I 'manifested on the Christian path', if you want to call it that. First of all because I really had no choice. Back in that time, back in the '50s in Philadelphia, there weren't at that point Buddhists and Sufis and Hindus running around where you could find them and consider those paths. The only question was what kind of a Christian were you going to be? Not were you going to get out of the religion altogether? The second reason was because of a real, kind of profound, you might call it *conversion* experience that happened to me when I was twenty. That really changed everything.

Renate: Yes. So that was when you for the first time had Communion?

Cynthia: Yes. I received Communion by accident. The Holy Communion, you know, the most sacred ritual of Christianity when you come up and receive the bread and the wine that has been offered and received as the living body of Jesus. Normally a very, very protected thing, you study and you work for a long time before you are initiated. Well I got initiated very, very quickly by total accident. In Christian Science, Communion did happen once a month but it happened in the church and we were only in Sunday school, so we didn't know about it – and Quakers don't do that sort of thing because they believe that every *moment* ought to be a full communion with Christ, so if that's happening who needs bread and wine?

So I wasn't presented with this and, when I was twenty I went with my college roommate to what I thought was a concert. [both laugh] The boy choir from St. Paul's Cathedral in London, England was doing a concert on Sunday morning at St.Paul's Anglican Church in London, Ontario. So all I saw in the newspaper was that they were doing the William Byrd *Mass in Four Voices*, one of my favourite, beautiful Renaissance singing pieces. I said, "Lets go!" So I dragged my college roommate with me and off we went and I was so enraptured with the music that I didn't even notice that there were long, kind of, talk breaks between the various movements.

Well, I come to find out it that was just music offered as part of the service and, the next thing you know, a very stern looking usher is standing in front of our row of pews and motioning us forward. So I said, "Oh! Oh! I'm in a Communion line! Help, help!" My mother, who was a Christian Scientist and had a profound loathing and fear of Catholic tradition, had warned me about terrible things that occur when this happens to you! [both laugh] But at that moment my fear of the usher was greater than my fear of eternal damnation! So up I went. And my roommate, who had fortunately been raised Catholic, said, "Just follow me and do what I do." So she put out her hands and I put out my hands and into my hands was placed this wafer and she looked over at me and said, "Don't chew it!" [Renate laughs] And then comes along this beautiful silver chalice of wine and she hisses over at me, "Don't touch it!" and I was about to say, "But how can you drink it without touching it?!" when it's put to my lips and I [mimes taking a sip].

So it happens, and I'm walking back to my pew thinking 'well, that's that'. And I'm about two thirds of the way back to the pew and all of a sudden I realise 'that's that!!!' And it wasn't like I'd met my risen Lord, there wasn't a big Jesus image in front of me, but there was just that ancient sense of familiarity once again. That this dimension that had been missing all my life, that I hadn't found in my 1950s childhood in Philadelphia, was there! This 'other intensity' as the poet T.S. Eliot calls it.

Renate: And how did you feel it? Where did you feel it?

Cynthia: It was right in the heart. It was very profoundly a sense that I'd met my path and I'd met my master. And that this master was a *someone*, not a theory to be mastered, not a set of creeds to be recited. So there was a deep sense of invitation to a path that was really an initiation. And I think that, over and over again, has been the reason I've stuck with Christianity through thick and thin with my eyes open. I've said many, many times that if I could have been a Sufi I would have done it in a heartbeat. But, when you receive what really your own heart-of-hearts receives as an invitation from a living master to come *this* way, you don't say, "Sorry, Jesus, I'd rather be a Sufi!" And I've worked closely with many of the religious traditions, I have a great belief that, like colours of the rainbow, they all belong together. And it requires every one of them to show the full spectrum of divine love. But the path that I've been plonked down on and called to manifest in and serve in is this particular ray of the rainbow.

Renate: Yes. So what does manifesting and serving mean for you?

Cynthia: Well, it really means a couple of things. One of the dimensions is to try, wherever you are, to be conscious, and to be grateful, and to be alert. And to see what needs to be done in the moment and to do it in such a way that you're moving in a direction of greater compassion, greater love, and greater understanding on the planet. So I would say that's the simplest version. I don't like to obscure it with devotion talk and God talk, and I don't have any sort of special notion of my importance or being in some sort of consecrated path. That's, sort of, too-inflated terminology. I mean every human being is consecrated just by the fact of being born. And we have our life to live and we either live it awake and consciously or we snooze through it. And if we live it awake and consciously, we touch other human beings who are trying that same way and we begin to touch a container and a shape of *awakeness* that's different from anything else on the planet. So that's where I work and, while I hold down the corner in Christianity, it really is a universal work. Each of the traditions participate in it in their own way. To reveal, I think, what divine love looks like in created form.

Renate: So tell us about that. [both laugh]

Cynthia: Well ... I would say that's one of the things that we tend to forget because so many, many, many, many thousands of years we humans have spent thinking that there's something wrong with being here, on this planet, that it's illusion, it's *maya*, it's sin, it's coarse, it's contaminated.

Renate: It's still in some teachings.

Cynthia: Yeah, it's still in most of the teachings. I mean that you just go from one teaching to another but they all start with the fact that there is something not trustworthy about the human condition, not good about it, and that spiritual transformation means getting out of it, leaving the whole thing behind like a dead booster rocket and boosting off into some spiritual world. But I think what we forget, and what's actually there in the heart of Christianity – although Christianity has forgotten it as well as all the others! – is this affirmation that 'God so loved the world'. That there is something very, very precious *here* in this dimension, in this form with purple sofas, and glasses of water, and bodies, and embodiment, and love, and rejection, and trial, and death, and suffering. Something in the mix of that that brings forth a manifestation of love that's so precious that it can be uttered in no other way. And we are here for a little while, as the poet Blake said, "To learn to bear the beams of love" and to manifest them forth as what the heart of God looks like.

Renate: Mm ... but this is quite a journey!

Cynthia: It is.

Renate: To come to this point where you are free to love. And so my question is: How does Christianity address our deep wounds and delusions?

Cynthia: Well, I think all the traditions address them or don't address them on two levels. The one level that's there from the beginning is in the great language and offering and energy of the whole world of sacraments and devotions. At this level, as things get offered up – like, in Christianity, the Eucharist, the Holy Communion – as the image gets lifted up, as ghoulish as it may seem at first, of the suffering Christ on the cross, there's actually a wisdom being conveyed there that does give comfort and healing. The problem is we don't mostly *get* that because something else has to kick in before any of this becomes really operative in our brains and our hearts and that's the path that begins to get opened up when we start to do conscious inner work.

Renate: So how did that start with you, Cynthia? How did you *get* it?

Cynthia: How did it start with me? Well, of course I had my first wonderful, rounded mystical rapture, you know, I had the Eucharist, I'd had this experience I told you of, I had the beauty of singing ... It catapulted me into wanting to be a priest and feeling that what I wanted to do was to serve up this Communion, and all the usual mystery and drama! So I did. I was ordained in the Episcopal Church in 1979. The Episcopalians were among the first of the mainline, the greater family, of Christian Churches, in that greater Catholic tradition, to ordain women. And I was among the first that was ordained in that tradition.

So here I am: a priest in my bright, shiny black suit and white clericals – and then I began to notice, to my horror, that no matter how much

I preached the scripture to people, no matter how much I offered up the Eucharist, people remained people! Gossipy, nasty, confrontational, divisive, always tending to splinter into small groups and to act out of their hidden agendas. And I realised 'Dear God! There's nothing we've got here that's actually getting people to change!'

So I went searching myself and it was about that time, that what fell into my lap – as things always fall into your lap when you say you are searching – was a copy of a book called *In Search of the Miraculous* written by P.D. Ouspensky in the 1940s. It was his record of the teachings of the spiritual teacher G.I. Gurdjieff, who was an underground spiritual teacher of the twentieth century and was the first to bring to the West a practice, which nowadays we call 'mindfulness.' They didn't have the language yet, and the Gurdjieff Work was a very, very, I would say, *cumbersome* early run-up on mindfulness training. But it did open the question of: How do you wake up? How do you pay attention? Do you even know that you are spending your life snoozing through on autopilot? Something pushes your button and you are off and running in that direction and something pulls your chain and you are running in this direction and yet you say you are alive?

So I entered the Gurdjieff Work and was a serious student for ten years, which really laid down in me the basis for understanding our own responsibility in waking up and making actual, confronting that vast maze of automatic, programmemed behaviours that keep us chained at a level that's lower than real human freedom. I worked in that for a long time. I still work in it, I have the deepest respect for this body of knowledge. But it led me forward and then, by the time I was really getting serious in that Work, in Christianity there were the beginnings of these wonderful paths of meditation, which hadn't been a part of normal Christian religious upbringing till that point.

So from my teacher Thomas Keating, the great Trappist monk, I learned a very simple form of sitting meditation called 'Centering Prayer.' Centering Prayer brings all the effects that have now been documented that meditation does for the brain and for the heart when you begin to meditate seriously. I also have this wonderful grab-bag of teachings from the Gurdjieff Work on conscious awakening.

Renate: Did you do the movements?

Cynthia: I did the movements, yes.

Renate: How was that?

Cynthia: Chilling, you know. The movements are, I would say, the great sacred liturgy of the Gurdjieff Work – the Gurdjieff Work wouldn't consider it that way. But, in these very, very simple 'dances', you can call them, although they're not that, they're more sacred gestures [demonstrates some of the gestures] that you learn to take in beautiful sequences, and pay attention in the middle of them; some of them very complicated, some of them heartbreakingly simple. And to music that is beautifully written to go *right into* the chakras that need to be adjusted and off it goes ... It leaves you writhing on the floor with just the wonder and the terror and the beauty of this whole journey in form.

Renate: You said that they are like rabbit holes and sometimes you were lying on the floor and crying.

Cynthia: You get sucked down into... and, of course, they pick you right up because those kinds of displays of being 'slain in the spirit' are not on. So you learn to contain your ecstasy and you learn to contain your anguish and move on and take the next position, but meanwhile something is being touched at a level that's so profound that ... again, you can only get a *felt* sense that life hangs together by some deeper coherence and compassion. And I think our theologies and our doctrines and our dogmas and our principles try and take that and put it in mental form, but the mental form never touches that sense that something holds together. And I felt that in the movements so profoundly.

Renate: And you cannot name it ...

Cynthia: Well, you can name it, but you name it in code phrases. That you 'feel the suffering of God', you feel your wish to 'relieve the sorrow of His endlessness', as Gurdjieff called it. You say the words: "Lord have mercy," and you realise that they are not about somebody getting down and begging for pity before a great God who's a judge. But a deep sense of remorse and seeing the vastness of the whole thing and the terror of the whole thing.

Renate: Yes, it is a terror.

Cynthia: Yes. But not the kind of terror that they put in the tabloids of three more people dead in the street, but the kind of terror that something so immense, that something so beautiful, that something so sacred and veiled in the heart of God.

Renate: And how beauty and suffering belongs together.

Cynthia: They belong. They are the two inevitable sides of the same coin, of the intimacy of God. So, you see this and you feel this as you dig the capaciousness of your soul, the capacity to hold this, this wine of yearning and suffering and beauty, without being destroyed by it.

Renate: So you must have quite an open heart to be able to do that.

Cynthia: Oh, on my better days! [both laugh]

Renate: To be able to hold the suffering and the pain and the sorrow, which is really running through the Earth.

Cynthia: Yeah, exactly.

Renate: Or, like Thich Nhat Hanh says, "Listen to the Earth cry."

Cynthia: Exactly, exactly. And these are all kinds of things that are absolutely real. But they make no sense on the level of the mind alone: 'What about the Earth crying? The Earth is rocks, they're not sentient!' It's when you calm down into the full embodied being that you begin to hear and you begin to see, and respond to these threads of coherence. Rather than having to project them out. You know, there's a huge, huge difference between explanation and meaning. And mostly the Church has tried to give us explanation, thinking that if we have explanations we'll say, "OK, it makes sense." But explanation is hollow, you know. What's the explanation for making love?

Renate: It's the left side of the brain.

Cynthia: Yes, the brain. It's the *meaning* that tells us, 'you belong, you are here.'

Renate: Beautiful. You said yesterday, at your evening in Westminster Cathedral, you said that this era is about embodiment. Can you say more about that?

Cynthia: Exactly, this era is about embodiment. It's so true. As we talked about earlier in this conversation, for about 2,500 years part of what's called 'first axial consciousness' really depicted the world as flawed and depicted the spiritual path as getting out of the body and the body was seen to be the seat of sinful self-will, the seat of delusion, the seat of coarseness. And everything was depicted as, you know, we were in a cave and we had to leave the cave and go to the light. So most spiritual practices were built on some variation of either gaining mastery over the body or even mortifying the body. But we're in the body for a good reason. And the body is our profound vessel of truth and spiritual exploration. And so coming more and more in the end of the last century and into this has been a renewed appreciation of the goodness and wisdom of the body.

Renate: Also within the Church?

Cynthia: It's getting into the Church but it's getting into the Church by the back door, not the front door. It's getting into the Church because, I think, a lot of the people in the congregations who are now getting old are realising that they need to do yoga to keep their bodies in shape and, if they're going to sit on a meditation cushion, they have to know how to bend their legs. So it's getting in through the portal of wellness. I think that still, in most Christian Churches, if you look at how a service is actually conducted, you might as well check in your body in the cloakroom when you go in because it's all just pitched at your head. You sit in a pew and you listen and you say words. But, I think, in other formats that are coming – our wisdom schools, and even in meditation when it's done properly – we're beginning to see more and more that we need to embody because the body actually reads spiritual gestures, spiritual wisdom and coherence *way* better than the mind does.

Renate: So the Gurdjieff dances helped you with the embodiment.

Cynthia: Exactly.

Renate: What else can we do?

Cynthia: Well, you know almost anything that begins to teach us to embody. Skiing! One of the most powerful lessons I learned about how the spiritual journey works I learned when I was eight-years-old when a beautiful life guard at a swimming pool taught me how to float. Like all children, I was scared of sinking to the bottom of the pool so I went like this [curls up tight], and she finally says, "Well, you're gonna sink to the bottom right fast if you do that!" She says, "fill your chest with air, put your head back, put your hands out and breath and you won't go to the bottom." This, little did I know, is a basic gesture of the spiritual life. It's the gesture of trust, it's the gesture of vulnerability, it's the gesture that some people say will open the throat chakra. You see Teresa of Avila in all the ancient art works, exactly that position: the rapture.

So from Gurdjieff I learned, even more from the movements itself, I learned the wisdom that the body understands the language of spiritual gesture. And that in the simple postures of life, in the simple taking your broom and bringing your attention to your hands on it as you sweep and being in the motion as you sweep the room – not just having someone else hired to sweep the room but participating deeply in the rhythmic nature of embodied life itself – you begin to learn something about your participation in life, your *belonging* in life that can't be had with the head, which can't belong to anything because it's always separating itself from things in order to 'see it'. So the world calls us to embodiment with every breath. We just have to learn to attune to it again and to value the body as a sacred temple of perception, not just as something that has to be kept well so we live a little longer.

Renate: I want to touch a little bit on the heart. There is a lot of talk about how the brain needs to sink into the heart. How do we do that? What does that mean?

Cynthia: Well, it's a beautiful statement. The statement is actually all over Eastern Christian Orthodox practice, 'Put the mind in the heart. Put the mind in the heart. The chief thing is that the mind should be in the heart.' And they speak over and over about something called 'attention of the heart', which is also known in that tradition as 'vigilance' and is touched in the Western Christian tradition as 'recollection'. I believe that I was saying, in the talk we did last night in London, that one of the really powerful insights that the Christian tradition brings to the whole spiritual playing table of transformation is that these higher states of consciousness, these states that we call non-dual or unitive or contemplative, aren't just attained by the mind alone. That they are attained by bringing the mind into the heart, which is not just a symbol, it's not just a metaphoric way of talking about things, but is an actual physiological event so that the brain waves entrain to the rhythm of the heart and they become a single perceptual unit. So how do you do it?

Renate: Yes, Cynthia, how do *you* do it?

Cynthia: OK, how do I do it? Well, you know, just buy my books and give me fifty-thousand dollars and I'll let you do it on the weekend! [both laugh]

It's a long, slow process. And it has a couple of component pieces. The core attitude that the Christian tradition works with is the piece called 'surrender' or 'kenosis'. Kenosis is the word in Greek which Saint Paul used to depict 'putting on the mind of Christ'. And it, basically, is pretty close to what the Buddhists mean by non-clinging. Doesn't hang on, doesn't insist, doesn't assert, doesn't grab, doesn't brace, doesn't defend, you know. It's the mind that [she sighs and relaxes outwards]. We try to put *that* mind on. In one of those ancient early Christian writings, the Gospel of Thomas, the students asked Jesus, "What are your students like, how would you describe them?" and He said, "They are like small children, playing in a field not their own. When the landlords come and demand, "Give us back our field!" the children return it by stripping themselves and standing naked before them." That's the description from Jesus of this process. So it's the lifelong practice, the core practice, of learning to recognise when you've gotten into one of these postures: tightened, urgent, angry, self-important, and in that moment …

Renate: Open to Him.

Cynthia: Open to Him. So that's the hang of it, that's the heart of it combined with a couple of complementary practices which come from the mindfulness sector. One – the piece that I learned from the Gurdjieff Work – is to learn how to even *notice* when you're getting into these states of constriction, and smaller-self urgency, and automaticity, because we don't notice that automatically. It's like you don't notice the moment you fall asleep at night. You sink into these lower, unfree, ugly states of being automatically. So you have to learn to even notice when that happens. And the second –

Renate: There is this point, I know this with myself, there is this point where you see you could go both ways, you could serve the ego or you can surrender. And you can decide.

Cynthia: Yeah. There is definitely that point. What makes it difficult though is that for a long, long time in the practice you can see that point. You can see yourself going over the waterfall, but you don't have the power to swim away yet. So what you have to do is live in the gap and say, "Oh my God, look at what's happening to me, I can see that I'm sinking but I don't have the force to stop." And it takes a long time until we have the force. And to be able to see that you're falling into a bad state doesn't, for a long time, mean you can do anything about it. I think that's a truism that disappoints many people, so the even more painful penance is you just have to sit there and watch it. Your only real choice is can you just see it, and the horror and remorse and helplessness, or do you just pretend, "Oh well, I'm really right! I'm going to fight for this for all ..." Can you just go with the lower state or can you wait in the gap? So for me that's brought a whole new meaning to that whole British cliché 'mind the gap'! [Renate laughs]

Because we sit there in the gap for a long time saying [gasps]. And that's when you begin to learn the meaning of 'Lord Have Mercy'. I can't do anything to raise my state but what I can do is stay honestly ahead of, in plain sight, what's happened, acknowledging. Here I am. And I think it's from that repeated acknowledgement of my own helplessness at that level, but refusing to simply hide from that helplessness, that *gradually*, gradually, gradually the energy that had originally gone into your, sort of, ego programmemes gets recaptured to begin to hold this other kind of field of awareness, of attentiveness, that's not identified with that small self acting-out and can begin to become a *nest* for that deeper and fuller and truer wiser self to live in. And then we begin to *Be*. Then we begin to have Being. And it's from that Being that sometimes we can pull ourselves out of that spiral we were heading into, and it's from that Being that we can begin to offer our force of Being to the world as love, as assistance, as a shift in the energy field for someone else. 'Baraka' the Sufis call it. But it comes slowly, because you can't just, kind of, click your heels together and have Being. It has to accumulate slowly in your being for a life of painfully bearing the crucifixion of inner honesty, and slowly it emerges.

Renate: One thing I like to also touch on is: If you look at the world it looks all very sad and you wonder where it's all going, and at the same time we say, "God is Love." And I remember I struggled with this question already as a child. What does it mean: God's Love? How do we feel it, how do we learn to feel it and trust it, despite of what we are seeing?

Cynthia: Well, to begin with, the sense that in which it's usually presented to you as a child won't work. Because we think of God as this big daddy out in the sky who has this kind of nature that He is love or He is wrath. He'll fling his fireballs or send his love. As long as you are holding that picture, it's impossible to understand that. It really breaks my heart to see children have to go through what you just described because you say, "How can God be love if this world is suffering, and cruelty and hatred, and people are dying in Syria and Iraq, and madmen are running planets and countries, and what's going on?! The planet is quickly warming itself into non-existence. How can God be love?" As long as you are dealing with that external God out there, who's presumed to be a first cause and could change things if he wanted to, then it's not going to make sense.

So you have to come back to that *felt* sense that we were talking about earlier, that very, very deep thing that happens in your heart-of-hearts when you know that somehow the whole thing hangs together in a field of compassion. The idea of a suffering God that doesn't make sense at all from a mental concept because how can a God that's almighty suffer? Not logical, right? But when you enter that with your heart, you understand the catch-22 that divine love is in. That, in order to manifest this most precious dimension of love, it takes form. And when you have form, there's suffering. Because things are broken, they're yearning for wholeness, they can't have it. There's cruelty, there's automatic-ness. And in the midst of this you yearn. And in the midst of it, you find that something holds together. And the fact that 'God is love'... it's true it doesn't depend on the world being bright and twinkly and sparkly outside; as a matter of fact, it's exercised and touched most deeply in those moments of *poignant* heartbreak. That somehow, yes, even *this* holds together and is the chalice of love poured out of God's yearning to touch the world and to hold it. It's like the sun yearning to hold a snowflake. He can't do it without melting it. And that›s the suffering of God. To let it be, to let it ... to let it *have* to shoulder its Planck's constant of horror and pain and to still love it, and to still be accessible in love.

So we grow, I think, as human beings in our own capaciousness – it's a word I've used before – to hold this every which way-ness of love.

This love that won't be killed in the midst of suffering, and yet won't make suffering go away. This love where you see hearts broken, lives touched apart and yet love holds. And when your own heart becomes deep enough to hold a piece of this, then you become part of the mystical heart of universal love. And it doesn't feel good, it doesn't feel blissful. You know, I think one of the clichés that's thrown about on the spiritual journey is that it's about making you feel blissful states all the time. No! When you open your heart to the world, what you can guarantee is that your heart is going to be broken. And to hear the pain of the world and to hold the pain of the world. So it's something *way* beyond bliss. It's that every which way-ness of the reality of love in the midst of brokenness. And as we begin to hold that, we sense the coherence and the cost by which everything holds together. But you never touch it with your head. You know, religion is not a philosophy, God is not a first cause. All that level is just explanation, meaning is something different.

Renate: So that brings up the question in me, what is then freedom?

Cynthia: What is freedom?

Renate: Because you go on this journey. We start out on this journey to become free, which we call enlightenment.

Cynthia: Well, you know, we have so many mixed metaphors as Western and Eastern ways of contexting reality come together like tectonic plates. And they don't often match up. I think, in a very obvious way, freedom is easy. At the obvious level, what it means is what you'd call 'freedom from the false self'. Most of us think we're free, and yet we are not free at all because we are under the absolute compulsion of agendas, addictions and aversions that have been programmemed into us from early life, and sometimes from the womb. We have our values, we have our triggers, we have our flash points, we have our agendas. And, as A.H. Almaas said so famously, "Freedom to be your ego is not freedom." Because that's slavery. You're being pulled around by a ring through the nose.

So part of the work of freedom begins when you can stabilise in yourself this thing that some of the Eastern traditions helpfully call 'witnessing presence', which is something deeper that's not dependent on the pain-pleasure principle, that's not attracted by attraction, or repulsed by aversion. You know, as my teacher Rafe, the hermit monk of Snowmass, Colorado, used to say, "I want to have enough Being to be nothing." Which means he is not dependant on the world to give him his identity, because he's learned his identity nests in something much deeper.

So that's the first level of freedom. But I think beyond that what makes it difficult is that old cliché that comes out of the Anglican tradition talking about our relationship to Christ 'whose freedom is perfect service'. It's the freedom you know when you fall helplessly in love with somebody – you're not free to walk away. Because you see the coherence of your life, you see the only pattern in which your life could fit. Like for me back then, I wasn't free to choose to be a Sufi or a Buddhist, because the path of coherence is *this* way.

And as you finally become free to follow what you might call the 'homing beacon of your own inner calling', you realise that it's only in that complete *obedience* that freedom lies. And, of course, the trick to that is the word 'obedience', which we usually thinks means knuckling under, or capitulating, really comes from the Latin *'ob audire'*, which means 'to listen deeply'. So, as we listen deeply to the fundamental, what you might call the 'tuning fork' of our being – which is given to us not by ourself and is never about self-realisation because the self *melts* as that realisation comes closer – you find the only freedom is to be your own cell in the vast mystical body of God.

Renate: Beautiful.

Cynthia: But you have to get free of the false self to see that. [both laugh]

Renate: So, you spend a lot of time in solitude. Three months a year, I think?

Cynthia: Well, that's the game plan – as they say in *Hamlet* 'more honoured in the breach than the observance'! Yes, I have spent some time in solitude.

Renate: And silence.

Cynthia: Mm hm.

Renate: And how does that work for you? What does that give you?

Cynthia: Honesty. You know that we often equate it with... You know, we go into silence to find profound states of Being – this will come around, but the first thing that silence does is it *ruthlessly* exposes the evasions, and the first evasion is simply our own – or my own – restlessness. You begin to discover how jumpy you are and then you begin to discover the evasion of time and how we set our life up with a schedule. We get up and we wake up at a certain time and we do our prayer practices and we have our meals then and we have a... In other words, we parcelled our day out on this kind of linear continuum and all of a sudden, you know, it begins to hit you like a freight train: there's simply this *now* and we're breaking it up into bits so that we cannot be squashed by it. You begin to see these evasions, you begin to see these screens that you put up to live in the world. You begin to see that so much of what you thought you were about is only being cued to that evasion you've already set in place. So the first is just falling through your own restlessness and beginning to develop a little bit of capacity to live in your own skin.

I think, for me, that this is really what incarnation, what solitude is about. It's about becoming more restful in embodiment, about being able to confront and fall through that ever, kind of, restless tendency. So many of us are fundamentally autophobic, we don't live comfortably in our own skin, we are always projecting it *out there*: my path, my enlightenment, my practices, you know, where I'll be next year. Stop! Be! But it's, you know, it's *squizzly* for a while. And then you finally drop through that. My hermit teacher used to say, "You have to endure the tedium until something emerges in it." And then what develops is an expanded capacity for restful presence in a larger field of the now. The nows get longer and longer and are not broken up into time things so much. So you don't do anything particularly *different*, you just do it with a deeper and deeper rhythm of being grounded in something beyond our, kind of, completely human artificial constructions of what reality actually is structured like.

Renate: Beautiful. Well our time is slowly running out.

Cynthia: Oh well, speaking of time ... ! So, if we were good hermits we'd just, sort of, relax and be here for another four months!

Renate: We can just be in the now and let it all unfold! Is there anything else, like one or two sentences, you still would like to say to our audience?

Cynthia: Well, I think that the one thing that I would say is that hermit work is not done alone. It looks like the ultimate 'well, she goes off by herself and nobody sees her ... ' But you really are in solidarity with the hearts of everybody. And my belief is that so many of the models we've used, in our spirituality of the past, are individualistic models even right up to enlightenment, my *personal* self-realisation. But what happens is, when we enter that deep, deep heart space, it's *transpersonal*. It's personal and it's transpersonal, it touches the heart space of everybody else, both living and beyond, I think. So it's ultimately a communal form and I do believe that, particularly in this next era of our spiritual unfolding, along with embodiment we're going to understand again much more keenly an era of human solidarity and a higher collectively, and my own work when I go and teach is always in the service of that union. Way, way back when I had that Communion at twenty, the words are 'this is my body given for you', and the sense that our whole common sentient being is the body of Christ, or the body of God, or the body of Buddha – pick your Bodhisattva! But we're forming something that's higher and deeper, which can more worthily and deeply bear those beams of love.

Renate: Thank you. That's a beautiful ending, Cynthia, thank you very much.

Gabor Harsanyi –
The Master of Silence

Interview by **Iain McNay**

*S*o then, the next "problem" that comes, the next challenge for me,
is that everyone misunderstands – they think that this nice feeling
that they have is like meditation. "Oh, it's just like a meditation
technique. I know. I did this before, you know." So the mind from memory
says, "Ok, this is this, and that meditation technique ..." and starts
comparing immediately.

So we are there, nothing else is needed, and if you can stay there, I am
not even needed. But they can't stay there, because the mind will start
coming at it. "Oh, it's just like meditation." But, no, it is not meditation.
Meditation has a beginning and an end. This is a feeling, a sensing of
existence. This is a sensing of your being. When your being recognises its
own being, you will not need me, and I don't want to call this meditation
simply because this is not in time. As soon as you enter this being state
– if I can call it a state – you are no longer in time.

Iain: My guest today is Gabor Harsanyi. Gabor is a Master of Silence. I think that's a wonderful title, and we're going to find out how he became a Master of Silence. He has really quite a story to tell. He's lived quite a life and he's been through a lot of things, and we're going to get a feel of that and also, obviously, a feel of where he is these days. So, Gabor, you were living in Hungary when there was the 1956 uprising, when the Russian tanks came in. That must have been very hard for you.

Gabor: Yes. Most of my childhood was spent in an upheaval type of situation. I remember when I was three years old, and there were flowers and plants next to our house, and I used to walk and be at total peace. And then, after that, a lot of troubles started. All kinds of trouble – the 1956 revolution came, and my father was part of that uprising, so we were pushed back and forth, back and forth. All kinds of emotions came up, all kinds of emotions. And then the revolution was beaten down, and my father was in and out of jail for a few years after 1956. So that was really dramatic and emotional shake-up.

Iain: And how do you remember that peace that you found when you were with the plants?

Gabor: It's not in memory. It's not in my mental memory. It is in some kind of other memory. There was this nurturing wonderful feeling that I felt at home between the plants and the grass. And very early I was wondering, "What am I doing here? Why are all these people so weird?"

Iain: So you didn't fit in somehow.

Gabor: No. I didn't fit in at all.

Iain: Ok. And when you got a little older you decided that you didn't want to stay any longer in Hungary.

Gabor: Yes. Well, when I was in Hungary, I was dreaming of going to America, and what America represented at that time was freedom. I didn't know that what I was after was inner freedom. That concept was not even available to me. I guess I just wanted the chain to be looser, or I wanted the chain to be made of gold, let's say. So, I was really desperately going for freedom, freedom, freedom! As to what it represented to me at that time – being able to travel, have enough money and do what you want kind of thing. That's when I escaped. I spent six months in a refugee camp in Italy.

Iain: Were you on your own when you escaped, or were you with some friends?

Gabor: I was with another person, it was the two of us who attempted to escape.

Iain: It must have been hard to leave your family.

Gabor: Yes, it was extremely hard. There was something inside me that yanked me out, if I may use that expression. There was some kind of power that helped me to make it. There was not much planning. It just happened. So the desire, the vision, actually happened – getting out and being free.

Iain: So practically, you had to go through Yugoslavia.

Gabor: Yes.

Iain: Then you mentioned you were in Italy.

Gabor: Yes.

Iain: So you were walking, were you?

Gabor: Yes.

Iain: And Yugoslavia then – although it was Tito in power – it was still a communist country.

Gabor: Yes. It was still communist at that time. It was easier to cross from Yugoslavia to Italy than, let's say, from Hungary to Austria.

Iain: Yes.

Gabor: So I decided to take that route. And I escaped from Koper, which was in Yugoslavia, to Italy, the side that's called Trieste.

Iain: And was that journey dangerous?

Gabor: Yes. Very dangerous. It was very dangerous. They were actually shooting, and dogs were running after us and stuff like that.

Iain: Wow!

Gabor: Very dramatic, again.

Iain: Wow! Yes.

Gabor: Even to remember it is kind of weird, you know.

Iain: But you were determined to make it

Gabor: I was determined to make it. I was running, running, and I walked, oh, I don't know ... about sixty Kilometres from the boarder to Trieste. Then I registered with the police. For two days I didn't know what to do, so I lived in a telephone booth. I didn't know what to do. I was eighteen with lots of testosterone, but with lots of fear also. I didn't know what's going to happen, "Are they going to ship me back to Hungary? Are they going to accept me? What's going to happen?"

So, after a couple of days I went to the police, and they took me to a refugee camp where I spent six months.

Iain: And, of course, now in Europe we have so many refugees. This is 2016 and there are so many refugees coming to Europe. So, in a way, your experience then is similar to what the refugees are experiencing now.

Gabor: Yes. And certainly my escape and my troubles were really nothing in comparison to what's happening to those people right now. I didn't have a child to carry. I was on my own. I was eighteen. And also, there were very few refugees.

Iain: Ok.

Gabor: Italy didn't have to deal with ten thousand of them a day.

Iain: Yes.

Gabor: So I was extremely fortunate to escape at that time and that I was a refugee at that time. I was well treated, and they didn't have the current refugee problems that they have now.

Iain: I understand. So then you were able to get from Italy to Canada.

Gabor: Yes.

Iain: And I guess you flew there and somehow that was financed.

Gabor: Yes. I flew to Canada. I landed and basically I ran out of the plane and said, "Ok, here I am come. I am ambitious. What do I have to do to become successful?" Success meant financial success.

Iain: Yes.

Gabor: I didn't care really what I had to do … within reason. And so reasonably quickly I became very successful financially, because that's really all I wanted, totally believing that that's what is going to give me the freedom that I was looking for.

Iain: Yes, but how did you do that? Here you are coming … you are a refugee … presumably your English was not that good. You get to a foreign country and pretty quickly you become a multi-millionaire.

Gabor: Yes. By the time I was thirty.

Iain: So how did you actually do that? I mean, truly, how can you do that so quickly in a foreign country?

Gabor: I would call that "creative stupidity." I was not educated enough to know what won't work. I quickly learned English. I worked for a British company for a couple of years – Gestetner – at that time. I was the only immigrant kid, so you can imagine how many jokes they made about me and things like that. I went to university. I took electronics engineering, but I never got a job. I immediately went into real estate. And I bought and sold, and I bought and sold land. I bought and sold land at the time that other people didn't, because the interest rates were so high. So I had no idea why I couldn't succeed. If there was a secret to that success it was: I didn't know I can't.

Iain: You had nothing to lose.

Gabor: I had nothing to lose. I didn't know what accounting meant. I used to think that "net-worth" was perhaps ladies' stockings or something like that.

Iain: [laughter]

Gabor: And so, the initial success was really raw trial and not thinking much about it.

Iain: Ok. So, you got this success. You're a multi-millionaire. In the notes that you gave me it said you got married to a beautiful woman and you had three children.

Gabor: Yes.

Iain: Everything in life seemed wonderful.

Gabor: Yes. Life was wonderful – great success, lots of money, lots of parties, the best cars, etc., etc. – just how I imagined success to be. Success meaning freedom. And yes, there was some freedom within reason, but when you make parties and have thousands of friends, they were mainly acquaintances. The true friends didn't exist at that time. I didn't know who was, or who wasn't, my friend. And so I used to go home every night and I used to drink two bottles of wine just to calm my nerves and to be able to go to sleep. Something was missing. Even though I was "successful," something was really missing. I had not yet gotten what I was looking for, which was freedom, but I had interpreted freedom as financial success.

Iain: Yes. So did you have, at that point, a feeling of what might lead to real freedom? Or, were you just in this position where you realised that what you've done wasn't going to work, or wasn't working?

Gabor: Yes. Knowing something was missing, I didn't know quite what the solution was, but I turned to so-called spirituality. I had seen a video tape at the time of Ramtha, and as soon as I saw it I thought, "Ok, this is exactly what I want to know." It was again such a power in me, such a desire to go and learn that. "That's what I want to know. That's kind of what's missing. That's the direction I need to go."

So I shifted direction. And the universe was very helpful and kind to me in shifting direction. At the same time I lost all my money, all my friends.

Iain: This was the '97 financial crash ... I can't remember ...

Gabor: Early 1990s ... '89 ... '90

Iain: But also you had studied some martial arts, like Karate, Kung Fu, and Kick Boxing. So you had some idea of how you could at least have some energy in the body to generate that kind of spiritual energy through the body, I guess.

Gabor: I know that now. At that time I did not know that, in my martial arts training they taught me something very basic that was extremely useful later on. But, since I knew it in the martial arts context, I did not know that that's going to be the key ingredient later on for being in the body or having inner peace. That came much later. And, of course, I did a lot of martial arts because, again, I wanted freedom and I wanted to protect myself. I was a very sensitive "soul," so I wanted to protect myself with martial arts, lots of money, better lawyers, etc., etc.

Iain: So you saw the martial arts as an outer success, in a way, protecting the outer success.

Gabor: Outer success and protection.

Iain: Yes. Ok. So you mentioned that you were pulled by Ramtha and I think at that time you had to leave your family for that.

Gabor: Yes.

Iain: Wasn't that difficult to leave your family and your children?

Gabor: The hardest thing to do in my entire life is that. Escaping from Hungary and doing all the other things - even depression – were not nearly as hard as that. Something, again, yanked me out and placed me in the West Coast of the USA. I started to live in a forest, very quietly, and every moment, every day, there was this mental emotional challenge about my family. "I should be with my family. I should be with my family." So, that was the hardest decision I ever had to make.

Iain: So you wanted to say "no" to civilisation somehow.

Gabor: Exactly.

Iain: So you were actually living in a forest. You were living in a hut or something. You weren't actually living in the open in a forest, were you?

Gabor: No. I actually build a small log cabin out of the trees that were there. I was totally self-sufficient with my own electricity and I had my own garden. I had food storage and stuff like that. So, I turned from so-called "civilisation" to a whole different direction. At least that's what I thought.

Iain: You were very resourceful to do that on your own, to build your own place in the forest and survive.

Gabor: Yes. I had lots of help. In a community like that there's lots of help available. I met the most interesting wonderful people, who were very different, who were very supportive of that kind of life style.

Iain: So what do you feel was changing in you at that time?

Gabor: In retrospect, what was changing was, I substituted one ego need – money – to another ego need – "I am now spiritual." I said "goodbye" to civilisation and "I am now a better person ... slightly better than you, because I am now spiritual and I am going in this direction." I didn't know that at that time, but in retrospect, that really is what it was. "Now I am collecting data and information." Instead of collecting information about how to make more money, I was collecting information in respect of spirituality – different types of meditation, different types of knowledge – the unseen, the chakras, and on and on and on ...

Iain: So, in a way, something at your core wasn't actually changing or wasn't challenged at that point.

Gabor: Yes. What shifted was, that a different type of ego developed. I still had the male ego and I had all those wonderful experiences with Ramtha – all those meditations and breathing exercises that made you feel so good. So, I was absolutely sure that, "I'm on the right track now."

176

Before, I used to feel good about my success. "Oh, I got this done!" Now I felt, "Oh, when is the next seminar? When is the next retreat?" So, for a while it felt so good, so powerful. I didn't know that I was still in the duality swing. Something felt so good, but then it goes away. Again, something felt so good, "Oh, this must be the right track, because I now have a kundalini experience. I am crying and laughing at the same time. That must be it." The amazing euphoria that followed some of the exercises … it was amazing … for days!

So I was absolutely sure that that was it. That was the right track. There's no right or wrong track. I'm just saying that that path is not the way to awakening, because you are still in the duality swing.

Iain: So, at that time, you felt that, because you had the highs, you were on the right path. So, how did the questioning start to take effect? How did you start to realise that you probably or possibly were not on the right path?

Gabor: I didn't question it and I didn't know that I was on the right path or on the wrong path. It was: I had an experience of business, and something was missing. I had an experience of spirituality – which I know means different things to different people – and I was not aware that there was anything else. There is this direction and there is that direction and something was definitely missing. I started to have depression. I started to be interested in other things now – other teachers, other meditation techniques. Also, I started building a condominium building with a friend in Puerto Vallarta in Mexico. So I got involved with a construction project in Mexico. If you are unprepared, I don't recommend it to anyone.

So, things started to change. I made moves again, not knowing where I am going or what, but something was still missing.

Iain: So you mentioned depression. What form did the depression take?

Gabor: It lasted for about twelve years altogether.

Iain: twelve years. That's a long time.

Gabor: Yes. I had to function while I was depressed. Hardly anyone ever noticed, but it was a feeling of – I get up in the morning and I don't want to live. Sometimes I bicycled to the beach, in one of the most beautiful areas of the world. I "should" be happy, right? [Gabor shakes his head] "No."

"Perhaps I should drive under the bus?" I mean, I had all those weird thoughts. So, the questioning of my own existence came into effect with the depression. Looking at it from my eyes now, the existential shake-up was necessary for me to even consider awakening. It is an existential shake-up. Depression is a very good existential shake-up. You just don't want to exist. So, now we are getting close to existence. So I think that's how the universe guided me to the existential question.

Iain: But did you see a way out of the depression at the time?

Gabor: No. I thought that that's just the way it is. I tried to get help here and there and everywhere, but the help I got was very temporarily helpful. I was fortunate enough to spend three and a half months with an Indian tribe in the Amazon in Ecuador. I took a trip to Ecuador and someone introduced me to a shaman of a tribe. And, although he didn't speak Spanish or English, he gave me permission to stay with them. By that time I was doing construction in Mexico, I had depression, so I had a lot of stress plus depression. Something was pulling me to be there.

My first impression was amazing. I woke up the first morning scratching like crazy because of the bugs. I was not used to the environment. The people were just sitting there. Just sitting. I was the only one – with all my spiritual experience and knowledge – that was pretending to be sitting. I was sitting, but inside my mind was going, "When am I going to learn something? Where is this going? When am I going to be initiated? Whoo ... whoo!! [laughter] So I can tell my friends, 'Whoo ... whoo ... I was initiated.'"

And after a week or so, the shaman took pity on me and made me some ayahuasca tea. I took that twice a week for three weeks and that helped me to calm down totally. I still couldn't just "be" like the rest of them and just sit. I still had anticipation. They were actually sitting with no anticipation, no expectation, nothing. I still had some expectation of the future, "I wonder what's next! I wonder what knowledge someone is going to impart to me." And, so, finally I was able to relax and stay with them, and be there. I could actually be there rather than think of something else.

The major, major realisation for me was that: in spite of all my "knowledge" about spirituality and many, many, many meditation techniques, many, many things – I didn't know anything. They knew something that I didn't. I didn't know what it was or how it was. I thought it was some kind of coincidence, but that left a major question in my heart, "Ok, I tried this, I tried that. There are these people who know nothing and I know everything, so how come they can just sit and I can't?"

Iain: So, the bottom line was that they were happy and you weren't happy.

Gabor: Well, you could call it that way. They were able to just "be." In the meantime, of course, I am having my existential shake-up with the depression. So, knowing that I don't know was very helpful. I was giving up on life, basically. The depression lasted so long. It took a toll on my body, my relationship, everything. And one day I was walking on the beach, and I just sat down and I remembered the martial arts tactic that I learned when I was in my twenties. When I received the so-called black belt, my teacher taught me how to be in the body, because we were demonstrating things to the public. For example, you can hold your arm out, and if you are inside your arm, they will not be able to bend the arm, or it will be very hard.

Those were the martial arts demonstrations that we were doing. And so, I remembered how to do that. It was easy because I learned how to do it then. So I said, "Ok, let me try that." Jesus also said, "The Kingdom of God is within," and "Seek ye first the Kingdom of God and all else shall be added unto you."

I said, "Ok, I tried all those things, so why not look inside, really? I actually know how. So, ok!" And then the mind says, "No, no, no, no … hold on … you've got to try that too (pointing away), because that's more exciting."

(Me) "No, no … I'm going to try this going inside …"

(Mind) "No, no, no, no … you must try first [pointing away] … let's go back to Ramtha and learn such and such … go to that level … and when you go to that level, then you try …"

(Me) "No, no, no … ok … Jesus said, you know, it's within, so let's go within."

Iain: "The Kingdom of God is within."

Gabor: Yes, within. I didn't know what the hell was within. What's within? Within what? So, in my desperation and in my existential

179

shake-up, in the midst of the existential shake-up – being close to existence – I go look inside. And looking inside is not a visionary thing, where you can say, "Ok, I am imagining looking inside." It's a feeling. It's a sensing of the inner body's nurturing. There is a "nurturing-intelligence-feeling" within the body, that runs the body, and we have access to that.

So, oops, I look inside. And all of a sudden, the waves from the ocean were different, mainly in what I was hearing. The hearing shifted. And I could hear the waves differently. So my ego right away said, "Oh, look at that! Look at that! Look at how it works."

(Me) "Ok, calm down. Let's just look inside."

It wasn't difficult to stay, because I had such an existential shake-up, that for me it wasn't difficult to just stay there peacefully. At that instant I realised what it means to be inside. It was instant. It wasn't gradual. There was an amazing amount of – I don't know what to call it – euphoria. Pleasure of, "Oh, ok, now I know what it means to be inside."

All along I had it right in front of me. [laughter] I even knew how to do it. It was right in front of me. It's simple.

(Mind) "No, no, no, no … I don't want to do this. I want to do that (pointing away) … it's more exciting."

Iain: But don't we sometimes have to exhaust what's on the outside? It's just the way it is, isn't it.

Gabor: Exactly. It was all exhausted. All these other trials went bankrupt. It didn't work.

Iain: But the whole of society is building this up for us. That's kind of the level of what we aim for. It takes a great courageous being, or desperate being, to really say, "This is all not going to work. I have to come back here [pointing inside]." It's very rare actually.

Gabor: Yes. It was a very fortunate-unfortunate thing. The desperation was so big, so high – my existential shake-up – that one little look, one little touch [pointing inside] … I call it a "touch"… was enough to have this instant realisation of simplicity, that's available to me and to everyone else.

Iain: And what happened to the depression when you did that?

Gabor: Good question. The depression that I felt at that time was instantly gone. It was an instant shift. It was instantly gone. But, it has tried to come back. It has taken a mental form. It had its memory now after twelve years, "Look at that. This is how you are ... and la id a id a ... " So, it, like any other mental memory tried to come back, tried to come back, tried to come back. But, now I was very aware to the simplicity of the "one touch" – paying attention [pointing within]. Just one small "paying attention."

And that small effort of "paying attention" takes care of one hundred depressions. Instantly you step out of the duality swing and it's no longer in my reality. It has tried to come back and has actually trained me to go deeper and deeper and deeper into presence. Because, occasionally, it would try to come back really hard. And when something really hard happens in our life, in duality, we just have to go in ... but just a little deeper, just a little deeper.

Iain: So depression actually was a catalyst for you to go even deeper inside yourself.

Gabor: Absolutely, yes.

Iain: There is a gift there somehow.

Gabor: It was a huge gift to me. Yes. Initially it made me try to look inside, and, secondarily, when it tried to come back, it helped me go deeper and deeper and deeper – realising the same thing deeper and deeper and deeper. There is no deeper, but it's just an expression.

Iain: No. I understand that. Yes. And I guess there are so many things in so many areas in life, and I include myself in this, where something goes what the mind thinks is wrong, or is difficult or a challenge in some way ... and, of course, that, in a sense, is the catalyst, that's the thing that's unsettling. Without that you wouldn't explore and you wouldn't end up going deep inside, because the motivation wouldn't be there.

Gabor: Exactly.

Iain: And people who often have fairly normal balanced lives often don't find this pearl that you found.

Gabor: What's really weird is – I don't know what word to use – that the opportunities are available to everyone consistently throughout our lives. One doesn't have to be depressed to get there. That was my path. Your personal path is your personal path. The realisation is instant, but the opportunities are consistently there for us to have this self-realisation, because life brings us situations, and the immediate response of the untrained mind – let's call it that – is to go and fix this – whatever this is. The situation comes, I go and fix it, which is the normal way to attend a problem.

The other way to do it, if someone chooses, is different. This "something" came into my reality. The universe, God, which is a lot smarter than me, put this in front of me. So why don't I just embrace this and be with it. It will actually help me "in-body" that situation. Not "embody" but "in-body" – "IN" body. When that – whatever it is – is in my body, now it is so close to me, that I have the ability to shift it. So this "something" that came into my reality became a catalyst for me, and in turn, almost always, the situation also shifts. So a human situation could be used that way. And that way, whatever life brings us is a consistent seminar – a custom-made seminar for us, because life knows a lot better, "What sort of situation do I need to deal with?"

Iain: How did this realisation change how you saw reality?

Gabor: The way I used to see reality is the way we all see reality. Now I see the exact same reality as is, except from a different context. The mind, which has been running, running, running – our mind has not been given the proper nurturing and the proper context within which it can operate properly.

Iain: So when you say, "The mind hasn't been given proper nurturing," explain that more ... what you mean by that.

Gabor: Very hard. We call it the mind, but our attention has been hijacked by institutional fear and all kinds of things.

Iain: And the speed of society.

Gabor: Yes. "Think of that, think of that, think of that. No, no, no ... don't pay attention here [pointing within]. It's over there. It's over there [pointing outward]. I will tell you exactly what to fear today."

Iain: Or the television does that.

Gabor: Yes. The television – whatever. So we are inundated with all that information. Our mind, our ability to function properly is totally hijacked. Even the synchronisation between vision and sound has been hijacked. They tell us what sound goes with what vision. So, all this God-given ability has been totally hijacked.

So the simple "touching" [pointing within], simple inner attention, gets my mind, and your mind ... everyone's mind, to be aligned with the body. The body was here [one hand held in straight vertical line] and the mind was here [other hand wavering back and forth]. Now it just simply lines up (the wavering hand slows down and lines up with the vertical hand) with the body.

Why is it good to line up with the body? Well, the body already has the innate intelligence. It's like a mini universe. It's a smaller fractal of the large universe out there. So why not use that intelligence? In many, many, spiritual circles the body is a "no-no" – "Oh, no. I am not the body. I've got to do astral travelling, and I have to step out somehow. I know I am not this. I am all that."

It's a half-truth statement. Yes, it's true. But here [pointing within] is the door. We knock on the door by paying attention – using the words of Jesus. We knock on the door, paying attention, the door opens, and instantly, I feel one with everyone. Now, back to your original question – how did it affect my outlook on life? Now the mind can function properly. Instead of functioning in a hijacked fashion.

Iain: What does that mean, "The mind can function properly?"

Gabor: It means that my capability of paying attention and all the information that I have learned so far, all the information that I have made a template of in life, which is important – how to build a bridge, how to play tennis, how to do this, how to do that – all the education I've had created this bunch of information, put them together in a template, or in a format, or in a thought stream. The problem is that if the mind is hijacked, it's just going to go like a loose cannon, "brrrrrr ... bang, bang ... oh, how about this, how about that ..." So all of that wonderful information is just about useless if the mind runs like an idiot in lunatic asylum.

However, if it is placed on its foundation, where it's supposed to be, and it is also nurtured naturally, the way it should be – now the mind is at home. First it rebels, because it's used to operating by itself, "no, no, no" (making hand gestures of fighting). First it rebels, but then, in time, it settles into this new foundation. And now, the proper use of mind is that "I can think of whatever I want to think of." It's like walking into a library, calm, and I can pick up any book. Before that, I walked into that same library, and the books were attacking.

Iain: Yes. And the mind becomes your servant rather than your master somehow.

Gabor: Yes. We can call it that way. And the mind is happy doing that, because it wasn't quite happy being hijacked, except it got used to it.

Iain: I just want to mention something ... I have these notes that came from Nurit, your wife's book – your final and actual realisations appear on their own, rather as subtle and uneventful happenings beyond the senses and are very difficult to describe. So it was interesting when you say, "The final and actual realisations appear on their own."

Gabor: Now, of course, we are into an area, where we don't have the words, and so, we are attempting to use words. How I handle it is that I usually use a metaphor and then we drop it, and then I use an explanation and then we drop it. But, initially, for everyone it's instant, because we are going beyond time. We cannot accumulate things and go in time and hope to be eventually beyond time. So it is instant. If we want to call it final, we can. Nothing is really final. It's instant. So, when the mind gets incorporated, when it gets used to operating in this new environment ...

Iain: Re-trained in a way ...

Gabor: Re-trained, Yes. When the mind gets retrained, it starts with the original instant realisations. The mind starts to get retrained and there are little final, little refined realisations in between. The initial excitement, the initial honeymoon of "Oh, my God! Look at that!" kind of starts to be over. So, refinements start happening. The practical end of it starts to happen, "Oh, ok, I can incorporate that too in this peace. Oh, that too I can incorporate in that peace, and that too I can incorporate into that peace."

So those are the final touches that are not describable until ... there is nothing final ... but it keeps on happening and there is a total relaxation into this possibility, into this context, knowing that the mind works just fine. Nothing that I have ever learned is lost. I don't have any ability that I have lost. Except now, when I am walking, when I am doing anything, the mind is not talking to me. There is no conflict within me.

Iain: That's a wonderful thing you said, "There is no conflict in you."

Gabor: Right.

Iain: And so many of us ...

Gabor: Right

Iain: The human world – we have the outer conflict and then there is the inner conflict, which, of course, contributes to the outer conflict.

Gabor: That's the reason the world is the way it is. I call it "The open air lunatic asylum."

Iain: Anyway. We've got about ten minutes left and I want to use that time as effective as we can to find out more about your work and how you do seminars and private sessions. You free people from thought addiction, as it's said in your notes. You protect someone from their mind, or you help them protect themselves from their mind and to know how to do that, and you help people go from a habitual thinking state to a non-thinking state, and they speak and act from a "Being" state instead.

I know you covered a little bit of it. So just talk more about – on a practical level – how that can manifest in people, where they go from this habitual thinking to a non-thinking state.

Gabor: The first thing I do – and when I say, "I do" it is a figure of speech – the first prerequisite to awakening is that a person understands that the way they have used their mind before, in an accumulative state, in accumulating information, in accumulating something to get somewhere – the way we've used the mind so far – is perfectly correct to use the mind that way to, say build a bridge or something like that.

Once they understand that a totally different approach has to be accepted and necessary even to try, to actually go through this – what I call "The eye of the needle"... so once a person has sufficient understanding that, "Ok. I know I don't know how this works, but I will not be able to understand it, and if I understand it, I will misunderstand it. All the truths that I have known to be true are maybe half truths, or maybe one hundred percent truths, but I cannot base my listening entirely upon those assumptions that I have assumed in the past."

There are like a million assumptions out there about spirituality, which are somehow connected to awakening. So, the first prerequisite is to understand that that kind of accumulative approach with assumptions is not going to work. Once that's understood, and at the same time we start with a personal session or with a group, a very simple thing happens. I am just sitting there "Being," and people are looking inside. People are guided to look inside. All you have to do is "touch" (pointing inside) for a second – no expectation! So, if I say, "You are looking at me but be aware of your hand, that's it ... no expectation." And then, "Look at me and be aware of your butt touching the chair."

And I keep on talking ... keep on talking ... And then, all of a sudden, the person gets how simple this is – that this simplicity, when the mind slows down and eventually stops, is the "It." What I mean by "It," is that that is the beginning of awakening. Now we can begin the awakening process. My whole explanation prior to that was coming to the simple moment so that you can please accept this simplicity. The Indians in the Amazon didn't need to learn ... didn't need to unlearn all these things. They were just sitting there.

So then, the next "problem" that comes, the next challenge for me, is that everyone misunderstands – they think that this nice feeling that they have is like meditation. "Oh, it's just like a meditation technique. I know. I did this before, you know." So the mind from memory says, "Ok, this is this, and that meditation technique ..." and starts comparing immediately.

So we are there, nothing else is needed, and if you can stay there, I am not even needed. But they can't stay there, because the mind will start coming at it. "Oh, it's just like meditation." But, no, it is not meditation. Meditation has a beginning and an end. This is a feeling, a sensing of existence. This is a sensing of your being. When your being recognises its own being, you will not need me, and I don't want to call this meditation simply because this is not in time. As soon as you enter this being state – if I can call it a state – you are no longer in time.

That expression we can also take further, but we don't want to at this point, because it's really absolute time, but that's another discussion.

Now, if we are staying here, the mind starts relearning to operate, "Oh there is this Being. There is this context. There is this nurturing foundation that I can use." But the mind will come up with all kinds of comparisons and I have experienced this hundreds of times from my students ... consistently. The mind has an amazing ability to come up and try to complicate this, try to compare it and put it away in the memory so it can access it later, because this feeling right now, this sensation right now, is not going to be the same five minutes from now. We can't recall it.

So what I do do, I do with nothing. The more nothing I do, the better. I am really providing the space. I just sit there, within which, if they wish, they can stay longer and longer and longer and longer.

Iain: And that, as you say, is the beginning of awakening

Gabor: Exactly. That's the beginning. So, unless someone starts to look inside, their awakening has not started yet.

Iain: Ok. I want to ask you one more thing before we finish: what's it like for you to be a master of silence?

Gabor: Well, I wish I didn't have to be called anything. To operate in this dimension we have to be called a something. So, a friend of mine called me in Hungarian a "Csendmester," which means "Master of Silence," and it kind of stuck. To operate as such, my life is not any different than anybody else's. My life is exactly the same. I no longer get excited about a profitable idea as much as before. My responses to things are very different, but I see the world as is. I don't see things and people and situations through the old bias I used to see through.

The normal mind looks at the world and says, "Ok, what filter do I bring in to look through? Iain McNay, British, friendly, nice guy ..." You know, I mean there is a filter of looking. While now, I just look at the way it is.

Iain: ... the way it is?

Gabor: The way it is. If I see anger, it's anger. It's not like I don't see anger. It's not like I see the world through pink glasses at all. Just the way it is! But coming from this nurturing foundation, looking out from this nurtured foundation, even the so-called "ugliness" – ugly is still ugly, misbehaviour is still misbehaviour, but there is no judgement or reaction at all. There is not even "no judgement." There is just ... love.

If I happen to be close to a reaction to something, I just go a little bit deeper.

Iain: And that's the key, isn't it. I think that's where you've been going right from the start ... a little bit deeper into your journey. And that's the journey. It's ongoing.

Gabor: Right. Yes. It's ongoing this way [pointing within]

Iain: Ok. I guess this is a great place to finish. Ongoing journey ...

Gabor: This way [pointing within].

Iain: This way [pointing within]. I am going to actually show Nurit's book, your wife's book, because it has a lot about your story.

Gabor: Yes.

Iain: This book –*The Blind Leading the Blonde on the Road to Freedom: Confessions of a Recovering Spiritual Junkie* – is written by Nurit Oren whom I am actually interviewing next, but the reason I am showing it now is because it also has Gabor's story in there and some conversations between Nurit and Gabor. So you might like to find this book if you are pulled towards Gabor's journey and are intrigued by what he had to say.

Thank you very much, Gabor, for coming all the way from Budapest, Hungary. It is very much appreciated.

Tess Hughes –
The Non-Event of No Self
Interview by **Renate McNay**

*T*o know that you are eternally. I suppose the test is the body sitting here, the voice and everything that is talking to you, that's just the instrument through which the 'I Am' functions in the world. In some ways I am much more me than I used to be. Even though I'm not here at all, I am much more me, I'm much more free and relaxed. I'm not trying to hold anything back from anybody, trying to be proper, or trying to ... whatever the things one would always be trying, some awareness of one's image. It's just gone.

It's totally natural. I used to hear about this before this happened to me and I used to think, "But you look quite normal." I don't think an outside person can see what's happening within one – what has happened. It's a transformation of consciousness. What one is, as consciousness, is different – much more spacious, open. I don't know what else to say.

Renate: My guest today is Tess Hughes. Tess arrived this morning from Ireland – that's where she lives – to just come and visit us here to be interviewed, which is wonderful.

Tess, you were born into quite a big Irish Catholic family with nine brothers and sisters.

Tess: Nine children in the family and I'm number two.

Renate: And your parents were farmers?

Tess: Yes.

Renate: You had your first existential crisis when you were eight years old?

Tess: Yes, about eight or nine; I was quite young.

Renate: What happened?

Tess: Well, living on a farm, there were always calves being born, pigs, chickens and new life coming all the time. In our house there was a baby every year or two. All the neighbours were having babies. So, there was constant new life coming.

I did know that older people and older animals died. But I thought, "That's just the way nature goes. You get born, you live your whole life, and when you are fed up living or you are old enough, then you are very happy to die." And, that's the way the world functions.

One day one of our calves died. I was really shocked by this because my world order was shattered. I didn't even know this could even happen. Then it struck me, "Well if a calf could die, a child could die. If a child could die, then I could die. And, I could die any time." I was really shocked by this; I was really upset by it.

I went and I checked with my mother. I asked her about it, "was this so ... ?" and she said "Yes it is." She said, "Everything that is born will die." It's extraordinary because I think it's the classic thing that the masters would say, but my mother just said it naturally. "Everything that is born will die." And, it could die any time, was my interpretation of it.

Renate: So, you had a lot of fear? You started to have a lot of fear around death?

Tess: Around death, I did have fear.

Renate: And that eventually became your driving force.

Tess: Yes, that's right.

Renate: To seek answers.

Tess: Yes, yes. I just couldn't dismiss it, ever. After that, of course, I began to see in my life plenty of evidence of people dying suddenly. Or, on the radio you hear of crashes and so on.

So, what my mother had said, about everything that is born would die – and it could die any time – there were mountains of evidence of that coming to me all the time. I won't say I was thinking about it all day, every day; I wasn't a miserable child or anything like that. I had quite a good life; but this was running in the background, always.

I could never fully shut it out. I did try to for many long years, and in many ways. But I used to think, "What's it all about?" Later, when I was working in a job, I'm working very hard and trying to get money together to get something. I would think, "what if I knew I was going to die tomorrow? Would I still keep working so hard today?"

Renate: What would you do?

Tess: There was something, a fundamental conflict going on. Nobody had any answers and nobody was interested in talking about it either. I can tell you people are not that happy with you bringing up conversations about death when you're in the middle of a party or wherever.

Renate: We actually see death as a failure.

Tess: Yes, but the evidence kept coming up, as I said, all the time. I couldn't deny it so I started reading and stuff. I started reading philosophy and psychology.

Renate: Earlier, you were a teacher?

Tess: Yes. After secondary school I went to university and I studied science, maths, and I became a science teacher. But I knew, when I went to study science, that I was trying to find out the secret of the world.

Renate: Right.

Tess: What was the secret of the world? What made it go? Really, in a way, I was trying to find out (about the) death problem that I thought science would somehow be able to explain that to me. But I found pretty quickly that it didn't. However, I got a job out of it.

Renate: Yes, and you started reading classics?

Tess: Yes, and philosophy, psychology – a lot of psychology and that kind of thing. I tried reading various philosophy books; I didn't get a lot out of them because I wasn't able to understand them.

Then, at some stage – maybe around the time I was thirty, this new generation of self-help books began to appear. They made a lot of money out of me because every new book that came out, I thought this would surely explain something of the fundamental problem.

By this stage, of course, I had realised that a lot of people were suffering from some kind of fundamental unhappiness. This is why all these books were coming out, that I wasn't the only one going around with this worry, fear, or whatever ... just dissatisfaction.

The thing was, on the surface, I had everything and I knew it.

Renate: But you still had this nagging feeling, something is ... ?

Tess: Yes, it was there, "What's the matter with me? Why can't I just accept everything as it is? Why can't I just be happy? I have everything that anybody could want." But still, there was something in the background bothering me.

Renate: But you had everything you wanted and you weren't happy.

Tess: That was it, yes.

Renate: And if you go out in the street and ask people, everybody really, what are you looking for in life? Everybody would say the same – I'm looking for happiness.

Tess: Yes.

Renate: Okay, so you started reading all the self-help books. Did you come closer?

Tess: I was attracted to books that were talking about this problem of unhappiness. So, along the way I did get ideas and new questions came up. I began to be able to question things and ask myself questions.

I remember at one stage, when I was a teacher, I must have been reading a book – I can't remember what it was – and the question of values came up. What do you value? Or, what's worth valuing? I thought about this. Somewhere in the book this idea was, what values are you going to take into your life? Consciously choose some value. I decided at the time that I would choose the value of kindness.

This was actually very appropriate as a teacher because I'm a science teacher and a math teacher and lot of the kids, they just don't care about it. They don't like it. It isn't delightful or interesting for them. But they were stuck with having me as a teacher and I'm stuck with having them in my class. I thought, under those circumstances, what is a good way for me to treat them? What can I do? So I thought if I had the value of kindness ... so no matter what was going on academically between us, that at least I would treat a child with kindness. Some of it was to just not be unkind, not to make a flipping remark or putdown remark – to be conscious of my words and to be sure they were at least nice; that some child wouldn't go away hurt because they'd been overlooked.

That was one of the things I got out of it. I actively took that on in my life, that that would be a value. So, I got things like that, which I think were a move in a good direction. At least it was a move towards a degree of consciousness, I'd say.

Renate: But this was not your goal? Consciousness was not your goal?

Tess: Well I didn't know about awakening or anything at that stage.

Renate: Yes, yes. You said – I was reading somewhere on your website or somewhere, your biography – you had thirty years of searching.

Tess: Yes.

Renate: Thirty years of searching on a psychological path?

Tess: I'd say between twenty and fifty. Even though as a teenager I was already very interested in things like Shakespeare or classical literature we studied at secondary school. It was very moving for me and did give me the clue that there was something serious to be thought about and discussed. Although I would have thought on an intellectual or abstract level ... I hadn't figured out to bring it right into myself.

Then, in those years between twenty and fifty, trying to understand psychology or psychotherapy ... the self-help books then were beginning to bring it more personal. What can you do? What values can you choose? It was beginning to become more personal about the thing and trying to interpret things in relation to myself during that time.

Renate: It seems that you started to adjust certain things? Started to integrate into your life, like being kind? I don't know what else changed in your life through ...

Tess: Yes, it was such a long, slow, gradual thing I suppose.

For instance, I, at some stage, remember reading and thinking about honesty and what did honest mean? Could you be one hundred percent honest all the time, with everybody? I came across a book written by a Harvard University professor; it was called Lying. The whole book was about little ways in which we are dishonest with each other. You can't really be totally honest with the world. I would even question if it's even worthwhile? You are not going to walk up to somebody, you notice they are very heavy or something, and say something to them about it.

Renate: You get food in America ... [laughter]

Tess: Yes, but it just isn't appropriate anyway. That may be practicing honesty; it's also very unkind. Do you see where a conflict of values would come in?

Renate: Right.

Tess: But I did decide that it would be very important for me to keep myself mentally clean. For instance if I went into a shop and the person gave me too much change. If I noticed this – I don't usually notice, I just put in my pocket – but if I noticed it, I could easily put it in my pocket and walk out; there would be no repercussions for anybody. But for my own self it was important that, if I noticed anything like that, that I would be totally honest. Basically, to keep my own mentality, myself, clean.

It may be something to do with guilt, to not create any situations that might, afterwards, produce guilt.

Renate: Right.

Tess: So there was a certain taking of responsibility for myself.

Now I wasn't in any way thinking that anybody else should do this or anything, this was me taking responsibility for myself. I felt this was an important value. Getting away with it wasn't ... didn't ... matter. It was keeping myself clear and clean.

Again, Shakespeare said, "suspicion haunts the guilty mind ... " So, not having a guilty mind removes all suspicion, which gives a great sense of cleanliness and contentment. Those kinds of things helped.

Renate: At what point did you become aware there is not only a psychological path but also a spiritual path? What was the shift?

Tess: The shift happened in a way that was very clear to me in 2003. My first boyfriend when I was a teenager was called Richard Rose. My mother had died earlier in the year. This is my home town where I was born and raised, and he didn't come to the funeral; he had been to my father's funeral a couple of years before. I thought, "Gee, Richard didn't come. I wonder if he's okay?" Because he had told me he was having health problems. I wondered, there was nobody who would tell me now if he died. So I Googled his name and I didn't get anything about him. But, I got this other Richard Rose, Zen master, in West Virginia of the United States.

When I looked at this website and started reading it, something really happened to me. It was like I just became clear and alert, right there. It was like, what is this? I would read the sentences and I would every single word but I would still think, "But I don't get what he's saying." I suppose I thought, "Well I'm going to challenge this." I should be able to understand any English sentence if I know all the words.

The next day I went back to the website, and for the next eighteen months I went to that website. There are a lot of websites linked to it and I started reading this kind of stuff. I was just utterly amazed because

195

they were talking exactly about the kind of things that really interested me. Gradually, I began to understand what they were saying. That was when I really began to get focused and get clear.

There is such a thing as an end to this suffering and to this anxiety and this ... whatever. There is an end to it. That was a new thing for me because I just thought I'd go on for the rest of my life trying to be as good as I could. That was the deck of cards I got, and be happy with them. But here was a group that were saying, "No, no. There is an end to this. There is a way to come to the end of psychological suffering."

Renate: It's interesting because a lot of people say there is nothing you can do.

Tess: I would have thought that.

Renate: But there was something prior to that, I think. Again, I saw on the interview that you did with The TAT Foundation.

You made this little diagram of two mountains – one was a hill and one was a bigger mountain.

Tess: Yes.

Renate: And then you found this article about Teresa of Avila and it said, "Right here in the middle there is hardly anybody to get across."

Tess: Yes.

Renate: The reason for that is? Would you like to pick up ...

Tess: ... Yes. I'll tell you the name of the mountain. The name of the mountain is Croagh Patrick. I was born and raised at the foot of it, about a mile from it. It's a very famous pilgrimage mountain. It was a place of pilgrimage from the time of the druids a couple of thousand years ago and when Catholicism, or Christianity, came to Ireland, this pilgrimage site was taken over by the Christian movement by Catholics. To this day, the last weekend of July, there is a big pilgrimage up there.

But, as I showed you, the shape of the mountain is lower and long like this. Then it takes a curve and goes straight up. It's a volcanic mountain.

I had read an article about Teresa of Avila. Now according to Teresa's system, there are seven steps in spiritual awakening. She was a spiritual director. Somebody asked her toward the end of her life, "What was the biggest obstacle that people encountered in spiritual development?" She said that, according to her system, that stage four was the single biggest obstacle. Everybody that came to the convent, they got through stages one, two and three – which I likened to the lower part of the mountain. And stage four is when it changes from being this shape, to going up. There are three steps up there and she said, "If people got across that fourth step, they had no problem getting the rest of the way, getting to the top." When she was asked, "What exactly is the obstacle?" what she said was, "If I could get people past self-esteem."

These two ideas of the mountain and this came into my head – happened to come into my head at the same time which is why I talked like that. But when that came up for me, I thought "self-esteem, there is something past self-esteem." I couldn't figure out what it was. There were no thoughts and no ideas coming to mind. So I thought the best thing I could do was start making a list of all the qualities of self-esteem that I had. There would be things like I'm well educated – that gives you a certain level. I'm a mother; you get a certain amount of status with having children. Just all the different qualities that we all know from a psychological level ...

Renate: But there's also another side, low self-esteem.

Tess: Yes, but there's still self-esteem.

Renate: Yes, it's the way you see yourself.

Tess: Yes, that's right. How you see yourself.

Then you ask – I asked the question, "Why do I see myself like this?" I see myself like this because of what the rest of the world has told me. My teachers told me, "You're quite good in school." Other people told me, "You've a nice personality; we get on." So you have friends. Other people say, "You've made an awful mess of your career. You didn't make a lot of money." So you don't feel so good in that.

The full collection of these messages that I got from the rest of the world are what make up self-esteem.

Renate: We could say your 'problems?'

Tess: All of our problems.

Renate: Yes.

Tess: But we got them from outside.

Renate: Yes, and we started believing them.

Tess: That's right. And, we started adding to them. You have low self-esteem about something and somebody says something, and it goes even lower.

Renate: Yes.

Tess: So they are basically all beliefs. I think I'm like this. I believe myself to be like this because this is what everybody's been telling me. And, along the way it gets tweaked and changed a bit. Being a sixty-year-old woman, the world treats you quite differently from being a twenty-year old, so it gets tweaked along the way too, to accommodate these changes.

But, what Teresa was saying is getting people beyond that. I was just going around, baffled. Get beyond ... what could be, beyond self-esteem? I wasn't getting anywhere with it.

Then, I remembered during a couple of days in which this was going out of my head. I would think about it and anything that came up, I would be checking this idea with it – would I get any clues as to what was beyond self-esteem?

I remembered one day when I was a kid, my mother used to say, "I consider all of you to be God's gift to us." This was now a small farm, with a woman with nine children and new babies arriving all the time. You are God's gift. I remember the feeling of her saying that, "I'm really precious. They consider me a gift, a gift from God. I'm beyond anything that they themselves could have created."

When my own children were born I really did feel that they were gifts from heaven or something like that. They were beyond anything ... So that feeling was renewed in me as a mother. The mystery was just a fabulous mystery, that these little babies and these little people would come into my life.

I started thinking, what if I am a child of God? A divine child? I don't know what language to use, but what if it is, that what I'm really created from is something other than this world? That there is something else there? Then I thought, if I'm a divine child, so are you. And you. So I'm not special in being a divine child. I AM special being a divine child but everyone also has this specialness.

What happened was judgment just fell away. How can I be criticising a divine creation? Who am I to be finding fault with something that is a divine creation? It's not my business to know why that creation was created or its purpose or anything in itself.

Renate: It's a huge step!

Tess: It was a huge step in feeling. It was a huge step in feeling. It was like my face fell with, "Yes!" There was a real shift that happened there and it was a feeling shift rather than a thinking shift because suddenly the world looked peopled with divine creatures, animals and plants. Everything created from something that I am also created from.

In a way, what cemented the idea for me was when I was looking in my jewellery box one morning. There were three pieces of jewellery that must have been there for years and I never noticed this: it just dawned on me, there's a brooch, there's a ring and I think it was a bracelet. They are all made from gold. And, I thought, "their value is in their golden-ness, not in the shape that they are, not in the form." I thought divinity is the same kind of thing, it's what we're created from–the form can take any form. Gold itself doesn't disappear when it gets melted down and put into another shape – it's water mutable or something like that.

That made it a concrete idea for me, this idea of something divine which I can't see or feel or anything. But, we all know it in ourselves. We know that there's something sacred in us, don't we, at some deep level. Regardless of what the world says, or ...

Renate: ... It's what we are looking for all the time.

Tess: It's covered up ...

Renate: ... Out in the world.

Tess: Yes, we try to find it out in the world. Well, Jesus said, "The Kingdom of heaven is within you." If I'm to take that statement clearly – this would have been part of my reading at some stage – saying, "Well, what did he mean?" He wasn't saying it for no reason. So, if the kingdom of heaven is within me, how can I find it? How do I get there? That kind of thinking, and that kind of questioning, is what got me on what I call 'self-enquiry.' Looking into what am I? Or, who am I? I was trying to find the kingdom of heaven.

Plus, the Buddha had said, "What I teach is suffering, and I teach the end of suffering." I would take that, that they are speaking about the same thing – the end of suffering and the kingdom of heaven. They are both trying to say the same thing.

So these great teachers – no just them, many hundreds of others have been saying this – there must be something to it. So, when I came across the TAT Foundation they said, "Yes, there is something to it. This is for sure and many of us have found it. You, too, can find it. It's available to everybody; it's your birthright. And here's how.."

Renate: Something earlier, which I just love, when you discovered or inquired, into is there free will? Or is there not free will?

Again, that came from your Catholic background. You worked with the phrase, "Thy Will be done."

Tess: I had spent years coming across lots of phrases and reading them on an intellectual kind of way, getting a certain amount and just glossing over other things. So, I would think that particular phrase, I had glossed over it a lot of times – seen it many times; it's quite a common phrase that people know.

Then, one day it struck me, "What does this really mean?" I started looking, what's my Will? And, thy Will? I didn't have a clue as to what it was but I thought if these two words are used, there must be a difference.

I thought I'd make a list of every kind of thing that is happening, events that are going on, and I kind of classified them as "my will" and "thy will." Having made that decision and taken out my piece of paper, ready to start making notes, the phone rang. So the phone in the house rang and I thought, number one for the "thy will" the phone rings because I hadn't done anything about that. So, thy will, the phone rings. [laughter] I went to the phone and answered it. It was somebody, a friend. We had a little chat and she said, 'why don't you come for dinner in a couple evening's time ... ?' and so on.

I'm there, at the same time, thinking 'Will I say yes or no? Because is that my will or thy will?' Part of my mind was, at the same time, thinking which way to answer? How would I know how to answer, whether it's my will or thy will? I was expecting a voice from heaven to shout from the corner [laughter]. Nothing was happening; there was just silence. I said, "Oh yes, I'd love that. We'll come whatever evening it is." That's fine.

In the meantime, I was writing other things. But in a couple evening's time we did go for dinner. When we got there, they weren't all that welcoming, just a little bit "so you guys decided to show up after all..." or something. We were like, what's this? So I got in, and it turned out, that I had agreed and they had invited us to come for dinner for 7:00 pm and we arrived at almost 8:00 pm. In my head it was almost 8:oo pm.

My will, thy will ... there is something going on here about my will and thy will. So, the thy will was that there was–this is how I figured it out in my head – The "thy will" was that there was a misunderstanding; and the "my will" was that I didn't want there to be a misunderstanding. I didn't like that that happened.

Then I asked the question, how will I know when it's my will or thy will and over a little bit of time what I found was, every time things went wrong according to Tess, that was my will. Every time there was resistance.

Renate: Yes.

Tess: So I became a bit smarter without having to go headlong into my will. When things were going against what I wanted, or my desires were not being met, or my wishes not being fulfilled, I began, "Oh that's my will in operation." The advice is not my will, but thine.

Another way you could put it, or often times, really it might be put to just surrender what is, accept what is ...

Renate: Also, what needs to come in is trust ...

Tess: Yes.

Renate: That is also trust in thy will, that this is right not matter how it looks.

Tess: Sure. First, for me, first of all I had to get an idea what thy will was and my will too. Remember I said from Teresa, that was step four? There were three other steps after that.

Renate: On the spiritual path?

Tess: On the spiritual path, up the side of the mountain.

What happened after I became aware of my will and thy will – my will was wanting its own way and so on – other things began to emerge.

At some point I came across of me taking credit for things and realised, actually, that was pride. Or, just not being grateful for things.

The following three steps, what would happen as I was doing this investigation, something would come up. I would look at it – I had gotten into the habit of looking at things, at myself. I think that's the crucial thing, to start looking at what's going on with yourself.

I remember one day thinking, "What do I really trust?" Do I trust that there will always be money in the bank to pay the bills? Do I trust that my children will continue to do well? Do I trust that my own health will hold up? At some point he question was, "Where could I put my trust?" Could I trust any of these things?

Again, it struck me that maybe the message was to put your trust in the divine. Put your trust in God. While I didn't feel it, when I thought that, I thought, "Okay. I'm going to put my trust in you now, Goddess, or God, because I don't' know what else to do with it." I don't feel awfully confident or anything but I'm going to do that. I'm going to try; give me a hand with it here.

The thing is, things then would emerge that would give you opportunities to reaffirm that you had made that practice. Opportunities would come up and I would see them through the filter of, "Well, I did say I would try to trust, and I will try to trust here."

I think sometimes people maybe have the idea that if you become trusting, that you become passive? There is no conflict at all between being trusting and being fully active in your life. Sometimes, for people, they might feel conflicts like that would come up for them intellectually.

Does that explain? Does that give you an idea ... ?

Renate: Yes. But, as I'm listening to you, one thing comes so strongly from your story is, how you took the time to attend to yourself. It's like almost consciousness was attending to itself and you took the time to inquire into things and to find out. It seems like you never had to rush through life. You never had stress in your life; you had this faith and the time to attend to yourself.

Tess: Yes.

Renate: Is this how you see that today?

Tess: Eh, yes and no.

Once I got in contact with The TAT Foundation, my group, and I began to read books. I began to hear things. They were about self-inquiry.

I really began to get some ideas at that stage about how I might do this and to personalise it. I had to do this for myself. I was fully responsible in doing this.

I would maybe read a little bit in the morning – or any time, whenever I had time. I was never really disciplined about anything but I would be standing at the kitchen sink washing the dishes, when I might think about something like trust. Or, I might think about my will and they will. I might be vacuuming the house and I'd be thinking about something like that. So, it came and went in between normal life.

The thing is we all have moments in our life, when we go to the bathroom, or when we're driving the car or whatever, when we do have plenty of time to think about things.

Renate: It's more like contemplating things.

Tess: Yes. I would say that ten years before that, what would I have been thinking about them? I am going down to the shop, now what am I going to get ... ? So I would have been putting my focus on the outside world and managing it. Now I began to have the idea of focusing within myself. There is plenty of time also to do the outside things.

So you actually don't need a lot of time. It's more that you need to get the idea that it's really important to look within yourself. It's well worth your while. What's to be found is the kingdom of heaven. Nobody can find it for you. You are one hundred percent responsible for doing this for yourself.

It's a goal ... that's really important. I can't imagine anybody who wouldn't be able to fit in time to think about it, to maybe read a little bit or anything.

I continued my normal life. I wasn't a good meditator. I wasn't a disciplined personality. So, I didn't do that a lot. A lot of people take half an hour out every day and meditate. Maybe this is consciously what they are looking at? But I can say that you can fit it into your normal life. Nobody need know a thing about it.

Renate: It needs to be a priority, then you find the time.

Tess: Yes, I think the first step is for somebody to realise that there really is an end to suffering. There really is a purpose to my life – it's mine and I have to find it. Other people are saying that they have found it and maybe I can trust them? Maybe, if somebody has the good luck of coming across people who have found this and one finds them trustworthy, then you begin to take the journey on for yourself. Nobody else can do it for you. They can, maybe, give you some hints or tell you how they did it. Then, you do your version of it, according to your personality and according to your circumstances and time.

But, it can go right along, right in the middle, of normal daily life.

Renate: What do you think about following a teaching, which was somebody else's path?

Tess: Yes.

Renate: Do you think that would work for somebody else?

Tess: It was very helpful to me when I came across the Richard Rose teachings. He wrote three or four books and when I read them, I felt there something to be very pure about them. I didn't understand a lot of them. He used phrases, and so on – backing away from untruth – well I didn't know what untruth was. I couldn't identify untruth so that I could back away from it – that kind of thing.

But then, in meeting some of his students, I went twice to the States for two weekends. Listening to them, I began to get a much clearer idea of what that was. It's what I would call self-inquiry, which is generating questions for yourself. Like you might ask yourself.

One of the things I did, one time, was I thought, "What's this thing about liking people and not liking people?" I know that there are some people I like and some that I don't. What is this in me that chooses to like and not like? And, do I have any control over it? Or what? Am I just a victim of liking or not liking or do I have any control of it?

Like that, I took out my piece of paper and wrote down the names of three people that I thought, honestly, that I liked. I looked at it and thought, is this a feeling? What is the feeling? Are these people I enjoy their company because there's energising conversation? Or because I feel not judged by them? There's a warmness or tolerance about them? So I wrote down characteristics like that, whatever list I got between the three of them.

Then I picked out three people that I really didn't like. I wrote down things that I didn't like. What I don't like is, I don't like being judged. I don't like them because they don't like me. [laughter) And of course the same would have happened to like ... you think if there's nothing more to it, are we nothing more than one mirror reflecting the other? Do I find them ... I don't like them because they are boring? What does it mean that somebody is boring?

Then, having got this bit of information from out there, I started looking at me. Looking within as to how I came up with these ideas or whatever. What was causing this filter of liking and disliking? Of course what I found was belief that are assumptions or expectation or needs that I had. I liked people that entertained me; I didn't like people that bored me – but that was my problem. I was projecting onto them something about that, if I'm spending time with you, you're supposed to be entertaining me. Talk about total selfishness. But, I wasn't aware of it.

What it is, it's about bringing what's unconscious into consciousness.

Renate: Yes.

Tess: That's what beliefs and assumptions are. We are all full of beliefs and assumptions from way back when we were children or from our culture. For the most part, we don't look at them.

People are afraid to look at them, actually. Because, if you look inside yourself and you think, "I'll write down the names of the three people I like most," it would be very inconvenient for you to find maybe that you didn't like one of your children.

So you have to be totally honest to yourself. There is no point in doing it at all if you're not going to be totally self-honest. But the thing is, I thought, "What if I find something that I come across, what do I do now?" Then what came to me was you don't act on it. You still treat a person exactly as is as appropriate and you don't tell anybody; it's nobody else's' business. This is a very personal journey, a very personal adventure. You must be able to be completely honest which is why you mustn't tell other people about it. Because the minute you start to tell somebody else, a little bit a guilt, or a little bit of shame, or something will come in. "I can't believe I feel like this about somebody." What if you find you like somebody better than your own husband?

If you are honest with yourself and find this, it's kind of like dangerous information, we think. But it's not, if you fit in the piece of you still behave absolutely appropriately, as you always did.

Renate: Yes, yes.

Tess: But now, you know something about yourself.

Renate: You somehow bring your unconscious into consciousness.

Tess: To yourself, for yourself. Purely for yourself.

You don't have to justify it to anybody or tell it to anybody. But you are on the path to finding yourself, getting to know yourself.

So, it does take a bit of courage.

Renate: It takes a lot of courage. [laughter]

Tess: Well, not really. The adventure is so interesting. What a shame to live your whole life without knowing who you are, especially when we have this opportunity to know who we truly are.

But, as I said, the way to deal with the courage aspect is to take it as a completely private, personal, business – not to be shared with anybody. Now if you feel sure it would be safe to share maybe with a teacher who has been through this because they know there isn't going to be any element of judgment. But I mean, in your normal circle of life, your spiritual path is yours, personally, and it is your responsibility. You can't let anybody else stop you.

We are so entangled with other people that we feel we are letting them down if we do something that is really important to us. But the thing is, the spiritual search is something you can do without letting anybody down in any way, or in any way changing any of your relationships with them.

Renate: So, as you were unravelling yourself, your unconscious, did your life change? Did people come up to you and say, "What's happening to you?"

Tess: No, nobody ever noticed a thing.

Renate: That's interesting.

Tess: I'd say things happened very gradually with me.

At some point, maybe five years ago, I had realised that I had become quite, maybe, eccentric in myself in so far as my values and beliefs. But I wouldn't necessarily be telling this to, of if I did it would be in a conversational way or talking about the way we had changed over time, maybe with friends of our own age.

What I realised, I was no longer a mainstream kind of person, which I had been. It happened gradually over time, so it didn't disturb anybody and it didn't disturb me much either. It went along fine. I mean, there were things that surprised me about myself but also, it's really an adventure. The adventure of yourself, it's the greatest adventure. And, that all of us have the possibility of this truly great adventure for ourselves is awesome beyond words.

Renate: I believe you lived for almost eight years in America.

Tess: Yes.

Renate: You did that to be close to the school or what was the reason?

Tess: No. When I lived in the States it was from 1986-94, long before I ever heard of The TAT Foundation. I was teaching in a school there. I did go to workshops of different kinds, maybe did yoga, did some meditation things, got into a twelve-step group for a while. I learned something from all of them.

I went to therapy a lot. When my marriage broke up when I was about thirty. It was the single worst thing that happened in my life; it was devastating. I lived in a country where there was a ban on divorce – not just that there was no divorce, there was actually a ban on it. So the concept of a broken marriage, you really had no options after that. It was just devastating. It was devastating for my ex-husband and it was devastating for my children and for all of our families.

So, when I went to the states I started going to therapy. We didn't have much therapy in Ireland at that stage, around the early eighties. Mainly, what I wanted to find out was what had gone wrong in this relationship because we had been madly in love. We went to college when we were eighteen, married as soon as we left college and we were madly in love. Ten years later, we didn't have two words to say to each other. I really wanted to know what had happened. How could this have happened? I just had no understanding at all.

During these years of therapy and counselling, questions were asked and I got to look at questions in myself. In a way, I guess, self-inquiry started by new ideas being brought up to me and maybe being introduced to different kinds of literature. That really helped.

Renate: Let's focus on the big event, which was in the year 2010. You went into a solitary retreat. No, the year 2009 somebody gave you a birthday present and you went on this retreat? And on the last day of the retreat, what happened?

Tess: You just said it there, something about this big event. It's a non-event!

Renate: We work all our lives toward this event ... [Laughter]

Tess: And it's a non-event. I have to say that because ... It's difficult to talk about it.

What happened in my case, was all week long there had been things happening. I thought there were things in front of my eyes. At one stage the whole world went completely silent and there was just silence – maybe for thirty seconds or a minute. So, there were things happening. "My eyes", I thought, I must get them tested when I go home and so on.

On the night, packed up and ready to go home from the retreat. I got into bed and as I got in I turned off the lights. I was in a rural area and I was going to look out the window to see where the curtains pulled, or whatever, and there was a light over this side of the room. I thought, what's that? I looked, and the light came closer. I still looked away – I don't know why or how, but I know but I'm checking out the curtains, this sounds extraordinary.

Then it came right up, it came right up into me, right up here. And inside, I don't know whether there were people, or what, but they were inviting me in. It wasn't just an invitation like, would you like to come in. It was an invitation that I could not refuse. So, I went in.

I don't know what happened then, but I'm sitting up in bed and there's a vision, we call it, going on at the end of the bed. And, I knew when this happened, I knew I had found what I was looking for. I think as soon as the light came or something. At some point, I was totally overwhelmed or overcome by, "This is what I have been looking for, for all my life." I would say my shoulders fell, it was like the relief of the world.

Renate: So what actually was it?

Tess: It was a vision. All I can say is it was an outpouring of creativity. An outpouring of visual creativity and I knew what it was. I recognised it and I knew it was what I had been before I was born into a body, and what I will go back into after I leave the body. I knew this. Nobody told me. There were no words, but I just knew this.

Renate: You said, "I knew."

Tess: I knew.

Renate: "I knew, and I knew that I knew."

Tess: Yes. It was just this huge relief?

Renate: Off your shoulders?

Tess: Just relief.

Renate: Of the world? What was it?

Tess: I don't know what it was. I suppose that all one's life, one is maintaining oneself. There is a certain energy or restriction holding you together, or keeping it all going, or something. It just went, like [sound of blowing air between her lips]. You know the way you can't say to somebody who's uptight, relax? Well something happened and, relax.

Renate: Yes.

Tess: That relaxation has remained. And, security. A sense of security.

Renate: So if somebody would ask you now, who are you, what would you say?

Tess: I know people always say that [laughter].

'I Am', is all I can say.

Renate: yes.

Tess: I Am.

Renate: That is beautiful.

Tess: That's enough, when you know that. To know that you are eternally. I suppose the test is the body sitting here, the voice and everything that is talking to you, that's just the instrument through which the 'I Am' functions in the world.

In some ways I am much more me than I used to be. Even though I'm not here at all, I am much more me, I'm much more free and relaxed. I'm not trying to hold anything back from anybody, trying to be proper, or trying to. Whatever the things one would always be trying, some awareness of one's image. It's just gone.

It's totally natural. I used to hear about this before this happened to me and I used to think, "But you look quite normal." I don't think an outside person can see what's happening within one – what has happened. It's a transformation of consciousness. What one is, as consciousness, is different – much more spacious, open. I don't know what else to say.

Renate: Would you say that everything that you did until that point – like your whole psychological past, spiritual past – made that moment happen? Or did that moment happen despite of all that? Or because of grace?

Tess: I don't know. I did not do that moment. I had nothing to do with it.

Renate: It sounds like something was preparing itself for this moment.

Tess: Yes, very much. I very much felt that for three years. It was like being let know that you are pregnant; the universe is pregnant with you and it will play out in its own time. In the same way, once one is pregnant, it will carry on at its own pace. You have nothing to do with it, really, once it's started.

I suppose I would be inclined to say that all the things that I was doing helped. Along the way they just gradually built up, or rather the ego just gets chipped away at, and chipped away at just from the various efforts and attempts.

Renate: And is the ego still sometimes present?

Tess: No. [laughter]

Renate: How does one know that?

Tess: I had read about this kind of stuff. I'd heard of it. So when this happened to me – and I told you about that night – so then the vision faded and I knew what had happened and I was as light as air. I turned over in my bed and I went to sleep; slept perfection – no dreams for about eight hours. I'm up the next morning and I'm standing in the kitchen making tea for myself. And, I think everything is so spacious, what is this? This little tiny kitchen is so bright and spacious; there is something missing. I wondered what it is.

I remembered leaving to go home to make sure I had my case and everything. I'm outside and I look inside to see what's missing, can I figure out what's gone. And, I just nearly threw up. I did that for a few times over the next week. There was something gone but I couldn't remember what it was that had gone and I couldn't remember anything about it. But, there was something gone.

Maybe over the space of a week or two, I tried a few times to look inside. Each time, the reaction was just one of nausea, so I stopped it. [laughter] Then, I think it was maybe after Christmas or around Christmas, I had a book on my shelf called *The Experience of No Self* by Bernadette Roberts. In the meantime, and I did have Art Ticknor, my teacher from TAT, and I would be able to ask him. I would say things and he would say things back to me. But I still didn't really get that what had gone was the ego.

I suppose I had no idea what it would be like. My mind wasn't functioning very well at that time; it took me a while to put the two things together. I started reading her book and I thought, 'Oh yes! That's what's gone!" It amazed me that I'd read so much about this and yet, when it happened, I didn't put the two together for quite a while.

Renate: Yes.

Tess: It seems to me that the personality remained exactly as it always had been.

Renate: Yes.

Tess: It didn't improve [laughter].

Renate: So the personality is how you move.

Tess: And how you talk, the kind of things you talk about, the kind of things you like and don't like.

Maybe I thought that the ego and the personality were the same, but they are definitely different. I've often looked to see how they are different but I can't remember what the ego was like, so I can't figure it out.

Renate: It shows how insignificant the ego can be.

Tess: Yes, but I see it in other people speaking to me and I see how domineering it is, and what suffering it's causing them.

Renate: Yes, if you believe in that, it's very domineering.

Tess: I can see it. I can see what's happening. It's the cause of all the suffering.

If there is any way that you and I, with the work we are doing right now, can do anything to alleviate the suffering or to even give people a hint that maybe there is something real that can be done about this. But, you do have to take responsibility for yourself and there is help, if you are willing to do that.

Renate: What a beautiful story.

Tess: Thank you.

Renate: So now you live quietly at home? You told me earlier that your husband has cancer.

Tess: Quietly at home, take care of my husband – my delightful husband.

I got a website up about a month ago, TessHuhes.com. I'm just learning how to manage it, technically. When somebody asks me a question I might right a little article and put it up on it. So hopefully I might be able to put some teaching or put, maybe, some useful thoughts out on it that may be of help to anybody. The internet is complete magic.

The internet is how I came across the group that I was helped by. I was nearly a year or two years reading their website, their links and all the rest, before I ever got in contact with them. But I was getting ideas. I knew they had come into my life by coming across it.

Renate: Would you say that life still has some challenges for you?

Tess: Yes. Life will always have challenges. Awakening doesn't spare you from any of the rough and tumble of life. I think what does happen, though, is you are no longer confused about the tragedy being you, or whatever is going on. It's like it's the movie; that's what's going on. It might be painful – if you are watching a movie and tears will come over poignant things. It's the same but you no longer think you're the character that's going to get mowed down or something.

There is also great humour. This is one of the things that surprised me – I call it divine humour. I just think divinity has a great sense of humour in its own way.

Renate: Well, I'm sorry Tess, we have to stop. But, I wrote down here, you were saying "one day we will all return to true nature." It gives us all hope.

Tess: Yes. There is no other way. Behind I, true nature – real true nature – we don't know that.

Renate: Of course.

Tess: The thing is, what can return to that, or find that, while they are still in a body and before they are faced with physical death. It makes it much easier for this.

Renate: Yes, yes. Thank you for coming, to share with us this courageous path.

Tess: Thank you so much for giving me this opportunity.

Philip Jacobs – The Pathless Path
Interview by Iain McNay

*T*he most amazing thing I've learnt about life, which is often quite difficult to convey is; at one time I thought that I was this separate person, weaving my way through life and you had to manipulate things or things wouldn't go your way or you might meet an accident and that's a very frightening view of life. The way it turned around and how it appears now is, there isn't a separate Philip trying to manipulate a separate life. It's like it's one immaculately produced movie or drama and I'm just watching it unfold as Philip. I'm not doing anything or creating anything. It's just like I'm amazed at the precision of how things unfold. Even the things which at the time that seem to be total absolute disasters, then I look back a year or two later and I think, 'My God, if that hadn't happened, this would never have happened.' And then once you've got that … it takes a while for that view to percolate down through all your Being, but once it does percolate, then you have a much lighter view of life. You're not pushing and pulling it and trusting it as it unfolds from moment to moment.

Iain: My guest today is Philip Jacobs. I first saw Philip a couple of years ago after I went to what's called a Turning Evening at Colet House in West London, and what that is kind of whirling dervishes and Philip is the Sheikh of the group in London and it was the most extraordinary experience. I had at the back of my mind to do an interview with Philip about his life and about the Turning and it's taken a bit of time but he's now here in the studio with me and I'm looking forward to this interview very much. To start with he's written some books, *One Self: Life as a Means of Transformation*, and *Being the Teaching of Advaita: A Basic Introduction*, and the one I like the most, *A Pathless Path: A Journey To The Place Never Left*, which is mainly autobiographical.

So, we're going to look at Philip's life and his spiritual journey and a little about the Turning and many other things that come up in our limited time of an hour.

So, let's start with your childhood where you had a great love of nature. You liked finding wild places. I think you lived by the Thames and you'd get on a boat, go in the middle of the Thames and find somewhere really quiet to hang out.

Philip: I grew up in a town called East Molesey. Our house was along a little river called The Ember and it was great because we had this great long river frontage as children. I had a brother and a sister and we all had our own boats so, all the time, all through the summer and the winter we used to go off and have these adventures. We used to have sea battles with children from further down the river. It just gave me such a love of nature seeing the way the river changed and the seasons changed and how the snow used to come and the frost and then the nettles rose up in the springtime. It just sort of got me off to being in such a lovely environment, it instilled a great love of nature in me right from the beginning.

Iain: Mm, and then you were given a book by a guy called Lobsang Rampa. I hadn't heard of him before, it was called *The Third Eye*, and that really opened things up for you didn't it in terms of the spiritual world?

Philip: It did, because at the time I was away at boarding school and boarding school is pretty dire (laughs), because it's a sort of world of getting up at seven in the morning and studying French verbs and nineteenth century English history and playing rugger out on the sports field, I'd been interested in oriental arts since I was about eleven,

216

my brother and I had both been buying Buddhas and Tibetan things with our pocket money. Then one day my mother sent me this book by Lobsang Rampa, called, *The Third Eye*. He was supposedly a Tibetan Lama but what I didn't know at the time was, he was actually the son of a plumber from Plimpton in Devon. (Philip and Iain laugh). But what he wrote was miraculous enough to inspire my fourteen-year old mind and it was suddenly like this whole new world opened up and I thought, 'Why, why didn't no-one tell me that this other world existed?' Reading the Bhagavad-Gita at that time wouldn't have had that much impression on me and it needed to be something very overtly miraculous.

Iain: Yes, and at fourteen that's quite something because most boys of fourteen are thinking of something completely different.

Philip: Well, you have to remember that in the 1960s and since the Beatles had gone in to Eastern mysticism, it was very much around everywhere and also my father had died of cancer at home when I was nine and that had sort of made me start looking in other directions. So, I was no longer just taking life on its surface value and I was wondering where he'd gone and what it was all about. So, I definitely started looking by that time.

Iain: I think your mother sent you a book by Frances Roles and that again opened something, didn't it?

Philip: Yes, that was because I wrote a poem inspired by Lobsang Rampa which got into the school magazine and then my mother, being a proud mother, showed it to all her friends and by a series of coincidences it found its way to Dr. Frances Roles, who had been a follower of a Russian writer, P.D. Ouspensky. He sent me this book called, *Waking Up*, which he had written about a system of meditation from the Advaita tradition. So, that sort of followed on from Lobsang Rampa and his waking up book became my bible for the next couple of years.

Iain: And you actually went to his centre in Colet House in West London and you started to learn meditation at sixteen-years-old.

Philip: Yes, I wanted to learn it when I was fourteen, when I first read the book, but I think they thought that I was too young so I had to wait till Dr. Roles agreed to initiate me when I was sixteen. Then I had to escape from boarding school because it wasn't popular thing to go off and learn a form of meditation in London. Eventually, I had to threaten my mother, I said, 'If you don't write to the headmaster a letter saying that I want to learn to meditate, I'm going anyway and I'll get into trouble.' So, reluctantly, she wrote a letter saying she granted her permission. Then, I went up to London and Dr. Roles taught me how to meditate.

Iain: But what does the headmaster of a boarding school say when a boy wants to go and meditate? It's an unusual thing for a boy to have that desire.

Philip: I think it was outside of their remit and I think generally they found me a bit difficult to understand. Two examples of that were after I'd learned to meditate the Prefects used to wake me up half an hour before everyone else so I could do my meditation, which was very nice of them. And when I had my own room a bit later, once the House Master came in early in the morning to wake me up and I was sitting in the half-lotus position, then the Deputy House Master came in a couple of weeks later and I was still in the half-lotus position and then they were overheard to say, 'It's best to leave Jacobs to himself.' So after that, I did get completely left to myself and I could really do want I wanted.

Iain: And did you find a lot of peace in meditation at that point?

Philip: I did! It was fantastic. I don't know if you know boarding school life? In the morning you're sort of fast asleep, having a lovely dream, but you're at home or by the river and suddenly a Prefect comes in and says, 'Right! Three to get out of bed!' and blows the whistle … and then it's down to lots of rows of wash basins and then down to a noisy dining hall. But getting up that half an hour before everyone, and initially I used to meditate down in the school chapel and then I went into the dining hall and it was like there was an inner glow. So, no longer was I a victim of the dining hall, it was like I was looking out on the dining hall from a sense of stillness. I'd also been a very rebellious adolescent and I was quite a troublemaker and I suddenly started to see from the teachers' point of view and started to realize they probably didn't want to be school masters and they were just trying to earn their living – so it was like there was this sudden shift in perspective to seeing it from other people's points of view. So, most of my adolescent angst started to evaporate at that point.

Iain: It was interesting, just to briefly cover what was happening at Colet House. Dr. Frances Roles. He'd learnt from Ouspensky and Ouspensky had of course been a student of Gurdjieff before that and there was also a connection with the Marharishi wasn't there and the Marharishi taught at Colet House one time when he was over?

Philip: Yes, and just to give you a brief potted history, Ouspensky had always been interested in the study of consciousness, and by consciousness he meant the awareness we have behind our thoughts and our feelings and our desires. He'd written quite an intelligent book right back at the start of the twentieth century and then he'd gone off to India looking for methods to access that consciousness more fully, but he didn't find what he was looking for. Then WW1 broke out and he had to go back to Russia where he was mobilized. He then met this enigmatic Greek teacher called Gurdjieff and for a while he thought he'd found what he was looking for in Gurdjieff's teachings but gradually their paths deviated and I think Ouspensky strongly disagreed with Gurdjieff's methods, which could be quite violent.

So Ouspensky carried on separately and he partly developed his own ideas and partly taught what he'd learned from Gurdjieff. Towards the end of his life, it was like he went right beyond what he'd been teaching, he went right beyond what he learned from Gurdjieff. Right at the end, he said, 'I abandon the system and you must reconstruct it all from the very beginning.' This threw people in to a bit of confusion because they'd become so dependent on the particular metaphors that he had been teaching. He privately prepared some of his followers, one of whom was Dr. Roles after his death, to find what he'd actually been looking for in the first place.

Ouspensky died in 1947 and it wasn't till 1961 that Dr. Roles made contact with advaita or non-dual traditions in India, which has existed for many hundreds of years as an advisory tradition. The Marharishi was a step in the process of that meeting. Ouspensky had told Dr. Roles to look for a method that involved repeating one word. Those were Ouspenskys' own actual words. So, when he met the Marharishi he realised that he'd found the method that Ouspensky had asked him to look for.

Iain: The Marharishi worked with a mantra, yes?

Philip: Yes, a mantra with meditation. A bit later the Marharishi introduced Dr. Roles to the head of his tradition. The Advaita tradition was originally founded by someone called Shankara. Somewhere around the sixth to the ninth century, no-ones quite sure when, he set up four seats of learning. So you have one of the North, South, West and East and the Marharishi introduced Dr. Roles to the Shankara of The North. He became his guide and Advaita teacher for about the next twenty years. So, it gradually started to evolve and in Ouspensky's day it was very strict. It was known as an esoteric school and when, just before Dr. Roles died he said, 'Our role as an esoteric school is over, no more secrecy. I want the Colet House of the future to be a place, like a cell of self-knowledge, that people can come to for rest and refreshment, and particularly for young people for whom life's very difficult today.' So it went through a path or process of evolution.

Iain: And one of the things that you learnt there, which I think was Ouspensky and Gurdjieff, was this Self-remembering. How was that to start with for you, Self-remembering?

Philip: Self-remembering was the cornerstone of what Gurdjieff had taught and what Ouspensky taught, but – obviously I never knew Ouspensky, because he died long before I was born – he found it very difficult to convey what he meant and at the time I think people had a lot of trouble understanding what he was trying to convey. I personally don't use the term any longer, it sort of belongs to history, but my understanding of it is; you have an identity in time, which in my case is Philip. Philip is a man, Philip is an artist, Philip does all the sort of Philip things and the Philip identity is always changing. So, when Philip was five, Philip liked certain things and then it keeps changing and evolving. But behind that, behind I am Philip, is just the pure sense of I Am, or the pure sense of Being. So, it isn't obscure, it is so universal. When you're five there's something looking out through your eyes, which is exactly the same as when you're fifty-five, it's totally timeless, it doesn't change, it's totally still. It's totally unaffected by what goes on in the changing drama. So, my understanding of Self-remembering is remembering that behind it all, I'm not just Philip, I'm this great stillness that lies behind Philip and which is universal and common to all of us.

Iain: Is that something you felt you were aware of when you started to meditate at sixteen years old?

Philip: When I was very young and when I was out in nature, I used to have these moments of intense happiness, when it was just like happiness would arise for no reason. It often happened like when I was … I remember one occasion when I was watching this raging storm at sea. I was just standing watching it and I was about ten years old I think, or nine, and I remember watching it and thinking,' Just remember this sensation that you're feeling now, remember it, remember it when you're at school and you're in a maths lesson.' (Philip and Iain laugh)

So that was my early understanding of Self-remembering, that it's just your natural state, it's who you are. The other state, the, *I am Philip*, is superimposed on top of that and it's a very fluid thing which just changes when you go to sleep at night, it completely disappears. So, I think more and more the deeper state is like the background and the *I am Something* or *I am Philip* is in the foreground but I think as life goes on there's a subtle switching between the two.

Iain: So, as we talk now, are you aware of the background? How is it now?

Philip: The background is always there. It's like, it's like you're looking out from the background.

Iain: So that's with you most of the time? This looking out the, what I would call, the vastness, what you would call more the peacefulness.

Philip: I sort of think it's with everyone all the time, they just don't know it …

Iain: They're not aware of it, yes.

Philip: It's what is looking out? What is seeing through your eyes? What is hearing? There's just this mis-identification of what's actually happening. Most non-dual teachings are simply pointing out what's actually happening now as opposed to what you think is happening now or what your mind's superimposed on that.

So it's actually happening to everyone all the time.

Iain: The other thing that you mentioned in the autobiography which reminded me of something I used to do when I lived in a Community many years ago, was the Stop exercise, where you ring a bell and everyone had to stop. I lived in this Community for a time in Northern Italy and that was so effective; you're busy doing what you're doing and the bell goes for thirty seconds you just stop and it reminds you, doesn't it? It takes you in to stillness you see the stillness or feel the stillness.

Philip: Yes, yes. Dr. Roles used to do that sometimes. He'd shout Stop! And we'd all freeze (laughs), but I find it's like when you see something incredibly beautiful in nature or a work of art, it has the same effect. It just suddenly the moving mind stops and you're in a state of awe at it. (Iain agrees).

Iain: Yes. I don't want to keep the whole thing biographical but I'm just getting some triggers here. The other thing that Ouspensky was really very committed to was Turning. Do you want to just talk us through that?

Philip: I'll talk you through that. In the early twentieth century Ouspensky had visited the Mevlevi Dervishes in Turkey, mostly in Instanbul, several times, and he writes about them in two of his books. He had meetings with some of the sheikhs and so he always saw dervish turning. He thought it was a method, again, for accessing this deeper sense of Self. In 1963, that was shortly after Dr. Roles had made contact with the Advaita tradition, one of the Colet House members had a Turkish boy working on her farm and he had an uncle who was a Mevlevi dervish out in Turkey. He invited some of the Colet House members out to a ceremony in Konya.

Because what had happened is, back in the 1920s, Kemal Ataturk, the then ruler of Turkey, had banned all Dervish orders and all Sufi orders and all fortune tellers and anything he thought was holding Turkey back from being a modern western nation. It was shortly after the Ottoman Empire had ended and he was trying to move Turkey on. So, prior to that most towns had what is known as a Mevlevi Tekeh, which is a place where the whirling dervishes whirled. After that it all had to go secret so the poor dervishes, if they were caught turning, could go to prison. So they had to draw the curtains and Turn secretly on their living room carpet.

In the late '50s it was just starting to be allowed again as a tourist attraction and they were having these annual ceremonies in Konya in Turkey, which is where Jalal al-Din Rumi had lived. Rumi was the founder of the Mevlevi Dervish order. So three of the Colet House members went out to the ceremony. They caught the eye of the Sheikh, who was presiding over the ceremony in Konya. He was a Mevlevihanesi Sheikh. He'd been a Mevlevi since he was a little boy and his name was Resuhi Baykara. Afterwards, he talked to the Colet House members and they asked him, would he be prepared to come over to London and teach the Turning to western people. He went and spoke to his Sheikh, who was a man called Munaichelabi and Munaichelabi said, 'Yes you must teach the Turning in London.' And so Resuhi came over and he was a civil servant, he'd only got a months' annual holiday, so he trained sixty people in a month to do this very difficult movement and to learn all the prayers and all the ceremonial. Then, by the time he went back at the end of it, the Turning and the Mevlevi tradition was up and running at Colet House where it's been taught and practiced ever since. But he was very radical and very far seeing at the time, because in Turkey, at the time, it was only taught to men and he came over and taught it to both men and women together.

Iain: Yes.

Philip: So, I think he probably got into a bit of trouble from hard-liners when he went home again.

Iain: And this Turning was something that was very attractive to you as well, wasn't it?

Philip: When I was sixteen, just after I'd learned to meditate on a half-term holiday, I went up and watched a public ceremony and watching it just made me so happy. It was a bit like watching a rock concert in a way. It was live music and I went away just beaming all over my face and I thought if it can do that for someone watching it, what must it be like to actually turn?

Iain: We were talking earlier, I want to make a separate programmeme about the Turners, so we won't go into too much detail on that but ... I was looking at my notes from your book and your life became very busy. You were up at five o'clock in the morning to learn the Turning, and then you had your full day and your meditation and earning your living and everything else. You said you had just incredible energy afterwards, with the Turning.

Philip: Yeah, when I was learning it, I was doing my degree show for my textile course in Liberty's of London in Regent Street, we were down in the basement. I used to go in about nine o'clock, all sort of beaming, like I'd been up all day and the other art students had just crawled out of bed. So it did give me this amazing energy just doing the training.

Iain: You also said around this time that, 'I began to notice that life appeared to be unfolding like a drama or a play, much like a multi-dimensional jigsaw puzzle, where everything appeared to slot together to form one whole.'

Philip: That's the most amazing thing I've learnt about life, which is often quite difficult to convey is; at one time I thought that I was this separate person, weaving my way through life and you had to manipulate things or things wouldn't go your way or you might meet an accident and that's a very frightening view of life. The way it turned around and how it appears now is, there isn't a separate Philip trying to manipulate a separate life. It's like it's one immaculately produced movie or drama and I'm just watching it unfold as Philip. I'm not doing anything or creating anything. It's just like I'm amazed at the precision of how things unfold. Even the things which at the time that seem to be total absolute disasters, then I look back a year or two later and I think, 'My God, if that hadn't happened, this would never have happened.' (Iain agrees) ... and then once you've got that ... it takes a while for that view to percolate down through all your Being, but once it does percolate, then you have a much lighter view of life. You're not pushing and pulling it and trusting it as it unfolds from moment to moment.

Iain: But you see, how does this fit in with being on a spiritual path and as many of us do, think,' Ahh, we're working our way towards clearing our personality, shedding traumas whatever, and one day we will be enlightened, we will be One. It's like the separateness is working towards the Oneness but from what you're saying, it isn't quite like that, is it?

Philip: I don't see it like that. I sort of see the two identities, *I am something* or *I am Philip* on the line of time and then there is the pure beingness – you might say it's here for convenience say. (Holds hand in front of him at shoulder height). On the line of time, (his arm moves from right to left at waist height), you're always going to be in process and so now you will have boarding school traumas that you'll process and relationship traumas that you process and probably when you're eighty years old, you get put in an old people's home and there's more trauma … (Philip and Iain laugh).

Iain: Even more traumas … laughing.

Philip: So at that level you're never going to resolve things. It's always going to be one process after another process. What I think you notice at a certain point is what you are is always there, independent of any process so, you can do all the spiritual exercises you want and that will happen in your particular drama or movie. Whatever's on your particular film, might happen to include being a Whirling Dervish, it might include meditating, it might include going to church. Whatever's right for you will happen but at a certain point you'll notice that what you really are has always been there, almost at right angles to that line of time.

The great stillness isn't along here, (his arm moves along an imaginary line from right to left), waiting to be realised. The great stillness was looking out from your eyes right from the beginning. So it's almost as if on the line of time you exhaust the process, you exhaust the process of looking for something in time, until you actually come to the realisation that it isn't time, it's always been looking out through your eyes.

Iain: Dr. Roles died and in the last year of his life you talk quite a lot in the book about how he saw things differently; it had been a bottom up approach and he now saw it as a top down approach.

Philip: Yes. I was sort of aware in his last year in particular, that he was getting very frustrated with us, because for a long time he had taught the Ouspensky system, the Ouspensky-Gurdjieff system, then he gradually introduced Advaita into it. For a long time I think he tried to look at Advaita from an Ouspensky point of view and then he suddenly realised that the Advaita viewpoint was completely different to the Ouspensky one. He described the Ouspensky teaching as a bottom up system and Advaita as top down.

So the more he went into this, the more he discovered, and the more he tried to convey to us something new he'd discovered but I could see him getting really frustrated because we kept going back to the old metaphors and then almost a day before he died, almost his last words were something like, ' We've had everything upside down and back to front. The need now is for simplicity, there's only one consciousness. The levels ... the levels of impediment to that consciousness is ... everything is that consciousness, that is what we have to feel and know.'

So, that was like his parting message; everything is that consciousness. There's only one consciousness. Back then it was quite a radical thing to say, nowadays, almost everyone is saying it (Iain agrees). So my particular interest back then, that was 1982, was what worked away in me, was to discover what he meant. I wanted to find what he had discovered.

Iain: One thing you talk again about in the book, is when you were writing a paper with Peter Fenwick and Peter Fenwick got you to be really precise with the language. Even writing one sentence, you can get caught and get the wording slightly wrong. I don't know whether you remember what that case was?

Philip: I remember it. I can't remember the exact words ... I probably can actually. I'd been working with Peter Fenwick for quite a few years, writing papers and doing meetings and we used to write the paper together. I used to go over to his house for supper and then by the end of the day we'd have a paper done. One day I wrote the paper before I went to him and I wrote, 'We have a responsibility to manifest the truth,' and he said, 'The paper's great apart from that one phrase.' So I was able to pick out that phrase that responsibility implied a sense of separateness, a dual-ship, so he made me find out what I'd done wrong and then I removed it. Then we never worked together again, because he'd played his role.

Iain: This precision of how you say, and how you think and how you write is so important, isn't it?

Philip: Yes.

Iain: And I'm just picking things out that interest me from the biography here and you started to research an aspect of the Advaita teaching known as Antahkarana which I haven't heard of before, but it's like the inner vehicle of the soul. Just talk us through that.

Philip: Yes, in the Advaita tradition, there are different levels of identity. For many people you don't need all these levels, you just need the sense of oneness and people get it instantly. But in most non-dual traditions reality is portrayed as manifesting through a series of levels, all be it metaphorical. It's a bit like from the bottom up, there appear to be lots of levels, from the top down there aren't any levels, there's just Oneness.

And, with the individual, again this is traditional Advaita, the way the one consciousness manifests as an individual is through what's known as the inner vehicle. So, *Antahkarana* – in India they have these big temple chariots called Kars and we get our word motorcar from it, which is a vehicle for a motor! Whereas *Aham* in Sanskrit, which means I, just the pure sense of I, so *Ahamkara* means vehicle for your sense of I. So inner vehicle is the Indian equivalent of the Christian concept of a soul, so, it's like, yes it's a vehicle through which consciousness manifests as an individual in the drama of consciousness.

If you're going for total Oneness then you don't even get stuck at the Antahkarana. It's quite a useful in life, it's quite a useful thing in understanding the mechanism.

Iain: So it's not who we really are ultimately …

Philip: It's not who you really are.

Iain: It's like a half-way house, is that right?

Philip: Yes. Some people need a half-way house, (Iain agrees), other people don't. But it's quite a useful way of explaining things to people who want explanations. Ultimately, anything less than the whole, the totality, is a limitation.

Iain: Yes, and in the school I've been in for many years, it's known as the personal essence. And I found that remarkably helpful actually and it took me a long time to realise that wasn't ultimately who I was, but on a human level it helps to take me away from the gross identification of the I. So, for me anyway, yes, it has a value, it's very useful.

Philip: In the Ouspensky tradition they had essence and personality you see. Essence is a deeper sense of Self but it's still not the ultimate.

Iain: Yes, and this book points out this thing here where you, after Turning, you would be having personal relationship problems with your girlfriend at the time, whatever (Philip laughs). You go in to Turning, you'd be in a curse, you would come out of it half-an-hour later and someone would say to you, 'Are you okay Philip?' And you would say,

'What a preposterous question! Of course I'm all right!' What would happen? Would it dissolve or would you realise who you really were or...?

Philip: That particular occasion was very powerful. It was when I was twenty-eight and I was always having romantic traumas back then. (Laughs). But it was after a big relationship break up and it probably was the worse day of my life, I think.

Then I went and Turned and the next day I went and Turned in the Mukabele Ceremony and by the end of it I just felt so happy and I knew I was having a trauma but the trauma was all going on over there somewhere, (points away from himself), and I was just in this great happiness and the lady, a good friend of mine called Annie, came up to me and said to me, 'Are you all right?' and I thought what a ridiculous question. (Iain and Philip laugh). The trauma was over there (again pointing away from himself), and it is Turning, which is such a lovely way of accessing the great stillness that then manifests in time and space as a great happiness.

Iain: And the way of course, the trauma is always over there. If it's anywhere, it's over there but we forget somehow, don't we? We get so absorbed in the trauma and the drama, the dramas of the situation, that it seems that we are consumed by it.

Philip: Yes.There's a lovely metaphor I heard Timothy Freke say, 'Life is like a journey from A to B, and on that journey you'll go through swamps and jungles and deserts and the open road and everyone sort of has that journey. And when you're on the open road and everyone thinks – you think –'Oh, I'm really enlightened and I'm doing really well,' and then suddenly you find yourself in the inevitable swamp again and things don't look so bright.' So, Life has a way, however much you think you've gone beyond it or you've transcended suffering, Life knows how to put you right back in it again. So, it's like, never get complacent about it. It can always draw you back in again, if that's part of the movie.

Iain: And you of course had a good example of this because you got very sick didn't you, you got Lyme disease, which really knocked you out at times.

Philip: Yes. I had about twenty-one years of illness. I remember a friend and I both got ill at the same time and we were probably a bit too blissful for our own good, I think. Then we suddenly got this illness, which was completely overpowering. Life could suddenly look very bleak and so it was almost like the non-dual realisation had to permeate down through all different aspects of life ... so ... you almost have to go into the bleak places, as the dark places as well as the other place, then you start to see them both as the same thing but you have to go there.

Iain: Yes, on a human level that's quite challenging at times ...

Philip: That's quite challenging ... it has been challenging.

Iain: Yes, and you talk about four levels don't you? Just explain the four levels.

Philip: That's in the Advaita tradition again. If you just want Oneness forget this (both of them laugh), just go for Oneness, but if you want to experience ... how consciousness manifests as a creation ... In the Christian tradition, in the early Christian church they had body, soul and spirit and that's a very good concept, because if you're just a body-soul, then God is (points upward) up there somewhere with body, soul and spirit, God and your deepest identity is one and the same thing. So, your spirit is the same as the universal spirit.

In the Advaita tradition they have Physical, Subtle, Causal and Divine. Physical is flesh and bones (he smacks his leg), body and world. Subtle is your psyche, so that's your feeling and thinking processes, so it's also, it's the dream world at night. So it's private to you and that's sort of what's often referred to I think, in Zen as the mind-body mechanism and for many people the identity stops at the mind-body mechanism. So, if somebody says, 'Who are you?' You will both identify with both body and mind, but when you're thinking and when you're feeling, there's also, an awareness behind that of the thinking and the feeling. It's what we talked about earlier. There's an identity behind the moving mind, behind the changing personality which doesn't change, which is always still and that equates in the Advaita tradition of the Causal level and it's also the realm of dreamless sleep. So sleep with dreams at night, when you're in this dream world is Subtle level and then at a certain point that disappears and there's total timelessness. When you go into deep sleep or meditation there's no time at all. So, you can fall asleep at midnight and wake up at seven and it's like it's almost instantaneous, no time has happened. That's referred to as the Causal level and the Divine level is really just a fuller understanding of that and the Divine refers to the ground of All Being.

With the Causal, it's like you've accessed this inner stillness and you're looking out on the world from the point of view of stillness, like I described in the dining hall at school, but there's still a subtle subject-object because you're stillness looking out on the manifest world. With the Divine, it's like the subject and object duality collapses and you realise that everything you perceive as external is actually taking place within this stillness, that is yourself.

Iain: I think that, that is also known as the Absolute – is that right?

Philip: Yes.

Iain: Yes ... and you find these four levels still helpful or do you feel that now that's not relevant to you?

Philip: I find them really helpful still, really helpful, and when you're explaining this again, it is a wonderful metaphor to use. And it's so brilliant at understanding different aspects of life and things like suffering and all the things that happen.

Iain: Yes, yeah, I almost feel we should make a separate programmeme about how you handled your illness because it brought up so many things and there's so much depth there but one of the things I really liked was the way that you and I think we all have that as part of the aging process too. For me, certainly, you can't do what you used to do and you find things that bring you joy. I love the stories that you talk about the two main things you found that brought you joy when you were so ill, if you remember what they are ...

Philip: They were dinosaur hunting ...

Iain: Dinosaur hunting! And there was one about things being swept down the river.

So, talk about the dinosaur hunting, that's tremendous stuff.

Philip: I love dinosaur hunting. I've always loved looking for things and finding things. It's a bit like a metaphor for the whole drama of consciousness, how consciousness manifests as apparent separateness and then it has to rediscover itself. When I was younger I used to love climbing mountains in the snow and things and when I got poorly I couldn't do that anymore, but I could still walk along my favourite bit of beach looking for dinosaur bones. This became such an absorbing passion that soon I was often discovering whole skeletons embedded in the hard rock.

Iain: That's right, you've got this story, you found this whole skeleton. Was it whole?

Philip: Yes.

Iain: It's a fossil, not the actual ...

Philip: It's a fossil. First of al I found lots and lots of bones, great limb bones and vertebra. Once I was walking along with a girlfriend on the beach and I just found this and I said, 'Oh, I've found a vertebra.' It was just a single vertebra in the clay and I got my chisel out and started hiselling away and then it became another vertebra, and then it became another one and it became another one and I thought, 'Oh, I've got a row of vertebra,' and then I suddenly found ribs were going off it and I thought, 'Hang on, I've got a skeleton here.' Then this very famous fossil hunter called Steve Etches came along, he caught me at it and he said, ' Oh dear,' he said,' you're doing what the Victorians do, you're just collecting the backbone.'

So then, he helped me excavate the whole thing and you have to chisel out a huge, huge great sort of slab. You have to dig a trench in the rock with chisels. It took about a couple of weeks to do and then you get chisels underneath the slabs and eventually it comes up in sections, then you had to get a boat to carry it back down the beach.

Iain: So, you've got a dinosaur at home now?

Philip: I've actually got friends looking after the dinosaur at the moment. (He laughs). I had to move house a couple of years ago to a smaller house, so most of my dinosaurs are being looked after at the moment.

Iain: And how old is that Dinosaur then?

Philip: She's 150 million years, give or take a million.

Iain: It's extraordinary.

Philip: I've got about, probably, bits of fifty different reptiles and dinosaurs. It's a wonderful thing to do. It's so wonderful, you sort of get the chisel under a slab and then you lift it up and you just don't know what's going to be underneath it. A bit like opening your Christmas presents.

Iain: And the other thing you loved doing was I think, it's the Medway, there was ...

Philip: Oh yeah, clay pipes.

Iain: Yes, clay pipes you used to find.

Philip: I used to stay with some friends in the Medway and they'd dug up several clay pipes in their gardens, beautiful things, like models, like acorns. So, I started researching, that how in Victorian times, rubbish was taken down the Thames in barges and then it was dumped into these muddy creeks in the Medway towns and places like Sittingbourne. So, I'd go off exploring all these muddy creeks and you'd find all the Victorian rubbish, just oozing out of the ground in the muddy banks. The thing I did love was the clay pipes, because in the late nineteenth century they were very ornate and they had famous peoples' heads as the bowl. So it was people like Lord Baden-Powell and Buffalo Bill. It was just so fascinating. (Iain laughs).

Iain: Yes ... Well I'm going to invite you back because in a way we've only covered part of your story and it's almost like the highlights. So, if you are able to do that I'd love to invite you back.

Philip: I'd love to, thank you.

Iain: Also we need to make a separate programmeme about the Turning. My idea was to get some fellow Turners and also some footage, just make a whole programmeme there. I'm looking at the clock and the element of time, which is the bottom of the four levels is unfortunately catching up with you ... catching up with us. So Philip, I want to thank you very much for coming in to Conscious TV and I'm going to show your two books again, *Being the Teaching of Advaita: A Basic Introduction* and *One Self: Life as a Means of Transformation.* I think from memory this is the one that has quite a lot about your illness and about how you handled that. Someone who is a bit poorly, as you put it and you were more than a bit poorly at times. This is such an insight in to how to handle very difficult physical situations. Thank you again Philip.

Philip: Thank you very much.

Igor Kufayev –
The Impact of Awakening
Interview by **Iain McNay**

*N*ow *I work with people who have found themselves in this condition and lived with that for many years without proper reconciliation. I am not speaking about hardcore spiritual circles, I am talking about people who experience what is commonly known as awakening. They "popped out" out of the blue, and suddenly they are having all of these experiences, and they don't know. "What is it? Why is it? Why is it happening to me? Am I going nuts? Am I going insane? Do I have to go to get checked?"*

Iain: Renate and I met Igor a few weeks ago at the European Science and Non-duality Conference in Holland, and we had a good connection with him. Even though we did a 'panel' with him at the conference, it wasn't appropriate for Conscious TV , so this is the first time he has officially been on Conscious TV.

Igor is an artist and an Advaita Tantra teacher. He has a book which will be out shortly, called, Flowing Wakefulness: Essays on the Nature of Consciousness. We're going to talk about Igor's life, hear some of his wisdom, and just generally see – as we always do on Conscious TV – where the adventure of the interview leads us.

Igor, when Renate and I first met you in Holland I was struck by a certain intensity you had, and a precision. Some remarkable and transformative things have happened to you, both in your career and in your ordinary, daily human life Let's just see if we can touch on some of the significant occurrences.

When you were a child, you had quite a lot of extraordinary experiences, didn't you?

Igor: Well, yes – you could say that. One of the most unusual was that periodically, especially from the age of where I can consciously remember my self-identity – maybe from about the age of four or five until my early teens – I had these spontaneous movements in the body. They would usually occur when I was lying down and completely resting. Sometimes I would even find it difficult to fall asleep; it was almost as if my body just wanted to move and that movement was obviously involuntary. It would always be quite surprising, because I was ready to sleep and my legs would start to twitch, and would even slightly jump. It would come to the point when my mother would come to the bedroom and try to pacify me, "Why are you still not sleeping?" She would sit with the weight of her body on my shins, on my legs, and in that state, press my body, and calm me into sleep. These are vivid memories of my childhood.

Also, it would be accompanied by some visions; visions of sudden flashes of light, or almost as if there was rain outside, but the rain was not water – it was almost as if the stars were falling. These were visual interpretations of this kind of liquid light. It was also often accompanied by sounds of different frequencies from very, very fine vibrations – almost like the buzz of the bee – to much more tumultuous sounds, like thunder, but, obviously, there was no thunder outside. I was quite aware that this is something that I should not really relate to other too much; on one occasion when I tried to talk about it to my mom, she displayed a bit of worry on her face – which made me realise, "Oops! Perhaps, this is something that I should keep close to my chest."

Iain: That is quite mature for a kid of four-years-old, to have this realisation that something is happening and you should keep it to yourself.

Igor: Well, this is as far as my memory goes; maybe it wasn't exactly like that. I should give credit to my mother; because she never mentioned this to anyone in our large extended family. If she had spoken about it am sure she would have been advised to take me to the so-called "specialists." I am saying that in quotes here, because later on I understood that these were not signs of some kind of pathology, but these were regular signs of what happens to the physiology when there is a stirring in Consciousness on that level when energetic transformation is imminent or in progress.

Iain: So now you can see it in a wider perspective and get it clearer, that was what was probably happening at the time

Igor: No doubt about it. Now I work with people who have found themselves in this condition and lived with that for many years without proper reconciliation. I am not speaking about hardcore spiritual circles, I am talking about people who experience what is commonly known as awakening. They "popped out" out of the blue, and suddenly they are having all of these experiences, and they don't know. "What is it? Why is it? Why is it happening to me? Am I going nuts? Am I going insane? Do I have to go to get checked?"

So yes, I had enough time, not only to reconcile and to understand what was happening to me early in childhood and throughout my teens, but I also came to realise later on, when I was going through the main transformative impact, that I had to develop an understanding from both perspectives: the classical (spiritual) perspective and the clinical perspective. They are not always the same although they share the ground, they share the territory. Spiritual experiences as they are described in spiritual literature, would fall into the category of classical. Clinical is that which has been recorded by outside observers just to give it bare facts, based upon what is happening to that person at any given time.

Iain: Okay, we'll come on to that later – a lot of things have happened to you. Let's give it a context where you were. You were brought up in Uzbekistan, and you lived in a sort of a ghetto, wasn't it, tall apartment blocks?

Igor: At the time I didn't know. At the time to me it was a normal environment, but when I came back to my homeland after living for many, many years abroad – as you know from my biography, I emigrated from the Soviet Union when I was in my early twenties – so when I came back to Uzbekistan, I already had something to compare it with. Obviously, with the knowledge which I got after living in three major capitals including London, I realised that I actually grew up in what would be classified as one of those ghettos – it was a Soviet ghetto.

Iain: One thing that intrigued me when we had a phone conversation three days ago, you said that from an early age you had a "witnessing state of consciousness." What does that mean in simple terms? How did you experience that as a child – a witnessing state of consciousness?

Igor: First I should give a direct example, and we'll roll into my understanding, how that actually functions. For instance, when I started to read more advanced or more demanding literature, I read compulsively, I read everything I would come across. I read all the Russian, French and English classics – in their English translation.

For instance, I read Shakespeare and he was one of my favourites from England, and then I moved on to reading more specialised literature, more philosophical literature. I do remember very vividly when I read Kierkegaard my mentor's brother asked me, "What is your feeling? Tell me how do you feel?" I said, "Whenever I come to a passage which obviously displays some profound wisdom, whenever that wisdom starts to resonate, all I experience is that someone is witnessing that fact that I am actually reading it. I am – as in that place in time – this teenager, this boy Igor, reading these passages of Kierkegaard."

That was very, very interesting, because it gave me a very, very palpable experience that it is now just this corporeal reality so-to-speak – and I would understand later what this corporeal reality really means – but this someone who I considered myself to be, is actually *not* in the full sense of that word, because there is another witness that is witnessing that, and *I am* that witness – or how else could that be put in the right context?

Iain: So you learned from that – as you say – you are not the person doing the reading, but somebody or something else is watching the person reading.

Igor: Exactly! Exactly! And what is more interesting – because I think it is very important to be specific – is that while the Igor so-to-speak is understanding what is being said in this or that passage, understanding in terms of processing through mental faculties, through intellectual capacities – that someone who is, let's say in an apartment above, is simply watching it in detachment, watching it as a pure observer. There is no need to understand, there is no need to qualify, quantify, or what have you – that was most peculiar, but I think when I related that to my mentor's brother, he totally dismissed that.

Iain: Yes, so it also means that any emotion or feeling that the ego is having, that is also being watched – or that *can be* watched.

Igor: That became more and more apparent as my life was unfolding.

As you know, I started painting at an early age, and I had a mentor. I was drawing professionally from the age of twelve; in a formal setting, preparing for the College of Art, and then it unfolded further on, and so forth. All through my teens, when I was working to perfect my skills, I found that the witness would become the most intense experience. Even if there was another person in the room it was as if I were alone with my work; I would find that a moment would come and – boom! The body just does it; the one who is drawing it, the one who is drawing lines, brush strokes, the one who is observing and trying to create some science on this two-dimensional paper or canvas – *is being watched at all times.* It was a very, very beautiful, soothing and calming experience.

Iain: My question then is, who is it that is aware of the one who is watching?

Igor: Well, I guess that's the whole theme, or the whole subject of what today is often called Non-Duality, isn't it? This whole spirituality business is to find out who is behind the scenes ...

Iain: Who is often pulling the strings ... ?

Igor: The puppeteer [*deep silence*]. Well, I think this is a profound subject, and obviously one can succinctly express that in one sentence, "That is Awareness." "Awareness" is a newly popular word, that is entering the collective unconscious now and almost has a different significance compared with its original meaning, a different texture to it, a different quality. When people say, "Awareness" in certain circles today, it immediately means not just awareness, as in, "Oh, I am aware of these flowers" – although that presupposes that too, but this word Awareness uses the capital A – and that is The Awareness, The Awareness which is prior to any other awareness, that only empowers these faculties which allows that very act of experience to take place. So in that sense, that *puppeteer* has already been identified ... and Awareness is one of its names. He is known by many, but that is one of His names.

Iain: So you also told me earlier that you had lucid dreams when you were quite young. First of all, can you briefly explain what a lucid dream is, and then talk about the effect that it had on you?

Igor: Maybe for some of the listeners it would be valid to mention very quickly, that Consciousness is experiencing itself through three relative states, known as waking, dreaming and deep sleep. For example, we are now both operating on the plane known as the state of waking consciousness, which is characterised by the acuity of the senses, all of the mental powers, and everything else. There is this cohesion, this complete seamless stream of awareness empowered by Awareness itself, where all the other faculties perform what they ought to perform in that waking state.

When the waking state of consciousness wanes, we get tired and ready to sleep, and we want to repose; basically, we want to rest. When we are about to drift away into the domain of dreams, another state of consciousness comes – the dreaming state of consciousness, the state of consciousness characterised by the cessation of sensory perception. It is like the tortoise drawing in its limbs; the senses withdrew themselves and the mind is left alone to abide on its own so-to-speak. So that is the phenomena of dreams. The mind no longer expresses itself through the senses, and it is coalesced in that sea of dreams and images and what have you – the phenomena of dreams.

Then, there comes a moment when we could say that the mind is also tired; it is a loose term for that – it doesn't really get tired, it is just that its vibrations simply ought to subside because the nervous system can no longer entertain that. Our body then moves into another state known as deep sleep. The deep sleep state of consciousness is characterised by a total withdrawal of the senses and of the mind. When that happens, it is a blank state; we know it because there are no dreams, yet awareness is present there because when we wake up we simply say, "I slept very well, I didn't dream of anything." We knew that this was our own dream, it wasn't the dream of neighbour.

So these are the three states of consciousness. In the phenomenon of lucid dreaming, the witness that is present throughout the day, throughout our daily activities when the senses are present, carries on as it were through the dreaming activity, and one has a total awareness of what one dreams about. Not only that there is a whole science of lucid dreaming which explains how we can navigate our dreams at will.

Iain: Was that something that you could do when you were a child? Could you navigate your own dreams?

Igor: I cannot answer that with any certainty, because I'm not sure if I had this as a goal. But I could say with certainty that the dreams were witnessed; the dreams were witnessed throughout, so there was this luminosity.

Iain: How was that as a child, because that's quite unusual, I would think, for a child to have the ability to have that experience ... ?

Igor: As a matter of fact, for children it is not that unusual. It becomes more unusual, though, as the child matures and nears puberty, particularly as the thyroid gland becomes more important in physical growth and development. When we say growth, it is not just the growth of the cells of the tissues of the body, it is also growth of awareness, as that very physical awareness, mental awareness, growth of the individual, growth of one's identity and it is all controlled and checked by the thyroid gland. I am almost certain that eighty precent of children probably lucid dream, but then most of them lose that by the age when the thyroid gland kicks in and introduces a very different process.

Iain: I guess the sad thing is that if they were to talk about it to their parents, most parents wouldn't remember that they had that ability when they were young, so there is no kind of recognition of it.

Igor: Exactly – there is no continuity. As we mature we lose that relationship with our childhood self and most cultures do not support the adult in maintaining this connection with the child's innate ability. I shouldn't even put it that way because it's not that the children have innate ability; it is Consciousness in that state, still in that very tender state as a child, has not lost the innate ability to know itself for what it is – it happens later – the so-called "fall from paradise."

Iain: Something else that you told me beforehand that was influential when you were young, was because you lived quite near the border with India, there would be Indian yogis who would come and they would do demonstrations. You saw these incredible powers that they had, and that seemed to trigger something in you, an interest for a deeper search.

Igor: I could say this was a turning point in making sense of what I was experiencing. because I was impressed completely to see these performances which took place when Indira Gandhi allowed... there was this warm relationship between our countries, so we would have this yearly festival. So, Indian culture was very present. Indian films, Indian popular Bollywood movies, food festivals, all would usually take place in the huge main square which in Tashkent, as they were known at the time as the Red Squares. There would be tents, there would be covered marquees set up, and in one of those places, the yogis were demonstrating their abilities, and my mother took me there. That impressed me a great deal, and from there on, I was completely driven. I compiled all the cuttings about yoga, from every newspaper and magazine I could find, and put them into my own handmade book. This was long before my experiences after I moved to West. This was a very different kind of yoga I am speaking about here; it would be very important to relate to the audience, to the watchers of our channel, that this is not yoga in terms of just postures. These were yogis from the Himalayas.

Iain: So what kinds of things did they do that really impressed you or triggered something in you at the time?

Igor: One of them was a yogi who was put in a huge glass container, and he was demonstrating how long he could go without breathing. The strict conditions meant there was no possibility that there could be any air that he could secretly breathe.

Iain: So that means that he was able to alter the state that his body needed oxygen to quiet the cells right, right down ...

Igor: Yes, we know that now. There were scientific studies made by the superpowers at the time in the seventies. Both the United States and the Soviet Union conducted a series of very serious investigations and experiments in that domain, because they wanted to utilise these powers for their own purposes. Science in these cases was unfortunately serving the perceived need for dominance in two countries, but much of the research found that this body and what this body can do exceed our wildest imagination.

So that of course made a tremendous impression on me, that what this body is, is not that obvious. Although by then I was very physical oriented – sports and other activities took over – I obviously realised what that this body could perform in terms of physical achievement, but more so, what is this body if it can do that? So that was a quest. A question mark was sown, the seed was sown.

Iain: Then you had a mentor whom you mentioned briefly earlier, that was very important to you too. Tell us a little about the mentor, what you learned from him, and what happened with him.

Igor: I was very fortunate that though I grew up in a relatively good school at the time, I was spending all of my free time on the streets with other kids, and most of the time we would get ourselves into mischief as you can imagine; boys left to themselves, running around at that tender age when there is a lot of competition going on, and you have to prove yourself – you try all of these substances that you shouldn't. When my mother noticed that this was happening, she was very concerned. She was introduced to a man who was running this art studio for different ages, and it happened to be on our usual route between her work and my school. So she took me there; at the time I was eleven, and this man became perhaps the turning point in my life in terms of understanding that this life is actually given for something tremendously important. I will explain why and how it happened; it didn't just happen on a mental level.

This man was an accomplished martial artist and a painter, so this is why I started to take professional lessons in art. He also happened to have an underground studio where afterhours he would have a gathering of various characters, of various beings who were involved in different practices. This was the first time that I heard the word "Buddhist" – people who were into Buddhism. I met other martial artists, there were poets, there were people who were in opposition to the government, there were people who you don't usually meet on the street so-to-speak – or you are not aware that they exist – at least that's how it was for me at the time.

He projected a lot of physical power and a lot of vitality, but as you know from the biographical notes, he was tragically killed. I was very close to him, because he brought me to that underground studio, where most of the people were much older than me. I was very privileged to know him, and there was a mutual trust, which I felt also mixed with responsibility; it was almost as if he instilled that trust into me, that I had to live up to.

When he was killed, it obviously shook my world to the very core. For me, it was the realisation that nothing is certain; this life is not going to be forever. I suddenly realised that through witnessing the death of my mentor, one could say I realised my own mortality – not palpably. I don't want to confuse the audience that there were these extrasensory experiences, but I would say on a very emotional level, I realised that this life is not going to last. For that early age, this was quite too much to stomach; it was quite a lot to handle. At the same time, it propelled me to this very different way that I handled my time and everything; my life suddenly had a purpose.

Iain: You had a focus.

Igor: I had a focus, yes. There was an inner regrouping, an inner realignment, where I realised I want to be an artist – I want to perfect myself as much as I can; I want to reach something which this life is for – and he was that example. And he was no longer there, so I was left to myself, almost as if the inner resources were drawn from within.

Iain: Yes, and I think after that you were actually in the army, weren't you? You had to go to the army for two years.

Igor: After, you mean … ?

Iain: Keeping it sequential and just the significant things that happened to you. And there, ironically, being in the army actually spurred something in you that encouraged you to take up an interest in theology and religion.

Igor: I have to say that because I never had a chance, but I have to say that very quickly. I was in the desert, in Turkmenistan – though I was in Uzbekistan, but the Soviet Union was one country, and it was during the Afghanistan campaign – the Soviet Union was carrying lots of heavy losses in lives, so everyone who was eligible was pulled immediately. So I was going through my training in the desert in Turkmenistan for the first six months, and the place we were – if there was a more desolate place even in the steppes of Mongolia, I would be surprised! There was absolutely nothing, but there was one shop; only one shop, and that shop sold various things. It had two or three long shelves, and on the top shelf you would have bread, on the lower shelf you would have a couple of bars of this very square soap, a pair of boots – like these soldier boots – and then, believe it or not, on that shelf where the bread was and maybe a couple of other very peculiar, surrealistic items put together, there was this enormous book – enormous. Guess what it was?

Iain: [*Shrugs to indicate he doesn't have any idea*]

Igor: It was the *Mahabharata*; it was actually the Mahabharata, it was surrealistic! A friend of mine who was a few years older, he actually said to me, "Do you know what this is? This is actually one of *the* most important Hindu texts, in terms of spiritual significance." I don't even know if he used those words, but he made it clear to me that something profoundly important is hidden here. So obviously there was this introduction, but with that there was this sudden interest, in the midst of what I could call... for anyone who has any remote idea of what military training is, would probably appreciate the fact that you live in very, very different conditions. Everything is encapsulated into this very primal, instinctual way, where the environment itself is very tough. You have to survive in that environment, let alone in that hierarchy that soldiers create within; there is this constant physical battle of the masculine energy of competition. If you fall down, it will be very likely that you will be walked over; so there was not an option to fall down, so you have to always be on guard. So life itself was tough. And yet, in the midst of that, what I was interested in was not, "How am I going to go through that?"

Fortunately, I was physically fit; by then I was doing boxing, running six miles in the morning for me was nothing, it was like a warm up, while some other soldiers were running out of breath. I was very physically fit, so the physical conditions for me were secondary, but what really occupied my mind is, "What is this whole thing about the spirit?" I could say this was the turning point. I started to show interest towards anything that has something which is what we call *beyond* – the Spirit, the Transcendence, the Godhead.

Iain: Interesting how that book was just sitting there waiting for you.

Igor: I know, it was like a message sent by the Divine Providence Itself.

Iain: I think that happens for people; we do hear that on Conscious TV, meeting people that say a book just suddenly just drops off a bookshelf, or it's where it shouldn't be, and that is the right time and that is what we all ...

Igor: It's not that I ever read that book – that is what is bizarre!

Iain: You didn't read it?

Igor: Where was the time to read that book? No, this was just a message! I flicked through, obviously with other soldiers and with that friend of mine who was already at the university. I was four years younger, and at that time, four years was a lot. I was nineteen and he was twenty-three. He said to me, "Watch carefully Igor, this is amazing!" He was also an artist, and so it was like, "This is funny, isn't it?"

I opened it, and there are no pictures; it is a very old book – none of these Hare Krishna colourful books – no. It is a hardcore, very old publication, small print – but I start reading one or two verses, and it is like, "Something *very* intriguing; something is [powerfully] drawing me in!" This book talks about something which all of this [*gestures to indicate the outer world*] makes it irrelevant and less important.

Iain: So we have to move on a bit, we have more stories to get to in order to get all of the important things in. You moved to London, and there was a time when your interest in the spiritual world and yoga began to increase. Your mother who was already doing Transcendental Meditation and she was quite keen for you to be initiated. There is quite a story around that.

Igor: Yes. Very quickly I should mention that being an athlete – and you can imagine after the army I was all 'meat and bones,' I was like this 'meat machine.' It carried on. I was really enjoying that strength, even though I pursued the career of an artist. If you had met me fifteen or twenty years ago, you would not recognize me at all; I was really built up, and I used to run in the morning, I used to do all of these exercises. Suddenly, in my late twenties, I pulled my lower back – but when I say, "Pull my lower back" – it was *it*. The third vertebrae went out of place, and I was in agony – I couldn't even put on socks in the morning – let alone doing any exercises – and it went on and on. I went to the chiropractor, and in one week it goes back out again. In one week, it goes back out again.

So what happened – obviously something was brewing, something was really getting ready – what it was, I was not yet aware, but in one of these moments of agony... and I was living in a different city, I was in London and trying to make a living as an artist and what have you, so what I find in myself, is that a degree of surrender takes place. "Whatever that pain is, whatever I need to learn, please let me know. Whatever that is." I wasn't even addressing anyone, but I could not go through the day.

So what happens is that in my dream, I have this act of initiation – there is various information elsewhere where I talked about this in great detail, so I won't go into it now – but just mention that that took place. There was this extraordinary power that lifted me up – literally – I sat down and suddenly I had no pain. I sat down in the bed in the middle of the night, and I was almost, as if I received the command to meditate, "That is what you are to do."

You have mentioned my mother, and Transcendental Meditation – all of her letters were all about that. I even wrote her, "If you mention Transcendental Meditation one more time, I am not going to write back to you, and I'm not going to call you!" I said, "I'm meditating when I paint. Please stop trying to convince me of what I need to do!" Obviously, these were messages on a much more refined level.

So this initiation takes place, and I go to sleep again; I wake up in the morning, and the first thing that I do, I climb out of bed, and I sit against the wall, I prop myself with a cushion, and I do what I was commanded to do in that dream state. From there on, for six months of meditation, amazing things started happening to me, and all this that I was experiencing as a child came back – all these movements in the body, all of these vibrations, heightened energy sensitivity, sounds, lights – all came back.

Iain: At this point you were doing TM meditation which is twenty minutes ...

Igor: Not yet. This was just a way that didn't come from any doctrine or any book. It initiated from a dream, you could almost say it was self-taught if you will and it all happened in that state of altered consciousness. When I shared that with my mother – and I thought that would make her happy – instead she said, "Fine, but now you still need to go and learn meditation, because that will take you to the tradition." I am forever grateful to her, because she is absolutely right; this is where the true spiritual journey unfolded for me.

So I went back to Uzbekistan, and I got initiated into Transcendental Meditation, and I practiced it without missing one meditation for a period of six years. To me, it was more important than brushing the teeth or taking a shower in the morning.

Iain: So you took the TM initiation, and then you did a Siddhis Course – is that right? You did a more advanced course?

Igor: Yes.

Iain: In my notes from when we talked on the phone, somehow the 9-11 date is in my notes, that that was a very significant day – and today is 9-11, again.

Igor: Yes, it is a bizarre coincidence.

Iain: Talk us through how 9-11 affected you then.

Igor: Okay.

So by the end of that summer, in the beginning of that autumn, I reached what I could call a personal crisis. I had been creative all of my life and knew how to express myself, I was a meditator, I lived in bliss already, I knew what the joy of creation and creativity is, I knew what the joy of relationships is, I knew what the joy of friendship is – yet I felt completely lonely, alone, and isolated. I felt as if the world was ending; there was this tremendous process of internalisation that coincided with my decision to go to Uzbekistan again and attend that advanced TM Siddhis Course, which was introduced by Maharishi Mahesh Yogi in the mid-seventies. It is an advanced meditation course – there is a lot of information available online to read about it in depth – but I felt that it is as if I am going to meet my end there. I literally felt that my life came to a point where it can no longer go the way that

I knew it; not just like I wanted some kind of refurbishment, not like I wanted some type of change in situation – it was not like that. It was existential, it was either–or. It was to be – or not to be; it was literally a matter of life and death.

As I am waiting for that course, nothing is happening because the course is being re-announced, re-announced, and postponed; announced and postponed. I keep changing the date of my departure, I am paying for this expensive studio in West London, and I am waiting for this course. Suddenly while I was working on a series of perhaps my last works, a series of pastels, and there is a date for my exhibition – as I was working, I was in the habit of listening to the radio in the background. As it happened there is literally a live broadcast where the commentator could not contain himself, his voice breaks, there is no longer a BBC diction, there is stammering, his voice trembles, and I actually felt in my heart, "Oh no!" He is probably watching it on the monitor live or what have you – I don't know how it all happened, but this is how the news came. It was all this very, very new age of media, when there is the news of what is happening at this very moment. I have a lot of friends, and there was this family of my patrons in New York, so to me New York is not just a city on the map; I've been there twice already and it is a very dear city to my heart, in the sense of people with whom I am connected.

So obviously I sit down, and I think, "My God, I am worrying about all this existential stuff, but the world is ending!" I literally thought that way. "How pathetic, all this! How pathetic, all this self-pitying, all this stuff that I am experiencing, when all around me is what looks like truly cataclysmic events." That is what it looked like; let's face it, it was out of the ordinary; out of the ordinary by any standards. Yet, that same evening I was discussing this with a family of close friends, who support my art activities and Jonathan Kagan, who's a great collector tells me, "Igor, carry on; just carry on with your work." What I said to him was, "What's the point of my exhibition, it's a new reality, who needs it now?" He said, "No, this is when the world needs it more than ever."

Literally, the time before I go to that TM Siddhis Course which was in November – and this event is in September – I am putting all of this energy into my artwork, as if I am kissing it goodbye. It is like bidding farewell to my activity as an artist.

Iain: Okay, so time is marching on and I wanted to get as much as we can of your story in there and what really happened. So when you went on the Siddhis Course, what were your experiences to start with?

Igor: This is it; everything happened there. The doors were unleashed.

Iain: Talk us through that.

Igor: I arrived at the course, and the course starts, and the course consists of two weeks of preparation when you learn certain *sutras*, and two weeks of actual practice on the mats. It was very demanding; you learn a lot, and you practice a lot. What we do, we meditate all day long; we meditate in the morning, we meditate throughout the day, we meditate after lunch, and we meditate in the evening. it's not like twenty minutes here and twenty minutes there – it's hours of meditation.

So by the time we've learned the *sutras*, and before we go into what is known as the main body of the course, these profound experiences take place, where basically the identity – what I knew of myself despite all of these experiences throughout my childhood, which I intuitively tapped into again and again and again with all the witnessing, with all the recognition that there is some greater reality, I'm not just the body – it's completely, completely experienced on the level where I actually become One with That Source.

Iain: So you become One with That Source ... ?

Igor: Shall I speak about it in more physical terms?

Iain: Yes.

Igor: So we sit down cross-legged, the programmeme goes on; the body goes into profound vibrations, profound *kriyas*. *Kriyas* are a Sanskrit term for involuntary movements, they are not self-made movements, your body is just on fire, your body is moving, your body is just experiencing powerful vibrations which manifest as physical vibrations. I reached the point when I feel I cannot take it anymore – the heat, everything, the nausea, I feel I cannot take it either emotionally or physically – I would rather die. You might say, "Well, why didn't you just get up and walk away?" That wasn't an option, but not because I thought I want to complete the course. It was as if I was driven, I was no longer deciding, "I want to go to this course, what is going to happen?" It had energy of its own; it has a vortex of its own. It's as if you entered the field where you no longer can move of your own volition ... the gravity is too powerful. It's important to note this and to understand why the only option I had was – no option. I am sitting there vibrating, and quite frankly, I cannot take it anymore.

Iain: When you say "vibrating" were you physically vibrating?

Igor: Physically vibrating, but there is also the sound. My skull is splitting from internal sounds. These visuals – these stars are bursting out of my eyes, it is as if my chest is being opened up like that [*gestures to indicate the chest being ripped open*], as if my chest is not being cut open, but more like opened from within, which physically was very painful. So when I felt that I can no longer take it, "Okay, let me die then. I would rather die. I will die here and now." There was a flicker of this thought, and in that instant, the face of the Master – in this case Maharishi Mahesh Yogi who devised this programme – comes in. I was nowhere a devotee before that happened, so it would be a mistake to think that. Yes, I was practicing his programme, I was very well participating in many of the activities of the movement – never working for the movement, never working with the movement – however, I couldn't call myself a devotee; I was a one-man band.

Iain: When you say "his face" – it was like a vision?

Igor: It was like a vision; an internal vision, and there is this firm look on his face with affirmation, confirmation, and reassurance, "Everything will be okay. You are not forsaken, you are not going to die – carry on." Instantaneously, this snowball-white, iridescent, huge ball descends down, and sucks my body in. When my body was sucked in, at that very moment my body literally hopped into the air – physically hopped into the air.

Iain: So you physically left the ground a few inches ... ?

Igor: Yes – the body jumped – it was not levitation. I don't want to confuse anyone, it wasn't like slow levitation – no. The body jerked up into the air, and from my own internal experiences then, it was when I entered that "placenta" of light – what I knew myself to be, burst and merged with that light. Later, I found myself panting, lying down, apparently I was hopping all over the place; those who want to find out about the TM Siddhis Course they will know, there are a lot of videos how men and women they hop on the ground – there are collective programmes.

So I was hopping there, but this programme coincided with my own existential process – what I call death, and which ushered a rebirth. I came out of there – apparently everyone was already circling me, and the administrators of the course asked me to share with everyone what happened. Apparently, what happened is very important, because they say the energy entered the course, so this will help others. So I go there, and I cannot find words, because this is an experience of bliss at its most extreme – to my knowledge, to the knowledge of that body – let's say to the knowledge of that being.

So when I try to open my mouth, I cannot. I come to the administrator's ear – an Indian couple – and I whisper, trying to explain, and he says, *"Ananda. Ananda*! Try to speak – try to speak." He speaks with this Indian accent, and so I go back in the centre and we are all surrounded by about fifty people – only twelve men, mostly women in the course. I start saying, "I feel like something profound happened to me. I feel that this is who I really am, this is my identity – not the identity of who I thought of as myself; and the joy is indescribable." It was coming palpably, probably through my eyeballs, and the three women on my right started crying; not just crying, they started sobbing, there is a lot of movement – very emotional. They are not saying anything special, it is just that resonance.

Iain: Yes. We only have about a three or four minutes left, and I want to bring it to a ... although Renate is going to do an interview with you afterwards, and we can talk more about what happened afterwards then.

So obviously you had this very, very strong opening, awakening, and did it last? Did that awakening, that realisation, did it last, or was it something that came and went in the next few weeks – how was it?

Igor: Well, all I can say, and I think is very important and we only have that minute or two left – is that this was the beginning. This was the opening. This was passing through the portal. Obviously, it will take years for me to fully understand why it was the beginning, because each time new territory will be gained, it would seem as complete – but it will still be a plateau, yet to go on. So for the next two to three months, the intensity only grew. The intensity was there – because before that there was no experience of anything to compare it with – but as the intensity grew, my body and my nervous system had more capacity to hold these descending higher states of consciousness, as I understood it later on. I am putting it in context now with how I understood all of these experiences of awakening took place.

For the next few months, this process continued, culminating with what is also known as a complete cessation, or complete mergence of the individual self with the Universal Self. This is something that hopefully we will have more time to talk about, but I would say that this was just the beginning. It is very important, because it was not something to experience, and then to refer to it as a memory; it is still a living, vibrating reality of my own. It has an infinitely more refined flavour to it – but it never stopped. It is as if I was born into another realm – from the realm I existed in or identified myself with prior to that.

Iain: Okay. Well, that's a great place to finish. Thank you very much for coming to London which I very much appreciate.

Igor: It was a great pleasure, thank you very much for inviting me.

CONSCIOUS TV – **THE IDEA**

It was approaching midnight on the 31st December 2006. My wife Renate and I were celebrating New Year's Eve on the island of La Gomera, in the Canary Islands. As usual, she was drinking Champagne and I was sipping my glass of mineral water. I had recently reached my sixtieth birthday and we were having a lively discussion about the things we hadn't yet done in our lives that we would still like to do.

"It would be great to have a TV station," I pronounced. "I could combine all my interests: consciousness, football, music, hiking – make some new programmes and broadcast some existing ones. We can get literally hundreds of channels on our TV at home and they are nearly all rubbish. I am sure I can do much better than that," I declared.

It was of course true that I had no experience in television at all, but on the other hand I had built a successful record label and music publishing company without ever knowing anything about music. I couldn't play any musical instruments and certainly couldn't read music. But I knew what I liked and I trusted my instincts. I had hired good people to work for me. I had learnt that if I couldn't do something then I had to find someone good who could complement me. "It can't be that hard to make decent, interesting television programmes," I added. I thought about it some more. "I could easily come up with plenty of programmes. I could start a satellite channel in the UK, and I am sure people would watch it." The mineral water was beginning to talk enthusiastically.

The next day we hiked into the hills behind the hotel where we were staying. Something was definitely brewing in me. The more I thought about the idea, the more I liked it. Soon after we arrived back in England, I made some enquiries and discovered that to start a proper satellite channel was going to cost getting on £500,000 a year. And that was just to rent the satellite space and the programme listing space. It didn't include the cost of making any programmes, or the overhead costs. That was definitely a step too far.

I also talked over the idea with various friends; they thought combining all my different interests wasn't going to work. "The channel would be too diverse, you would confuse people," most of them commented. "Why don't you focus on the consciousness side? No one else is doing that and there is plenty of football and music on TV already." Life went on, but the idea lingered and often surfaced in my mind. I lowered my sights a little. Maybe I could piggy-back on someone else's channel and just show a few hours of programmes a week. That seemed much more realistic. I found out that this was called a micro channel and other people were doing it. I had a few meetings, but I still felt it was working out too expensive. I was happy to spend money, but I wanted to spend it effectively.

It was now late in 2007 and Internet TV was just beginning to be established. By this time I had thought up a name: Conscious.tv. I liked it, registered it, and decided to make some programmes. I rang a few TV studios and couldn't find anything under about £3,000 a day; and then, of course, there were editing costs afterwards. That was still too much. My music company had started in 1978 and was born out of the first wave of punk music. Punk was a revolution; it quickly turned a boring stagnant music industry upside down. It wasn't just about the music, it was also about the way the music was sold, promoted, and marketed. Records that cost very little to make started to sell in decent quantities. People were ready for something new. The music industry was stuck in a groove and needed a kick. I felt television was the same. People were spending fortunes making programmes that just weren't very good, in my eyes anyway. Persisting, I found a TV studio in Acton, in West London, that would do me a deal for a day: they would record the programmes as if they were live, and I could pretty much walk out with the finished programmes. This was more like it. This was what I was used to. Something that was more instant.

On 2nd November 2007 I made four programmes. I was the interviewer as I didn't have anyone else to do it. None of the programmes were very good (and I have taken them all down now). But I was determined to learn fast. Three weeks later I was back in the studio for another full day of making programmes. I had coached myself and was much better as an interviewer this time; I felt I was getting somewhere. I had also remembered a spiritual retreat that I had attended a few months earlier. We had spent four days listening to everyone else's life stories. That was seventy stories in four days. It was an extraordinarily powerful few days. I had known all those people for twelve or thirteen years, and to hear the detail of their lives was a revelation. It was very moving and touching at times. I realised that with conscious.tv I wanted to create something similar. I wanted people to learn, to be stimulated, to be encouraged, and to be touched. I was also enjoying the challenge. I liked creating something from nothing and seeing where it could go. I would book the studio for an eight-hour day, 11.00am to 7.00pm, and then invite five or six people to interview. To start with, it was mainly friends and people I already knew as I didn't feel confident enough yet to invite people I hadn't met. Conscious.tv was a free service and I wasn't in a position to pay any fees or expenses, so I was really asking people to take part in an experiment in a new form of TV: making programmes cheaply for a niche viewing audience. Having said that, I felt the programmes were technically reasonable enough. We had three cameras in a proper studio, and the director would switch from one to the other so it gave the feel of a proper programme, which of course it was. I was learning a lot, and fast.

By April 2008, I felt I had enough interviews to launch the channel on the Internet. People's response was slow to start with, but I wasn't going to do any marketing as such. The phrase 'build it and they will come' was rooted in me. I felt what I was doing was interesting and different. The word would slowly get out there. For the first few months, I didn't even check how many people were viewing the programmes. I didn't want to depress myself if the numbers were very low. I just wanted to keep going. I was enjoying the project and felt the programmes were getting better and better. And then four months or so after we started, three emails came in one week, from people I didn't know, who had found the channel and enjoyed it. Something was starting to happen.

Around this time, I was talking with an old friend, Kate Parker, who suggested, "You should make some programmes on non-duality. Talk to Julian Noyce at Non-Duality Press. He'll have some idea of who, amongst the authors that he publishes, might be willing to be interviewed."

I called Julian and explained my idea. He mused for several seconds before suggesting Jeff Foster and Richard Sylvester. And so Jeff and Richard came along to the studio in Acton one afternoon and the Non-Duality section was born. Within a few months, it became the most popular section. Renate started to help me by doing some interviews herself. People seemed to like our style. Something was now quickly building. We were soon receiving emails daily from people with suggestions of people to interview or indeed, people who wanted to be interviewed themselves. Although our interview style may look casual, we actually do a fair amount research for most of our interviews, and that takes time. We quickly learnt that we needed to be pretty selective about who appears on Conscious.tv. We decided the solution was simply to interview only people we personally find interesting. People would sometimes object, "You should interview so and so; lots of people will watch it. You will find more viewers." But we weren't to be swayed. Conscious.tv is an integral part of our own personal journey, and all the interviews in this book have been important for us.

As I update this in 2018, we have made nearly 500 programmes. Apart from being available on www.conscious.tv, all the programmes are on YouTube; we now get many thousands of programmes watched each day on the Internet. We also have our micro channel on Satellite TV (via SKY and FreeSat – check www.conscious.tv for up-to-date details), with programmes broadcast daily in the UK. Our adventure is ongoing, and while we still enjoy it we will continue.

Iain McNay
iain@conscious.tv
Oxfordshire, Summer 2019

ACKNOWLEDGEMENTS

And a very special thank you to the many people have helped in the preparation of this book. Hopefully none of the key people have been forgotten.

Julian and Catherine Noyce put an amazing amount of time into the editing.

Niya Shambler helped with the coordination.

Eleonora Gilbert was so helpful with the running of conscious.tv at this time.

And the following transcribed the interviews as volunteers; many, many thanks to you all for your time and your dedication.

Karin Apoundek
Judi Appleby
Pamela D'Ambrosio
Dawn Cheers
Jonathan Daniel
Mike Hogan
Beverley Huish
Jayant Kapatker
Augie Monge
Thomas Nicholson
Gloria Oelman
Nurit Oren
Steve Taylor

Heath Thompson
Andrea Vachon
Carole Wilding

And last of all a thank you to publisher extraordinaire, Jon Beecher.

ABOUT CONSCIOUS TV

Conscious TV is a UK-based TV channel broadcasting on the Internet at www.conscious.tv. Our programmes are also shown on SKY TV and FREESAT from time to time.

Our aim is to stimulate debate, question, enquire, inform, enlighten, encourage, and inspire people in the areas of consciousness, science, non-duality and spirituality.

You can also find on our website the transcripts of many of the programmes under the Transcripts section. There is also an audio section where the audio only versions of the programmes can be streamed or downloaded.

We have two email newsletters. The first is a general newsletter that we send out every three months, and the second is our 'New Programme Alert' list where you will be notified every time a new programme is available to watch on the channel.

Email us at info@conscious.tv if you would like to be included on either or both of these lists.

We are always open to ideas for interesting people to interview. Do let us know if you have any suggestions.

We are run by a team of volunteers and are not a commercial business. If you would like to help us in any way, then do contact us at info@conscious.tv and let us know your skills and how you feel you could help out.

WEBSITES OF INTERVIEWEES

A.H Almaas	www.diamondapproach.org
Jessica Britt	www.diamondapproach.org
Sheik Burhanuddin	www.sufiway.eu/sheikh-burhanuddin-herrmann
Linda Clair	www.simplemeditation.net
John Butler	www.spiritualunfoldment.co.uk
Billy Doyle	www.billydoyle.com
Georgi Y Johnson	www.iamhere.life
Cynthia Bourgeault	www.cynthiabourgeault.org
Gabor Harsanyi	www.treeofsilence.com
Tess Hughes	www.tesshughes.com
Philip Jacobs	www.studysociety.org
Igor Kufayev	www.igorkufayev.com

OTHER CONSCIOUS TV PUBLICATIONS

Conversations on the Enneagram
Edited by Eleonora Gilbert
ISBN: 978-1909454347

There are nine basic personality types, and we are all predominantly one of them. Once we find our Ennea-type we can start not only understand why we are the way we are, but also begin to explore our true potential. There has been increasing interest in the Enneagram over the past few years and it is now regarded as a very useful tool both in Psychology and spiritual development. *Conversations on the Enneagram* is a unique collection of transcripts of in-depth experiential interviews with panels of individuals of each Enneagram type which were recorded for conscious.tv.

Also included are interviews with six of the world's leading experts on the Enneagram, Tom Condon, Ginger Lapid-Bogda, Sandra Maitri, Faisal Muqaddam, Claudio Naranjo, and Helen Palmer, who share not only their wisdom and insights, but also their personal experiences. Between them these six authors have had over twenty books published. All are well known and respected in the Enneagram community.

OTHER CONSCIOUS TV PUBLICATIONS

Conversations on Non-Duality
Edited by Eleonora Gilbert
ISBN: 978-1901447675

A fascinating compilation of life stories of perfectly ordinary people, all of whom have been through extraordinary experiences leading to amazing new perceptions. Some have been seekers from a very young age, whilst others had previously never even though in terms of seeking. Nevertheless, all shared a common sense of dissatisfaction with their lives. This collection of stories explores the means by which each individual went about achieving an end to their suffering and achieving non-duality.

Includes interviews with David Bingham, Daniel Brown, Sundance Burke, Katie Davis, Peter Fenner, Steve Ford, Jeff Foster, Suzanne Foxton, Gangaji, Richard Lang, Roger Linden, Wayne Liquorman, Francis Lucille, Mooji, Catherine Noyce, Jac O'Keeffe, Tony Parsons, Bernie Prior, Halina Pytlasinska, Genpo Roshi, Florian Schlosser, Mandi Solk, Rupert Spira, James Swartz, Richard Sylvester and Pamela Wilson